THE "I AM" DISCOURSES

The Magic Presence

THE "I AM" DISCOURSES

BY THE ASCENDED MASTER
SAINT GERMAIN

SAINT GERMAIN PRESS
POST OFFICE BOX 1133
CHICAGO, ILLINOIS

AUTHOR'S APPRECIATION

IT IS, with sincerest gratitude, that I acknowledge the blessed assistance of Lotus Ray King, whose untiring effort has enabled me to bring forth "Unveiled Mysteries," "The Magic Presence" and the "I AM Discourses," in their present, splendid form.

All credit is given Lotus for editing these books; by her great tenacity, in holding so closely to her "Mighty I AM Presence," she has called Perfection into action.

I wish to thank Max Gysi, Betty Mundy and David Livingston for their gracious assistance in perfecting the manuscripts.

I am also grateful to the many Students, who have so earnestly called the "Mighty I AM Presence" into action, for the success and Perfection of this transcendent Blessing to mankind.

GODFRE RAY KING.

Long Beach, Calif. July 20th, 1935.

v

DEDICATION

This series of books is dedicated in deepest Eternal Love and Gratitude to our Beloved Masters, Saint Germain, Jesus, the Great Divine Director, and also to the Great White Brotherhood, the Brotherhood at the Royal Teton, the Brotherhood at Mount Shasta, the Great Ones from Venus, and those other Ascended Masters Whose loving help has been direct and without limit.

EDITOR'S NOTE

THE words of Jesus, as quoted throughout this series of books by Godfré Ray King, are the authentic statements He uttered, although they do not always agree, verbally, with some versions of the Christian Bible.

This fact should not surprise the Truth-Seeker, who understands the difficulties encountered in translation.

Jesus has spoken again, on the Visible Light and Sound Ray, and made this point clear, saying:

"It is unfortunate indeed, that some of the Scriptural statements have been clouded by HUMAN CONCEPTS; *yet I am thankful indeed that many have remained unaltered."*

LOTUS RAY KING.

TRIBUTE

A T the present time, the attention of mankind is being drawn to the *conscious understanding and use* of the words, "I AM," by the Ascended Masters, Saint Germain, Jesus, and others of the Ascended Host, who are pouring out ceaselessly, the Great Light to release Freedom, Peace, and Perfection. The Cosmic Command for the permanent Golden Age has been given and must now manifest on this planet.

The Great Ascended Masters have worked for centuries, preparing for the expansion of Light that is now flooding the entire system to which this earth belongs. The Great Cosmic Law has begun the release and increase of *That Light* which compels all things to come into Perfect Divine Order wherever it flows.

These Great Ones have always been the Custodians of the Eternal Inner Understanding concerning the use of the Great Creative Word, "I AM." They, and They alone, have been able to give the *complete understanding* concerning what occurs when those two words, "I AM," are used.

They have been the Elder Brothers, Protectors, Guardians, and Infallible Teachers of mankind throughout the centuries. The Ascended Masters are the Only Infallible Source of instruction to the humanity of this earth, because *They are Wholly Divine and One with the God-Self* of every individual. They are the Living Fulfillment of the Law They teach, and are the Only Ones who have manifested *Complete Victory* over so-called death.

They are the Full Manifestation of That Light and Love which rules the Universe, and maintains divine order throughout Infinity.

The release of Their Combined Light is taking place and flooding the earth at the present time. All that is not of the Light is consumed thereby. Their Light will continue to expand throughout this planet until all its humanity has made the Ascension also, and the earth itself becomes a Blazing Sun whirling in its appointed path in space.

To These Great Ascended Masters, mankind owes all the good it has ever received or drawn forth, because they are the ways and means by which the Infinite God-Self expands Its Perfection through the finite activity of personalities.

This earth and its humanity are entering into "The I AM Age," and therefore the *full use* of this "I AM Knowledge" must be understood and utilized by the individuals who live here, in the present and near future.

The Great Cosmic Beings, the Ascended Masters, and Angelic Hosts have given tremendous protection to America and her people over the year just past, and to all individuals, who will call unto Them in the Name of the "Mighty I AM Presence," keep their feelings harmonized, and pour out intense Love *continually* to their own "Mighty I AM Presence," They will give assistance without limit.

This book is especially charged with Saint Germain's Ascended Master Consciousness and Love and that of the other Ascended Masters concerned with this activity, to bring protection, freedom, illumination, and Perfection to all who read or contact it, that all may express Mastery and also make their Ascension.

It is the privilege of every student of Light, at this time, to call in the Name of "The I AM Presence," with all earnestness and Love, to These Great Ones to protect America, the land, and her people, to *illumine* all officials of the government, to *perfect all* within her borders and to *compel obedience* everywhere unto "The Light of God that never fails."

GODFRÉ RAY KING

FOREWORD

THE thirty-three Discourses contained in this book were dictated over a *Visible* Light and Sound Ray in our home during 1932 by the Ascended Master, Saint Germain, and those other Ascended Masters directly concerned with this activity. The sound of His voice was physically audible to everyone in the room. At times *His Visible, Tangible Presence* also stood within the room, when He radiated the Power and Energy of the Light Rays to accomplish special work.

The training and preparation for him to do this, at the present crisis of the outer-world, was given us over a period of thirty years, that it might be accomplished at this time, and assistance from the Ascended Masters comes forth in this way to protect and free all individuals, who make conscious effort to correct themselves and attain Mastery over all things on this earth.

Never before, except in the Retreats of the Great White Brotherhood, has such intensified, transcendent instruction concerning the "I AM" been given to individuals. Not for thousands of years have the *True* Inner Instruction and Use of the Sacred Flame been taught to mankind, as Saint Germain and Others of the Ascended Masters have revealed. Permission for them to be explained to students as given forth in these discourses has been granted to us by these Great ones. Such instruction, as is herein contained, has never been given to students until after a three year probation in the Retreats.

The condition of the outer-world at the present time is such that those, who sincerely seek the Light and want the Constructive Way of Life, *must have more than human help,* if they are to survive over the present period of chaos, which is the accumulated discord generated by humanity en masse through the centuries, that is pressing heavily upon the outer experience of individuals today.

The need of protection and help for the children of earth is so great, at the present hour, that the Great Ascended Masters and Legion of Light have let the bars down, so to speak, and have released this Inner Understanding of the "Mighty I AM Presence" into the outer-Life of mankind, that all who want the Light and will make conscious effort to attain their own freedom and Mastery may have the assistance which will give them the Eternal Victory.

Only fragments of the real understanding of the "I AM Presence" have been given to the outer-world until now. The Ascended Master, Saint Germain, says: "It is *the most important* understanding mankind can ever have, and there is no freedom nor Perfection for the individual, except through this conscious application." He considers it of such paramount importance that He dictated more than thirty-three discourses in which he explains what happens in the outer-Life of the individual when one says, "I AM." He also says: "Nothing will bless the individual to so great a degree as the *conscious understanding* of this 'Creative Word.'"

When the phrase, "Mighty I AM Presence come forth," is used throughout this series of books, it is always a call to the God Presence to pour forth or release the out-pouring of Perfection, which the one making the call desires.

It is *always* thought, felt, written, or spoken with the *feeling* of intense LOVE. It is *always* a *call* to God, the "Mighty I AM Presence" to establish Perfection everywhere, and thus let God's Will—Perfection—be made manifest on earth. When a command is given, it is *always* the outer-self calling unto God and, in the Name of "That Mighty I AM Presence," commanding substance and energy to obey the decree given, which is the Self-conscious effort required in order *to open the door* for the Intelligence of the "I AM" to release Its Perfect Manifestation.

This book not only carries the Ascended Masters' Understanding of the "I AM" but is charged with Saint Germain's Ascended Master Consciousness and the Ray of Light and Love from His Heart which is the Ascended Master's *feeling and comprehension* of Its Full Power forever Self-Sustained.

May this book of "I AM Discourses" anchor the attention of all who read or contact it, so powerfully upon each individual's own Divinity, that the Full Ascended Masters' Consciousness of the "Mighty I AM Presence" shall fill the earth, and release with the power of a thousand suns, the Eternal Dominion of "The Light of God that never fails."

GODFRÉ RAY KING

CONTENTS

THE "I AM" DISCOURSES

By THE ASCENDED MASTER, SAINT GERMAIN

———————— * ————————

DISCOURSE I

October 3, 1932

SAINT GERMAIN

INVOCATION: Thou Infinite, Mighty Presence—Thou All-Pervading Principle of Life! we give praise and thanks for Thy Wondrous Activity, through all outer Presence. Out of Thy Mighty Essence comes all that is, and Oh! that humanity might understand, Thou art ever and forever Self-sustained. Thou Mighty, Active Principle of Life, surge forth in the outer activity of mankind, manifest Thy Supreme Justice *now* in all places.

Mighty Presence of Light—God in Action! govern the minds of mankind, holding them to Truth and Justice, and see that Thy Messengers are placed in all official positions; let naught of the outer interfere, that none of humanity may accept any thought of deception.

Mighty Presence of God in Action, surge forth in the minds of all, expressing Thy Conquering Presence.

GREETINGS: I bring you greetings from the Perfected Ones, who are watching closely over, and ministering to all.

THE DISCOURSE

Life, in all its activities everywhere manifest, is *God in Action,* and it is only through lack of the understanding of applied thought and feeling, that mankind is constantly interrupting the pure flow of that Perfect Essence of Life, which would, without interference, naturally express its Perfection everywhere.

The natural tendency of Life is Love, peace, beauty, harmony, and opulence, for Life cares not who uses it, but is constantly surging to pour more of Its Perfection into manifestation, always with that lifting process, which is ever inherent within Itself.

"I AM"

"I AM" is the Activity of "That Life."

How strange it is, that students with sincere interest, do not seem to get the True meaning of those two words.

When you say, and feel "I AM," you release the spring of Eternal, Everlasting, Life, to flow on its way unmolested. In other words, you open wide the door to Its natural flow. When you say "I AM not," you shut the door in the face of this Mighty Energy.

"I AM" is the Full Activity of God.

Having placed before you so often the Truth of *God in Action,* I wish you to understand Its first expression, in individualization. The first expression of every individual, everywhere in the Universe, either in spoken word, silent thought, or feeling, is "I AM," recognizing Its Own Conquering Divinity.

The student, endeavoring to understand and apply these mighty yet simple laws, must stand guard more strictly over his thought and expression, in word or otherwise, for every time you say "I AM not," "I cannot," "I have not," you are, whether knowingly or unknowingly, throttling that "Great Presence" within you.

This is just as tangible, as if you placed your hands about the throat of an outer form, only with the outer form, your thought governing the hand, you can release it at any time, but when you make a declaration, using the words "I AM not," you set in motion Mighty, Limitless Energy, that continues to act, unless it is recalled, consumed, and transmuted.

This shows you the enormous power you have, to qualify this Mighty Energy of God, and I tell you, beloved students, dynamite is less dangerous, for that would but liberate you from the body, while these thoughts, sent forth ignorantly and ungoverned, bind you upon the wheel of re-embodiment indefinitely.

Thus you can see, how important it is for you to

know, what you are doing, when you thoughtlessly use wrong expressions, because you are using the Most Divine Principle of Activity in the Universe—"I AM."

Do not misunderstand me, this is no idle, foreign, or Oriental expression, but the Highest Principle of Life used, and expressed throughout every civilization that has ever existed, for the first expression every Self-conscious form of Life gives is "I AM." It is only afterwards, in its contact with outer, wrongly qualified activity, that it begins to accept anything less than "I AM."

Now dear students, do you not see, that when you say, "I AM sick," you are just reversing this Principle of Life, which is naturally all Perfection, thus requalifying it by your wilful ignorance with something which it never naturally possessed?

Through long centuries of wilful misunderstanding, humanity has charged the very atmosphere about them, with falsehood and unreality, for I need not say to you, that when you say, "I AM sick," it is an abject falsehood in respect to your Divinity, which cannot be sick.

Does this sound harsh to you?

Then I say, think it over, and you will see what a blessing and release it can be to you.

I say to you dear students—in the name of God, stop using these wrong expressions of your Godhead

—of your Divinity—for it is impossible for you to have freedom as long as you continue to do it. I cannot speak of this to you too often, that when you *really* recognize, and accept the Mighty Presence of God in you, there are positively no adverse conditions.

STOP! I say to you, giving power to the outer conditions, persons, places, or things, and in the name of God every time you find yourself starting to say, "I AM sick," "I AM broke," "I AM not feeling well," instantly reverse this fatal condition to your progress, and declare silently, with all the intensity of your being,—"I AM"—which is all health, opulence, Perfection, happiness, peace, and the power to recognize Perfection in yourself and everywhere else.

When you think of the expression, "I AM," it means that you know you have *God in Action,* expressing in your life. Do not let these false expressions continue to govern, and limit you. Continually remind yourself:—"I live, move, and have my Being and all outer expression in the full opulence of God, made manifest every moment."

In thus reminding yourself of this Invincible, Unconquerable Presence you keep the door open for Its pure, Invincible Essence and Intelligence to weave into your outer expression, that wondrous Perfection.

I plead with you, dear ones, everywhere, do not

continue to use these wrong expressions, thinking that in some hocus-pocus way, you may slide past reaping the result: IT SIMPLY CANNOT BE DONE.

Many of you know that they use the branding-iron on the Western Frontier as a recognition of ownership by the ranchmen. So great is my desire to have you recognize, and hold fast to the active Presence of God in you, that I almost long for a branding-iron to brand those words—"I AM"—into your consciousness for constant use, that you could not be drawn off the recognition, acceptance, and use of that Mighty, Glorious Presence of God,—which you are.

I trust that all, who may hear or read these words, will feel the power and the Mighty Conviction of this Truth, that goes with them, leaping into action wherever expressed.

If at any time, anything less than Perfection attempts to make an appearance in your experience, declare *vehemently,* that it is not true, and that you accept only God, which is Perfection in your Life everywhere manifest. As long as you give way to accepting false appearances, you will have them expressed in your Life and experience. It is not, dear student, a matter of belief on your part, whether you accept these Truths or not, but they are The Law, proven through long centuries of experience, and are placed before you for your freedom.

Awaken to the fact that your thought and feeling in the past have built—created—the inharmony of your world to-day. Arise! I say, Arise! and walk with the Father—the "I AM"—that you may be free from these limitations. There is only one thing in this Universe, that can surround you with limitation, and that is accepting the outer appearance, instead of the Mighty, Active Presence of God in you.

The Western World likes to fool itself with the idea that it refuses to accept the ancient and Eastern idea of sorcery, in other words, the misuse of the spiritual powers. The worst kind of sorcery is being used in the political fields to-day, that has ever been known in the history of mankind, through the use of mental power—wrongly qualified.

If this same, tremendous mental force were used in just the reverse way to know that, *There is only God in Action, in every individual filling official places,* the sender of that quality, or Truth, would not only be free himself, but the political world would be filled with freedom and justice. Then, we would experience a natural world, a world of *God in Action*—everywhere present.

It is to-day, as it was at one time in Egypt. Those who misuse the mental power are binding themselves to the rack of inharmony, embodiment after embodiment.

Take the stand:—"I do not take on conditions from

anybody or anything about me, but God—Good and I AM always God-commanded." You need to acquire the habit of stilling yourself. Sit down three or four times a day, and simply still the outer self. This will let the energy be supplied. Learn to command and control the energy in your body. If you want the energy still—be still. If you want the energy active—be active. You must stand up, face a thing, and rise above it. There is no other way.

The student should watch in every way for habits and break them up. He should not have to be told, but must look within himself, and uproot whatever is not Perfect. This brings a freedom, not possible in any other way.

The holding on of old habits is just like wearing old worn-out garments. The student must not wait for someone else to think these things out for him. He must do it himself. It is not possible for anyone to do it, but himself.

In this work and under this radiation, everything that is latent in the individual is being brought forth to be consumed. Watch—that the attention does not become fixed on the thing you do not want.

It is perfectly ridiculous to keep reverting back to things which have not worked out. If you have built your limitations for centuries and can, by this attention and self-effort, free yourself in a few years, isn't it worth it? Is it not marvelous?

A humorous sense of getting away from a thing is sometimes the quickest and most powerful way of doing it, for a buoyant, joyous feeling releases the energy, that many times enables a very wonderful manifestation to take place.

If one will buckle down to brass tacks, and call on the Law of Forgiveness, he can then consume all past creations in The Consuming Flame and be free. You must be conscious that The Flame is the Active Presence of God doing the consuming.

The Freedom of God is here in action.

When you have a feeling to do a certain constructive thing, go ahead, stick to it, and do it, if the heavens fall. Whether the manifestation comes now or not, should not enter into your consciousness at all.

Even when students only know a thing intellectually, they should not allow the mind to keep reverting back to wrong conditions, when they know what this activity does to their success. It is unbelievable that people will not conquer this enemy in their consciousness. No student can ever gain the victory, until he stops reverting back to the old negative conditions he is trying to get rid of.

The whole work of a teacher is to get some means and explanation over to the student of the activity of acceptance. What the mind accepts is that which the individual agrees with, through his *attention,* by letting the two become one. When the mind accepts and agrees with a thing or condition, the individual decrees it into his world. Whatever you let the attention rest upon, you are agreeing with and accepting, because through the attention you have let the mind become one with it.

If an individual were to see a rattlesnake coiled, would he walk right up to be struck? Certainly not, yet this is what students are doing when they let their attention revert back to their troubles. Such habits are only past momentum given a specific quality.

There are only two activities in Life, and if you will not let the Inner govern according to Its plan of Perfection then the outer must.

When a constructive picture is flashed to your mind, it is a reality. When you recall it as a mental picture, and hold it again, it calls forth the reality.

One can become so aware of his own God Presence, that at any time, he can see and feel Its Radiance pouring out to him.

For things it does not want, the outer has all the confidence in the world. It is up to the student to compel it to have the same confidence for the Perfection of God that it has for the imperfection of the senses.

The student must always rely on himself. He must always think, "What can I do to intensify this activity from the hints given?"

BENEDICTION: Mighty Perfected Ones! as we receive Thy Magic Circle of Protection, as we receive and are enfolded in Thy Mighty Opulent Presence, Oh Master Within! we accept fully that opulence made manifest in our outer experience and use. We give praise and thanks for Thy wisdom in its use. We give praise and thanks that we have the full strength to accept only Thy Mighty Active Presence at all times, and to refuse acceptance to anything unlike Thee.

546

DISCOURSE II

October 6, 1932

SAINT GERMAIN

INVOCATION: Thou Infinite All-Pervading Presence—Thou Mighty Master within each human form! we acknowledge and accept Thy Full Presence manifest within these forms, and within the human form of every individual that God has sent forth. We give praise and thanks that at last, we have become aware of this Mighty Presence to Whom we can turn and recognize the Fulness of God's Activity, the "I AM" of all things.

GREETINGS: to you all.

THE DISCOURSE

When Jesus said: "I AM the resurrection and the Life," he gave forth one of the mightiest utterances that can well be expressed.

When he said, "I AM," He did not refer to the outer expression, but He did refer to *The Mighty Master Presence—God Within,* because he repeatedly said: "I of my self can do nothing, it is the Father within—the 'I AM'—that doeth the works."

Again Jesus said: "I AM the Way, the Life, and the Truth," giving recognition to the One and Only Power—*God in Action within him.*

Again he said: "I AM the 'Light' that lighteth every man that cometh into the world," prefacing every statement of vital importance with the words— "I AM."

Contemplating "I AM," as *anything* and *everything* you wish to be, is one of the mightiest means of loosing the Inner God Power, Love, Wisdom, and Truth, and setting It into action in the outer experience.

Again, let us refer to His mighty utterance, perhaps one of the greatest ever spoken into the outer expression: "I AM the open door, which no man can shut." Do you not see how very vital this is, when you come to review understandingly, these Mighty Statements?

When you recognize and accept fully, "I AM," as the *Mighty Presence of God in you—in action,* you will have taken one of the greatest steps to liberation.

Now mark you, in the utterance of the Truth that, "I AM the open door which no man can shut," if you can but realize it, you have the key that allows you to step through the veil of flesh, carrying with you all consciousness, that you have generated or accumulated, which is imperfect, and there transmute it, or in other words, raise it into that Perfection into which you have stepped.

Too much stress cannot be laid upon the importance of contemplating, as often as possible, the "I

AM," as the Mighty Active Presence of God in you, in your home, in your world, in your affairs. Every breath you breathe is *God in Action in you.* Your ability to express or send forth thought and feeling is God acting in you. You, having free will, it is entirely up to you, to qualify the energy sent forth in your thought and feeling, and determine how it shall act for you.

No one can say: "How shall I know how to qualify this energy?" for everyone knows the difference between destructive and constructive thought, feeling, and action.

The student, in receiving instruction, should constantly analyze the motive back of the question, to detect if in that motive there is a feeling of intellectual pride, arrogance or stubbornness in the outer mind and body. If there is within the motive, a lurking desire to argue and prove the instruction wrong, rather than receive the blessing and truth intended, the individual has unknowingly shut the door, for the time being, to his ability to receive the good offered.

Again may I remind the students, regardless of their personal opinions as to what the Truth shall be, I have proven, through many centuries, these condensed instructions now being given forth. If one wants to receive the greatest benefit possible and the comprehension, that will be their absolute certain freedom and liberation, listen with an entirely open mind, with the consciousness, that the "I AM"—the Active Presence of God in you—is your certain ability to receive, accept, and apply without limit, the instruction which is being given forth with an accompanying radiance, which will enable certain students, at this time, to comprehend these simple, yet mighty, assertions of Truth to their great blessing and freedom.

The admonition has been before humanity through many centuries: "Ye cannot serve two masters." Why is this so? First: because, there is only One Intelligence, One Presence, One Power that can act, and that is the Presence of God acting in you. When you turn to the outer manifestation, and give all kinds of expressions and appearances power, you are attempting to serve a false, usurping master, because the outer expression can only find an appearance, through the use of God's Mighty Energy.

Your ability to lift your hand and the Life flowing through the nervous system of your outer form, is "God in Action" in your body, through your mind.

Dear students, try to use this simple means as a reminder of *God in Action in you.* When you start to go down the street, think for an instant: "This is God's Intelligence and Power, by which I walk, and this is His Intelligence by which I know where I AM going." Thus, you will see, that it is no longer possible to go on without understanding, that every move you make is God in Action. Every thought in your mind is God's Energy, which enables you to think. When you know this is a fact—and there is no disputing it—why not adore, give full confidence to, trust in, have faith in, and accept this Mighty Presence of *God in Action in you;* instead of looking to the outer expression, which is clothed, qualified, and colored by the outer or human concept of things, regardless of the One Mighty Presence which enables the outer to express?

All outer form and its attendant expression is but the experience of Life by which each individual may learn—through his own experiences—the True Source of his Being, and come again into the Fulness of Perfection, through the Self-conscious knowing thus attained.

The outer experience of Life is but a constant, changing, passing picture, that the outer mind has created in its pretense (imagination) of being the Real Actor. Thus is the attention so constantly fixed upon the outer, which alone contains imperfection, that the Children of God have forgotten their own Divinity, and must come back to It again.

God is the Giver, the Receiver, and the Gift, and is the Sole Owner of all the intelligence, substance, energy and opulence there is in the Universe.

If the Children of God would learn to give for the

joy of giving, whether it be Love, money, service, or whatever it may be, they would open the door to such vast opulence that it would be impossible to want for a single thing in the outer expression.

The unfortunate thing in humanity, which has caused such rampant selfishness and unprecedented condemnation of each other, is the idea of claiming ownership to these wonderful blessings of God, for there is but One Love acting, One Intelligence, Power and Substance and that is God in every individual. The Warning that should be placed before every student and individual, is to guard against the desire of the outer-self to claim power of its own. If in every act of the personality, God were given full credit, transformations unbelievable could not help taking place in the one thus giving full credit and power where it belongs.

There has rarely been a correct understanding of supply and demand. There is positively abundant supply omnipresent, but the demand for it *must* be made before the Law of the Universe permits it to come into the expression and use of the individual.

The individual, having free will, must consciously with full determination, make the demand, and it cannot fail to come forth into expression, no matter what it is, so long as the individual holds an unwavering, determined consciousness.

This simple statement, used with sincere determination: "I AM the great opulence of God made visible in my use right now and continuously," will bring to the individual all he can possible use.

The limiting element, so many students seem to be aware of, is that they start out declaring the Truth, for instance, as in the above statement, but before many hours have passed over their heads, if they were to analyze themselves conscientiously, they would find in their *feelings* lurking doubt or fear, for both these are feelings. Naturally, this neutralizes to a large extent, the constructive force, that would quickly bring about the fulfillment of the desire or demand.

Once a student can become fully aware, that every right desire or wish is *God in Action,* propelling his energy forth to full accomplishment, and is always Self-sustained, he would become aware of the Limitless Love, Power and Intelligence he has with which to accomplish any given purpose.

With this simple understanding, the word failure would be completely wiped out from his world, and in a very short time from his consciousness, because he would see that he was wielding intelligence and power that could not fail. Thus, students and individuals come into their Full Dominion as God intends. It was never intended by the Great All-wise, All-loving Father, that any of his children should want for a single thing, but because they allow their attention to become fixed on the outer appearance, which is like the changing sands of the desert, they have knowingly or unknowingly, cut themselves off to a large degree from that Great Opulence and Intelligence.

This Great Opulence is their birthright, which everyone can have, who will again turn to the "I AM," the Active Principle of God, forever within himself, as the Only Source of Active Life, Intelligence and Opulence.

All through the ages, there have been certain standards of conduct necessary for the student, who desires to reach beyond certain attainments. This is the conserving and governing of the Life Force, through the sex.

For an individual, who has been using this energy without any thought of governing it, to suddenly say: I will cease this, cut it off as it were, without understanding the correct attitude of consciousness, would be simply supressing a flow of energy, which he has caused to flow in the wrong direction. Any student, who wishes to govern this, will find this simple statement the most efficient—if used understandingly—of any one particular thing, that can be given. This will normally and naturally govern the flow of the Life Energy and bring it back into its natural channels. It is the Mighty Statement of Jesus: "I AM the resurrection and the Life."

This statement, will not only purify the thought, but is the most powerful, lifting, adjusting force, that can be used for the correction of this greatest of barriers to the full height of spiritual attainment. Anyone, who begins to feel the Inner Impulse to correct this condition and will use this statement earnestly and continuously, will raise this marvelous current of energy, to the highest center in the brain, as was originally intended.

He will find his mind flooded with the most marvelous ideas, with the abundant sustaining power and ability coming into expression and use for the blessing of all mankind. I ask any student to try this, and watch the results in his own mind and body.

Feel deeply this statement of Jesus: "I AM the resurrection and the Life." Repeat it three times, either silently or audibly, and notice the lifting of consciousness, which you will experience. There may be some, who will need to try this several times, in order to feel the amazing uplift, that others will experience at the first trial. This will show you in a small way, what can be done by its continued use.

There is only one means of overcoming or rising out of anything, and that is, after you know what it is you are to rise out of, to take your outer attention completely away from it, fixing it firmly upon the above statement. Any condition in the outer experience, that one wishes to overcome, can readily be accomplished by the use of this statement, as well as using it to change the flow of the misdirected energy.

I had one student, who felt the Inner Impulse to re-direct this Mighty Energy and the use of this single statement alone, enabled her, with little assistance, to raise her body. In one year, a marvelous transformation took place in her entire outer appearance.

It seems incredible, that in the recorded state-ments, accredited to Jesus, which were only a part of what he really gave forth, that so few of humanity would receive the mighty import of those wonderful words of wisdom. At no time in the history of the world, have so many Mighty Statements been given, as he taught. Every one of these, when conscientiously used, holds within it the attendant radiance and ac-complishment with which He attained. You not only have this power of the "I AM," but His individual assistance also, when these statements are used. One should often contemplate the true meaning of these Mighty Statements of Jesus. When once you under-stand that your thought, feeling, and expression of "I AM," sets the Mighty God Power in you into ac-tion—without any limit—then you receive that upon which the desire is fixed.

It should be no trouble for the student to see and understand, that the outer appearance is but man's distorted creation, by claiming the outer as a source of power, when a moment's contemplation will cause him to realize, that there is but One Love, Intelligence, and Power which can act, and that is God.

The human, or outer defects, or discrepancies, have nothing to do with the Omnipresent Perfection of God, for anything imperfect is the creation of the outer concept of mankind.

If man will turn to the "Mighty I AM" within, knowing that God is all Perfection and that all outer appearance is but man's creation, through the misuse of the God Power, he will see at once, that if he sincerely contemplates and accepts the Perfection of God, he will cause to come into manifestation in his Life and experience, this same Mighty Perfection.

There is no possible means of bringing this Perfection into your mind, body, and outer experience, except by knowing and accepting the Mighty Active Presence of God in you. Such full recognition will cause this Inner Power to propel this Perfection of God into your outer visible experience.

I AM putting forth, as a Messenger of this Truth, statements of Truth, which will positively produce results, if unwaveringly held to and used. Students think things do not work, because they do a thing to-day and forget it all next week.

The *desire* for Light and Truth, is the *Presence of God in the desire,* propelling Itself forth into action. For illumination use the statement:

"I AM the full comprehension and illumination

of this thing I want to know and understand."

The day your eyes are opened to see some of these Marvelous, Ascended Beings, the joy will last through eternity.

If one does not take the attitude, that: "I have the ability to do this, he never in the world can accomplish the thing he wishes to do."

The moment you express, "I AM the resurrection and the Life," in thought and feeling, it immediately turns all the energy of your Being to the center in the brain, which is the Source of your Being.

You cannot overestimate the power in this statement. There is no limit to what you can do with it. It was the statement that Jesus used most, in his most difficult trials.

Always know, that when you decree a constructive thing, it is God in you propelling you to do it.

It is the most foolish question imaginable to ask: "Have you proved this in your own experience?" Each individual has to prove it for himself, or it will mean nothing to him. Nothing ever really means anything to anyone, until he uses it.

The feeling carries with it a certain co-existent sight. One often feels a thing with such clearness, that he really sees it from the Inner Standpoint.

As you enter the Ascended State, thought, feeling, seeing, and color are almost simultaneously manifest. Harmonious sound is quiet. This is why ravishing music is the most quieting in its effect, while bombastic music is just the opposite.

BENEDICTION: Thou Mighty, Majestic, Conquering "I AM," we give praise and thanks for our comprehension of Thee, as God Acting in us, and with thy Mighty Presence and Radiance, cause us to feel the Mighty Import of Thy Mighty Truth and Wondrous Presence. When we contemplate Thee, let Thy Mighty Radiance fill us with that comprehending consciousness to know and apply Thy assertions of Truth more and more perfectly. We give praise and thanks for Thy Mighty Perfection and Truth for all those, who look unwaveringly to Thee.

DISCOURSE III

October 10, 1932

SAINT GERMAIN

INVOCATION: Thou Infinite All-Pervading Presence! with Thy Mighty Radiance surging forth throughout the atmosphere of earth, we give praise and thanks for the on-rushing Christ Power of Love and Wisdom, which, with no uncertainty, is raising the consciousness of mankind, above the sordid selfishness of the activity of the outer-self.

We give praise and thanks, that we have become conscious of Thy Mighty Active Presence at all times, and that in the conscious recognition of Thee, Thou dost charge our minds and bodies with Thy pure Presence forever.

I Bring Greetings from the Radiant Host to you all.

THE DISCOURSE

From within the radiance of the Great Electronic Belt I AM projecting this to-day.

From the heart of the Golden City the Twin Rays come forth, upon which are the speech, the Light, and the sound.

The time has rapidly enfolded us, when we must be more aware of the Great Electronic Belts, encompassing all creation from the Godhead to the individual.

The Etheric Belt around the Golden City is impenetrable—far more so than a wall of many feet of steel would be.

So in a lesser degree, may the individual, with sufficient comprehension of the Active Principle of the God Self, surround himself with an Electronic Belt or Circle, which he may qualify in any manner, he may choose, but woe be unto the individual, who qualifies it destructively.

If anyone should be foolish enough to do this, he would find this Belt of electronic force closing in upon his own outer form, and it would be consumed; but those, who with wisdom build and qualify it with God's Mighty Love and constructive power, will find themselves moving in a world untouched by the ignorance of mankind.

The Cosmic Period has arrived, when those, who have attained a certain degree of understanding, must create, apply, and use this Wondrous Electronic Circle. Every creation, that is Self-conscious action, has this Circle of pure electronic force about it naturally, but to a large degree its force is ungoverned, therefore dissipated.

In consciously creating this Mighty Ring of pure electronic force, you stop all leaks in the generation of this Limitless Essence and hold it in reserve, for conscious use and direction. After a few months of this conscious creative activity of and within this Electronic Ring, one will need to be very careful in loosing or directing this force in any manner except by Divine Love.

In the beginning of man's individualization, he was naturally surrounded by this Magic Circle, but as the consciousness was lowered more and more, rents were made in this Great Circle of force, causing leaks as it were, until it has almost entirely disappeared. This, however, was not a conscious creation of the individual, but was a natural enfolding circle.

Now students of the Light must go to work, with no uncertainty, and consciously create this Electronic Belt about themselves—visualizing it perfect—with no rents or breaks in its construction.

Thus, it will be possible to consciously reach within the Electronic Belt of the Godhead, and there receive Limitless Wisdom, Love, Light, and the application of simple laws, by which all creative power is possible.

While the student is admonished to look always, and never forget it, to his own God-Self, which is the Creator of his individualization, yet never has there been a single attainment in which there has not been given the assistance of those still in advance.

There being but the One God, the one Presence

and His All-Powerful Activity, then the one more advanced than the other is but more of the God-Self in action. In this recognition, you will understand why you can feel, "I AM here and I AM there," for there is but the One God-Self anywhere.

When the student can once understand, that the Ascended Host of Masters are but the more advanced consciousness of himself, then he will begin to feel the unquestionable possibilities within his grasp. Whether he speaks to the Godhead direct, to one of the Ascended Masters of Light or to his own God-Self, in reality it makes no difference, for all are One.

Until one does reach this state of consciousness, it does make a difference, for the individual is almost certain to feel a division of the One Self, which is not possible to be made, except in the ignorance of the outer activity of the mind.

When the student thinks of the outer expression, he should at all times be aware, that it is but the outer activity of the One Intelligence, guarding himself at all times, against trying to divide in his own consciousness this One Mighty God-Power, centered in him.

Again I must remind you, that this Limitless Mighty Power of God cannot intrude its wondrous powers into your outer use, except by your invitation. There is only one kind of invitation, that can reach it and loose it, and that is your *feeling* of deep devotion and Love.

When one has generated about him this Electronic Belt or Ring, there is no power that can penetrate it, except Divine Love. It is only your consciousness of Divine Love, that can penetrate within this Great Inner Blazing Belt of the Godhead, through which the Godhead sends back to you,—mark you,—through His Messengers, Transcendent Beings so far surpassing anything of your present conception, that it is not possible in words to convey to you the Majesty of the Love, Wisdom, and Power of these Great Ones.

At this point, let me again remind you, that the student, who will dare to do and be silent, will find himself lifted into the transcendent radiance of this Inmost Sphere; then by experiencing and seeing, will he comprehend this of which I have spoken. The soul, who is strong enough to clothe itself in its Armor of Divine Love and go forward, will find no obstruction, for there is naught between your present consciousness and this Mighty Transcendent Inner Sphere to obstruct the approach of Divine Love.

When you have touched and seen within this Inner Circle you will then understand how imperfect is the present expression of Divine Love. Once one becomes consciously aware of these Great Spheres, to which he may reach, he will find himself fearlessly reaching deeper and deeper within the radiance of this Mighty Intelligent Hub of the Universe, from which all worlds, all creation have proceeded.

There are among you, strong, dauntless, fearless souls, who will understand this, and be able to use it with great blessing to themselves and others. There are those, who will understand and see, that the Presence that beats each heart is *God in Action;* that the activity sending the circulation through the body is God; that the Essence charging forward to vitalize the outer form is *God in Action*.

Then, O beloved students, awake to this—now. Do you not see how great a mistake it is to sink under the ignorance of the outer-self, feeling pain, distress, and disturbance, all created by the ignorance and activity of the outer-self, when a few moments of earnest contemplation will cause one to realize, that there can be but One Presence, One Intelligence, One Power acting in your mind and body, and that is God.

You see how simple, yet powerful, is this Consciousness within you, to loose the full recognition of the Great Pure Activity of God into your mind and body, and let its Wondrous, Transcendent Essence fill full to overflowing every cell.

It seems to me beloved students, that you cannot fail to grasp this simplicity of your true God-Self acting in you. Ever turn to It, praising It, loving It, demanding and commanding It to surge forth into every cell of your body, into every demand of the outer activity, in the home, in your affairs, in business. When your desire is sent forth clothed in The God-Presence, Power, and Intelligence, it cannot fail. It must bring to you that which you desire. Desire is but a lesser activity of decreeing. Decreeing is and should be the recognition of the accomplished desire.

Beloved students, do forever put away any fear of the use of this Great Power. You know without being told that, if you misuse it, you will experience inharmony. If you use it constructively, it will bring such blessings untold, that you can but give praise and thanksgiving for the moment, when you *awakened* to the fact, that this Limitless Power is omnipresent, ever awaiting your conscious direction.

The individual, who has said, that you cannot add one cubit to your height by your thought, has stifled the activity and progress of the individual, for thought and feeling is the Creative Power of *God in Action*.

The uncontrolled, ungoverned use of thought and feeling has brought about all kinds of discord, sickness, and distress. Few, however, believe this, and keep going on and on continually creating by their ungoverned thought and desire, chaos in their world; when they could, as easily as a breath, face about, using their thought constructively, with the motive power of Divine Love, and build for themselves a perfect Paradise within the period of two years.

Even physical science has given proof that the body or outer form completely renews itself within a few months. Then you must see, that with the conscious understanding and application of the True Laws of your Being, how easy it is to cause Perfection to manifest in your entire body, and every organ to leap into its perfect normal activity. In a short time it would not be possible for inharmony to enter your thought or body.

Oh children reaching to the Light! this great privilege is the Open Door of God before you, which none may shut but yourselves. None may obstruct or interfere with it, but yourselves. Fearlessly use your God-given Dominion and Power, and be free. You cannot attain and hold this Perfect Freedom except through consciously applied knowledge.

Now I shall give you a secret, that if understood by the angry or discordant individual, would tear him or her from that destructive activity, even from a purely selfish standpoint.

The angry, condemning person, who sends out destructive thought, feeling, or speech to another—who is poised in his own God-power—receives back to himself the quality with which he charged this power, while the poised person receives the energy which serves him, and which he automatically requalifies by his own poise. Thus, the creator of discord through anger and condemnation, is consciously destroying himself, his world of activity, and his affairs.

Here is a vital point, students should understand. When one consciously reaches within the Inner Electronic Circle of God, he makes his outer expression and activity a channel for the ceaseless outpouring, of the Pure Essence from the Godhead. This in itself, even though he be entirely silent in the outer expression, is one of the greatest services to humanity, which but few not arisen are aware of what it means to mankind.

The one reaching within the Electronic Circle becomes a continual outpouring, and this very radiation alone is a tremendous blessing to all mankind. Thus, aeon after aeon, have there been those unselfish Messengers of God, through whom was poured for the Blessing of those not understanding, the uplifting Presence of this surging energy. When there is one or more found, who can be an outpouring for this great welled-up Presence, it is likened unto the first trickling of a leak in a dam.

As the consciousness is held steady and firm, and as the rent in the dam increases, greater volume of water comes forth, for at last all obstruction is swept away, and the whole force back of it, is poured forth into use. Unlike the water dammed up, that rushes forward dissipating itself—because it is without direction—the God Power, thus loosed, goes direct to the channel of consciousness most receptive, and there builds itself up, awaiting the opportunity to rush forward more and more. Thus, the student of Light, aside from his activity in dispensing the Truth, becomes as it were an artesian well, from the depths of which flows this Mighty Essence of God.

The students should at all times remember, that no matter what their mistakes may have been, God never criticizes or condemns them, but at every stumble which is made, in that sweet loving voice says: "Arise my child, and try again, and keep on trying, until at last you have attained the True Victory and Freedom of your God-given Dominion."

Always, when one has been conscious of having made a mistake, his first act should be, to call on the Law of Forgiveness, and demand wisdom and strength not to make the same mistake a second time.

God being all Love, must have Infinite Patience and no matter how many mistakes one may have made, he can always, once again, "Arise and go unto the Father." Such is the Love and Freedom, within which God's children are privileged to act.

There is only one mighty, invincible, evolving process and that is through the power of consciously generating Love. Love, being the Hub of all Life, the more we enter in, and use it consciously, the more easily and quickly we release this Mighty Power of God, that is always standing as a dammed-up force, waiting to find an opening in our own consciousness, by which it can project Itself.

For the first time in many centuries, the searchlights or Rays from the Golden City over the Sahara Desert, are set into active operation over America and the earth. There may be some individuals, who will see these Rays, not knowing what they are.

Mankind need no longer think that personalities can continue to generate their destructive forces and long survive. Those, who can use this knowledge of the Electronic Circle, should no longer be deprived of its benefits. Give it forth and the warning with it.

Use this statement: "I AM the fulfilled activity and sustaining power of every constructive thing I desire." Use it as a general statement, for the sustaining power is in everything that there is. "I AM here and I AM there" in whatever you want to accomplish, is a splendid way to feel that you are using the One Activity and you thus rise above the consciousness of separation.

BENEDICTION: O Mighty Ones of the Golden City! Glorified are we in Thy Wondrous Radiance. Privileged are we in the use of Thy Great Rays. Blessed are we in the conscious recognition of Thy Mighty Presence. Enfold us forever in Thy Transcendent Light.

DISCOURSE IV

October 13, 1932

SAINT GERMAIN

INVOCATION: Thou Mighty Consuming Flame of God! we bow before Thy Mighty Majestic Power: we rejoice in Thy Directing Wisdom: we rejoice in Thy Presence in the heart of every one of God's Messengers that go forth to direct His Service and Energy to the blessing of mankind. We give praise and thanks that Thy Presence has changed the tide of things, and that Thou art as always, The Mighty Governing Intelligence.

We give praise and thanks that Thy Consuming Fire and Thy Creative Activity, dwelling in the heart of every one of us, is ready to be loosed by the conscious desire into action. We give praise and thanks that Thou art the Consuming Presence everywhere; that "I AM there and I AM here, and I AM the power that makes all things clear."

"I AM the Majestic 'Presence,' " "I AM the Conquering Power," "I AM thy 'Mighty Energy,' " Thy Consuming Flame each hour.

I bring Greetings to you all from the Heart of the Creative Fire.

36

The Creative Fire that I AM is the Flame of God, His Master Presence, anchored in the heart of every-one of God's children. While in some it is but a spark, yet with the right touch that spark can be fanned into a Creative Fire and Consuming Flame.

This Mighty Presence, God, in Its myriad activi-ties, is the Omnipresent Activity that all may use without limit, if they only will dismiss from their recognition the outer appearance, which is but an appearance, and take their attention away from that which has bound them through endless years.

To-day the Scepter of Power and Authority stands in the atmosphere before the Single Eye of every advancing student. At first, they may reach up mentally and take the Scepter of Authority, using it in this way, until before they are scarcely aware of it, they will find it tangible and visible in their use at times.

It is no idle promise that those seeking the Light, may again receive this Dominion. When we go through a footpath in the forest, we know we may re-turn the same way, if we wish, but *we* must make the decision. So after hundreds of years of search in the outer for power and authority, we find that anything that seems to be so is but shifting sand, and to-morrow it may be gone.

By the rejoicing acceptance of your God Do-

minion, you may step firmly upon the sure foundation of the Rock of Truth, which is God, from which
no outer disturbance can ever shake you, once you
know from actual experience.

Students of Truth wonder why they cannot hold a
firm anchor in their decision to hold fast to the God
Presence, which is their Dominion. They do not
analyze their outer expression to see what is lurking there to cause disturbance, question, and doubt,
but for those who will take the authority which is
theirs, and probe deep into their motives, it will be so
easy to pluck out the tares from the Golden Grain,
and soon be free from that disturbance that causes
them to doubt themselves, and the very Presence of
God which beats their hearts.

When students will be honest enough with themselves and their God, The I AM Presence, to pluck
out by the roots anything that is causing disturbance
within them, and be able to feel the Mighty Light
and Radiance of the Great God-Self, will find little
effort in loosing the Great I AM Presence in Love
and Intelligence, that is an ever-sustaining power in
strength, assurance, or whatever you may need, in
order to hold your feet firm upon the Rock of Truth,
which is one of the Great Jewels in God's Kingdom.
Its Dazzling Radiance will enfold you upon the
slightest invitation.

Oh students of to-day! Hold fast to this Mighty

Presence, that beats your hearts, whose Life flows through your veins, whose Energy flows through your mind; you have free will, and can qualify and bless it to your Perfection or imperfection. Always remember—by your failure to turn to this Mighty Presence, when you find you have created inharmony and disorder, you must give yourselves ample time to gain the full recognition of this Mighty Power and give It full activity in your Life.

Do not become impatient because things do not work out as rapidly as you would like them. They can only work according to the speed of your acceptance and the intensity of your feeling.

The Mighty Energy that surges through your mind into your body is the Pure Electronic Energy of God, the Mighty I AM Presence. If your thought is joyously held upon your God-Self as the Source of your Being and Life, that Pure Electronic Energy continues to act unabated, uncontaminated by human, discordant qualification, but knowingly or unknowingly, if you let your thought begin to gather from the discord by which it is so often surrounded, you change the color and quality of this Radiant Pure Energy.

It must act, and you are the one who shall choose how it shall act to you. Don't ever think you can get away from this simple fact. It is an Immutable Law of God, and no human being can ever change it.

Students must understand and maintain this attitude, if they wish to make steady progress.

I tell you beloved students, you may rage and doubt and fear and rebel all you please at self-correction, but it is the open door to your Mighty Illumination and Freedom from all limitation in the outer world of activity.

There are a great many students, when they come to a certain point of understanding—where all the results of their activity are revealed to them, and they look upon the many mistakes that have been made which must be corrected—become despondent, critical, and condemnatory to themselves and God. This is a great mistake again. Everything that is revealed to them, in which they find they have been making a mistake, should make them rejoice exceedingly, that the things are revealed which need correcting. Knowing that God is the power to think, then they know they have the power to correct this, and should joyfully set to work to do so.

The Power of God's Life which beats their hearts is absolute proof that they have the Intelligence and Power of God within them, by which they may dissolve and consume all the mistakes and discordant creation, they have consciously or unconsciously drawn about them. They may say to this undesirable creation: "I AM the Mighty Consuming Flame that now and forever consumes all past and present mistakes, their cause and effect, and all undesirable creation that my outer is responsible for."

It seems so strange that students seem to have such difficulty in fixing the anchorage and recognition of the Limitless Power they are wielding when they say "I AM." When the intellect which is the outer activity knows this, then the students should intensify it with all their power, by the intense feeling of the Truth of this. Then, they would find greatly added speed and power in their active use. I tell you dear students, you have come to a time—when you can use this power with great authority—to free yourselves from the claims of limitation that have bound you so long.

Set about it with joyous determination to put your house in order. If you were going to have a distinguished guest, I doubt not that you would spend days working earnestly, cleaning, washing, polishing, and preparing for this guest. How much more important it is to prepare for this *Great Prince of Love and Peace—The Prince of Consuming Fire,* that dwells within you, and controls the element of fire.

When one thinks of Oromasis, Prince of the Firey Element, it is the Flame of Creative Fire within, that is calling to Him for assistance in the quickening of this Creative Power and brings results unimaginable.

There has been no time in my memory, when there was so much natural assistance at hand for the student of Light, for his use, as there is at this time, and the students should take advantage of this with joyous intensity.

When you speak in the Name, Power, and Authority of the "Mighty I AM" you are releasing limitless energy to do your bidding, to fulfill your desire. Why longer allow doubt and fear to beset you, when: "I AM the open door which no man can shut, into the great opulence of God waiting, surging to press forward to heal, to bless and to prosper you abundantly." Dare to be, to feel, to use this Mighty Authority—God in you.

Beloved students, do you not realize, that you can express Perfection by taking your determined stand with sufficient intensity, that: "I AM the Mighty Electronic Energy flowing through, filling, and renewing every cell of my mind and body—right now." Do you not see, with sufficient intensity of this, in a few minutes or hours you could dispel any disturbing condition in the mind or body, and allow that Mighty Pure Energy to do its work, uncolored, unaffected by any discordant element in your own thought?

You *can* renew any nerve, any organ, and build any member of the body into its Perfection almost immediately. Oh, why not *feel* this, apply it, and as you begin to experience the remarkable results, your confidence will leap into its Perfect Activity, and your mind will have all confidence in this Mighty Presence and Power and its omnipresent limitless use.

When there is a seeming lack of energy, take your determined joyous stand: "I AM the Mighty Presence of this Alert Radiant Energy surging through my mind and body, dismissing everything unlike Itself. I take my stand in this Alert, Radiant Energy and Joy for all time." You can pass this Pure Energy through your mind and body, as I would pass my hand down before you.

At first, because you do not seem to feel any great magnetic electronic force pass over you, does not in any way indicate that you have not received this Mighty Energy that you have commanded with authority to flow through your mind and body.

One may say the same thing to his affairs that may not be according to his desire for Perfect Expression. The student can stand, and call forth the "Mighty Presence of the I AM," send It forth into his business and world, command it to consume everything unlike Itself, and replace all with the Mighty Perfection of God—which I AM. Command it to be Self-sustained, and cause that Perfection to manifest his unceasing authority and power, and cleanse his world of every discordant thing for "I AM the Supreme Authority—*God in Action.*"

We do not need to do this with any tension or to

the extent that we create tension in the action of our bodies, but we can rise in the Supremacy and Dignity of the Authority of God, and cleanse everything needing it. In doing this, one need not speak in a loud voice, but in a very low, masterful tone.

Stand in the room by yourself, and declare: "I AM Master of my world. I AM the Victorious, Intelligence Governing it. I send forth into my world this Mighty, Radiant, Intelligent Energy of God. I command it to create all Perfection: to draw to me the Opulence of God made visible in my hands and use. I AM no longer the Babe of Christ, but the Master Presence grown to Full Stature, and I speak and command with authority."

Thus, one may consume the mistakes and imperfection he may have created, and in the authority of the "I AM," recreate—immediately—the Perfection he desires. Know that it is constantly Self-sustained, so long as you do not intrude upon it the discordant activity of your thought and feeling.

I want so much to have you *feel* that you are the Only Authority in this world or any other so far as your world is concerned. Do not ever fear that the Perfecting of your world is going to disfigure anyone else's world, so long as your intent is not to harm any one. It does not matter what the world about you says, or how much they try to intrude upon you their doubts, fears, and limitations. You are the Supreme

Authority in your world, and all you have to do is to say—when you are beset by those conditions: "I AM the Mighty Magic Circle of Protection about me, that is invincible and repels from me every discordant thought and element, that seeks to find entrance or intrude itself. I AM the Perfection of my world and it is Self-sustained."

Oh beloved ones! it is no longer necessary to wonder, waver, and question: "I AM the Authority." Go on—dare to be—and use this Authority of God, which is expressing in the "I AM" of everything. Why not be fearless. You have been wanting the Presence of the Great Ascended Ones: "I AM the Visible Presence of those greatly beloved Ascended Masters whom I wish to have appear here to me, and whose assistance I desire."

You have come to the point where you can dismiss all discord from your minds. Fill your minds with this Pure Electronic Essence and no discord can enter so long as you keep it filled, with this "Presence." I tell you again, you are the Authority in your world, and if your thought is filled with this Essence, then no discord will touch it. We are going to take this Authority and use it, clear away all discord, and declare with no uncertainty: "I AM the Supremacy of man, everywhere I go—I AM *God in Action.*"

BENEDICTION: Mighty Creative Fire, we give praise and thanks for Thy Great Omnipresence to-day, to heal, to bless, and to prosper everywhere. Enter into the hearts of mankind with Thy Creative Presence and Genius, and let the Full Divine Justice of Thy Supremacy reign throughout the land in all official places.   See—that all authority is in the hands of Thy trained and trusted Messengers, that they may govern fully all governmental offices in America, and be ever divinely sustained—that America be healed, blessed, and forever prosper; that all sinister influence be consumed and forever repelled from within the borders of America.

NOTES

The Host of Angels rejoice at the return of the wanderer who has come back home—who has sought authority so long in the outer, and found only husks.   After his energy is wasted, he comes back home, and there is the Fountain to recharge, rebuild all the discrepancies called old age.   Then, you can stand forth renewed again in the fulness of youth and power, for such is The Way of Life—God's Life.

It keeps the most marvelous vibratory action expressing for each one to speak gently.   It is perfectly wonderful, if you could see the Inner action of it.

Let each one enter into the happiness and Love of Perfect Obedience and liberate the Great Power of God.   If one just lets go of the outer, and enters into the Inner; every discord lets go at once.

ETHERIC CITIES

Over the principal deserts, there are Etheric Cities.   Over the Arizona desert is the Etheric City in America.   There is one over the Sahara and one over the Gobi.   The one over Brazil is the Etheric City for South America.

Humanity should know, and be made to realize that again, again, and again, the inhabitants of cities pass out through so-called death, and re-embody in that same place; because attachments have been formed that draw them back into the same environment again. The student who has to re-embody, should take the command that: "The next time I will be born into a family of Great Light." This would open the door to great speed in his progress.

DISCOURSE V

SAINT GERMAIN

INVOCATION: Thou Mighty Infinite Presence—Thou All-Pervading Healing Presence! descend, and do Thy work. Thou Mighty Infinite Intelligence! give forth Thy Confidence and Strength—fill the mind and body of each one with Thy Radiant Presence—Fill every cell with Thy Radiant Presence. Prove Thy Presence in Thy conquering Mastery and power. Mighty Master Presence within each one—come forth! Erase this outer human-self and hold Thy Dominion now and forever. There is but One Intelligence, Presence, Essence, and Love, and this Thou art. Pour forth Thy Radiance through these outer cloaks of flesh and command Thy Perfection to thus be sustained and manifest.

I bring you greetings from the Great Host ever shedding their Radiance and Intelligence.

Take the Command: "I AM the Pure Electronic Essence that fills my mind and body, and I brook nothing else." God in you is Master of all conditions at all times, say often: "I AM always the Victorious Presence of the Mighty I AM."

Feel the mighty current of Electronic Essence fill

your mind and body, erasing instantly all inharmonious activity and giving you the consciousness of Mastery and Victory.

Command: "Divine Presence! pour Thy Radiance through this mind and body, and see that Thy Wisdom directs always in every outer activity."

THE DISCOURSE

Let us be conscious of the Healing Radiance filling this home. The great need to-day is the healing of the nations and of individuals. As the individual is given assistance through the out-pouring of the Electronic Energy through the mind and body and filling every cell, so in an expanded degree is the nation treated likewise. The nation is a great body of individuals and of Nature's creations. We have the same power, being the individualized Presence of God. Then we know: "I AM everywhere present, and when my consciousness takes on this expansion, I know its energy leaps into action everywhere; in the cells of the body of the world, as well as in the body of the individual." We must come to know that the active Presence of God, All-Powerful, is everywhere present, that there is not a single nook nor corner anywhere that the Active Presence of God is not, and that this Active Presence seizes and binds all human creation, and consumes instantly everything of an inharmonious and undesirable nature.

With the use of the Electronic Belt surrounding the individual, he must understand that he can make this an absolutely invincible protection. Through Its protection Divine Wisdom acts, repelling everything through our conscious action that shall not be taken into the system; and that this Omnipresent Wisdom and Intelligence is always prompting us to refuse acceptance of anything into the system, either through feeling, thought, or food that would in anywise disturb its harmonious activity.

The natural activity of the Currents of Life play everywhere like the play of a searchlight. The outer activity should at all times be an invitation to the receptivity of the Currents of Life which are Pure Cosmic Energy and which are ever flowing through the atmosphere of the earth.

It is true that where there are conditions too dense for It to penetrate, It goes over or under them, so to speak, and finds Its way onward just the same. Every individual, since the beginning of this year, should come to understand that he is walking and moving constantly within the reach of Mighty Healing Currents. Through the power of Cyclopea, the Secret Love Star, and the Rays from the Golden City, currents of Healing Force of tremendous power are consciously directed through the atmosphere of the earth. These, you will understand, by their very nature,—being the Energy of God in Action—are therefore Self-sustained. The consciousness in the individual of their presence will enable him to contact these Rays at any time.

Students who have a feeling of patriotism and who wish to help the nation, should take the stand that these Healing Currents, reach not only individuals, but carry into conditions, environment and official places like an Intelligent Flame, and are doing a work for the protection and uplift of the children of earth, not heretofore set into such powerful action since the creation of this planet.

The more individuals become truly and sincerely conscious of this operation, the more can they become mighty Messengers of assistance in this most unusual work.

Through the conscious manifestation of the mental forces back of the communists is the sinister influence with which we are dealing in this activity. Those, who wish to be true Messengers will meditate upon this idea, until they have grasped the full import of it. They will use their conscious effort, knowing that these currents of Consuming Electronic Energy, consciously directed through the atmosphere of the earth, cannot be interfered with, and that in every sincere, conscious effort of the individual, in his desire to give his assistance, there will flow a consciousness of this Energy that he has not hitherto possessed.

Sometimes there are individuals of such a nature,

that while wonderfully kind and willing, the sudden consciousness that they need to let go of certain kinds of food or other activity is a sort of shock to them. I would say to these individuals that the Divine Intelligence within each one will cause them to naturally let go of the things not in accordance with this Great Presence at every step of the way, when it is necessary. In order for an individual to consciously let go of a thing, he must have something that he feels is stronger to anchor to. As students become conscious of this, the confidence and strength will come to them to take the step.

As I suggested once before, I would consciously, at least once or more a day, stand on the floor and charge the home with this Pure Electronic Energy and keep it charged so that God's very Presence will keep out of the home, food, thought, any kind of presence, and everything that is not in accordance with the desires here.

I would suggest that whenever you find someone is coming, you take the consciousness: "I AM the Pure Radiance of Love enfolding these individuals, and this garment enfolds them when they come and when they leave." When you are conscious of this, you clothe them and they will wear this garment into the home and out of it, and for them it will be a sustaining power.

Those who come into your home are deserving of

assistance and this will enable them to receive the full assistance they desire, and you will love to give.

No matter how great the knowledge attained, we at no time ever have the right to force either the knowledge or the discipline upon anyone. Only as students apply what they hear and receive can they ever know the Reality.

When you say "I AM," you acknowledge the power that breaks down all barriers and conditions of opposition. This human self is just like a starving lion in the jungle. It will tear anything to get what it wants to eat. In this state, the human consciousness will tear its best friend to pieces to get its own way.

In any astral element, there is that human desire element, through which, unless one shuts his mind entirely to the astral world, he will constantly find himself interrupted in a good decision; because he has left that door open to a force far more subtle than is ever found in the outer world. Many think there are good forces in the astral world. I tell you, no good force ever comes from the astral world. Any good force that seems to come from there, must come through it, but it makes its own Tunnel of Light through which it comes.

In the first place, what makes the astral world? There is only one place where the undesirable creation can find a home, and that is the next step to the human activity, which is the astral realm. This realm of astral activity has within it all undesirable creation, accumulated through the centuries. Therefore, it is easy to see at once that no good comes from the contact with the astral realm. IT HAS NOTHING IN IT WHATSOEVER OF THE CHRIST.

There is as wide a difference between the astral realm of activity and what some call the Star Astral, as there is between Light and darkness. However, the so-called Star Astral is again misunderstood. It is really called "Star Astrea." It is really an activity— not a realm, and it is from the fourth sphere. The "Star Astrea" is a Cosmic Being Whose work it is to consume all possible within the astral realm, and to reach individuals whose attention seems to be drawn there. This Great Being will sooner or later clear the understanding of such individuals, and consume their desire for any contact with that unhappy realm. No little children remain in the astral realm. The home of children who leave the earth is in the etheric realm. People who are in the body are in the same sphere when they sleep, as the disembodied. There is a Sustaining Consciousness of the "I AM Presence" that, if one goes forth with it on going to sleep, through that sustaining power one can reach unbelievable heights. If you have the consciousness through the outer expression of this "I AM Presence," and you take this consciousness with you as you go into the other realms, it is a Sustaining Presence that is unbelievable.

There is an activity in the experience life that demands the conscious recognition and use of the "I AM Presence," of *God in Action*. When we take that Consciousness with us through the veil of sleep, the soul is able to function out of the body with almost limitless power.

Suppose there is a seeming need in the physical activity. Before going to sleep we can say this: "Through the Mighty Power and Intelligence which I AM, I go forth while my body sleeps, make conscious contact with, and abundantly fulfill this requirement, no matter what it is."

Knowing that this activity is Self-sustained, it cannot fail in any way. It is a mighty way of setting into motion the "I AM Presence." Whatever the "I AM" commands while the body sleeps must be obeyed.

I knew of one instance of this kind, when there was need of protection. The one using it had a certain consciousness of this Presence. The individual was falling over a cliff, and this "I AM Presence" instantly built up a form, caught the individual, and took him back to safety.

When we enter the conscious path, and we go into any environment, where there might be danger, one should always do some quick definite work on his protection, for until one raises the body, he is always functioning more or less where he is contacting the outer thought of humanity. If the student be climbing the mountains, he must do conscious protective work. *He* must do the protective work, and do it *consciously*.

If the student will always keep up his conscious protection, he will be able to avoid the destruction of other individuals.

Steamship Protection: "God is the Almighty Power protecting and directing this steamship, therefore, it moves in a zone of absolute safety." On the conscious path, you must be up and in action all the time. There are some who might think this is a suggestion of fear, but it is not. It is a recognition of the Omnipresent Protective Power.

Autos: "God is All-seeing and All-knowing, sees ahead, and will naturally avoid undesirable contact." When you say: "God is driving this car," the Vision of God goes ahead, sees blocks and miles ahead, and the prompting will come to go to the street which is clear: "Because God is driving this car, our path is unobstructed in every way."

There are two reasons why students have accidents. First: because they have become angry and opened the door. Second: because the student has laid down on the job.

Whenever we do a thing with a positive dynamic attitude, it gives a confidence to the outer, and it can't fail.

To project an Electronic Belt around another, say:

"I AM the Protective, Electronic Belt around——."
When you say, "I AM the Protective Ring or Belt,"
it means that the Electronic Belt is *instantly*
formed—invincible. Realize that when you say, "I
AM," whatever is commanded is all-powerfully, instantly done. You cannot use the "I AM Presence"
without having instantaneous activity.

Often say: "I AM the Omnipresent, All-powerful,
Protecting Intelligence governing this mind and
body." It is instantly omnipresent there in action
when you say, "I AM." The "I AM" which is everywhere present, is at that point doing the work that
moment. This is the way you set into action, by the
most direct means, the All-powerful Action of the
"I AM," which is *All in All.*

Constantly remind the outer consciousness that,
when you say, "I AM," you have set into action *all*
the attributes of the Godhead.

You are now at a point, when you should have instantaneous activity. When you say, "I AM" in any
condition, it means that instant action is taking place
there by the Greatest Power in the Universe. The
moment you become conscious that "I AM" is the
Full Activity of God, containing all the attributes
of the Godhead, you do that moment have the full
use of that Mighty Power.

Use often: "I AM the Presence producing this
Master home." Get the consciousness of the Mighty

Presence you are using when you are using the "I AM." I have always loved to specify what I wanted to do. If I want health in my body I say: "I AM the Presence charging this body with Pure, Electronic Energy."

When you say: "I AM the Ascension of this physical body right now," then you have accepted, and entered into that action right now. When you are striving for the Light in unlimited action, you are striving for the greatest thing in the world. Fill your world with the "Presence which I AM" and when you do this, feel you are doing it consciously.

If one will take the consciousness: "I AM the Perfect Activity of every organ and cell of my body," then it must manifest. You have but to be conscious of this, and it must be.

Use often: "I AM perfect health now manifest in every organ of my body." Put your confidence in your "I AM" instead of something. Suppose you want great, intelligent activity, say: "I AM the Perfect Intelligent Activity in this body." You cannot do this looking to something outside.

To clear the mind, eyes, and ears:

"I AM the Perfect Intelligence active in this brain."

"I AM the Perfect Sight looking through these eyes."

"I AM the Perfect Hearing through these ears."

Go at these treatments with determination and they cannot fail. You have the reins. Now use them. Avoid all use of words that seem to be a reminder of limited conditions.

When you are conscious of the "I AM" you don't care what anyone in this world does. You must not be concerned about anything but your world. For squaring the circle, use the "I AM" activity. Pay no attention to what anyone says. Just say specifically what you want to produce.

Say again and again: "I AM the only Presence acting in this."

Say: "I AM the only Presence acting in my world."

For finding things: "I AM the Intelligence and All-Seeing Eye which finds this."

You will be amazed at the feeling that grows within, when you do not have to look to anything but the "I AM."

Wipe out of your mind everything but the conscious operation of the "I AM" for It is the most Potent Power possible.

Get the sense of ease about producing these seeming miracles.

Suppose you want to illumine a room, say: "I AM the illumination of this room."

Then you act upon the electrons in the room. The illumining of the atmosphere of a room is as easy as raising your hand. Your ability to illumine a room is just as easy as physically illumining it through the electric lamp. You can just as easily plug into the Universal current of electricity as through the wires.

To make visible the illumination within your own body say: "I AM the visible illumination through this body now." Right within yourself is a focal point.

The "I AM" in you created everything in the Universe.

When you enter into the confidence of the "I AM" It will soon do away with all obstruction.

Use often: "I AM the Consuming Power and Presence of every bit of fear, doubt, and questioning in my outer activity concerning this Invincible Activity of the 'I AM.'" Keep this up, and you will always know instantly what to do. You can take this and use it, and thus remove every obstruction to the "I AM Activity." When you operate consciously, you know positively it is done.

The consciousness of an individual clothes the form with that individual's own concepts of it. When these are drawn about an individual, who has generated a certain energy, they impose upon him nothing but the things in his own world.

Whenever you feel a sudden joy impulse, grasp it, use it, and decree.

BENEDICTION: Thou Mighty Infinite Intelligence! We give praise and thanks for Thy Mighty Comprehension and Mighty Manifestation in the consciousness of those present. We give praise and thanks, that: "I AM the Perfect Understanding in operation and that, I AM everywhere present, performing all required to be done. I AM the illumination of everyone who looks to me. I AM the radiant intelligent activity in the minds of all mankind. I AM the Master acting in the brain of everyone of humanity, causing Love, justice, peace, harmony, and Perfection to manifest to our beloved America."

DISCOURSE VI

October 20, 1932

SAINT GERMAIN

INVOCATION: Thou Mighty, Infinite Presence! Creator of all that is, always majestic in Thy Conquering Presence, we give power only to Thee. We forever withdraw all power we have ever given to outer things, and stand serene in Thy Majestic Presence, Love, Wisdom, and Power. Knowing that, "I AM here and I AM there and I AM everywhere, then I AM serene in Thy Majestic Presence, manifesting Thy Love, Wisdom, Power, and Judgment: that I have Thy foresight and see far beyond human possibilities." I give praise and thanks that I, now and forever, acknowledge and accept only Thy Mighty, Victorious Presence in all things, in my Life, my world, my mind, and my body.

I give praise that I have placed about each form, Thy Magic Circle, invincible, impenetrable, to anything unlike Thee. I stand guard over my Life, body, mind, world and affairs, that nothing manifest unlike Thee. We thank Thee.

THE DISCOURSE

Keep reminding the outer activity, the outer consciousness, that when I say, "I," I AM using the

62

Infinite God-Power. When I say, "I AM," I have set that power into motion to successfully accomplish whatever the idea is, that has been held in consciousness, or whatever idea the attention has been held upon. Sincere students should not forget this for a single hour, until that Truth becomes so fixed in the outer activity, that it automatically acts.

Therefore, you will see how perfectly ridiculous it is to say: "I AM sick, I AM financially embarrassed," or that there seems to be a lack of anything. I tell you, that you cannot possibly be affected, if you will hold fast to this idea. Then use it.

When you seem to have a cold, you do not need to be told to use a handkerchief. Then why do you need to be reminded that the outer activity has but one power by which to move itself about, and that is the "I AM Presence," God in you? The unfortunate thing about sincere students is, that they will not meditate often enough upon this Truth, for its marvelous Presence to come into activity.

Know that: "I AM the majestic, victorious Presence, filling all official places," and know it with certainty in your minds. If any of the students will sincerely take hold and use this, they will be blest for so doing.

Guard yourself in the outer contact constantly, that you do not unknowingly accept the appearance of things or the fear of so-called financiers. God governs your world, your home, your business, and that is all with which you are concerned. Do not ever fear that you are running amuck with your imagination, when you sense and feel the nearness of the full manifestation of that Mighty, Individualized Presence. Rejoice! believe in the Mighty Presence that holds in its embrace everything in this world, that you can desire or use. You are not dependent on the outer things. With the joyous entering into this Mighty Power and Presence that contains all, do you not see, how you would be provided for, if everything were cut loose?

I want you to feel, joyously accept, and with all your Being know, that the power of precipitation is no myth. It is real. Those who enter into this feeling, deep enough, will have the precipitation of anything they want.

Children have been chastised for seeing Angelic Beings, and for manifesting an Inner Perception. It is the parent of that child that should be chastised, and well at that, for daring to interfere with the God-given freedom of that child. If grown-ups would live more, in that conscious imaging and acceptance of these Mighty and Great Presences, of whose very existence most of humanity doubts, they would feel their Presence and uplifting, sustaining intelligence.

My Beloved Ones! if suddenly, we find ourselves needing courage or strength: "I AM there surging forth, supplying this instantly." If I need harmony in my mind or body, then: "I AM there, supplying it instantly," and I do not need to wait.

Do not give a thought to the world or individuals, who do not understand these things. Go right on, rejoicing in the visible, active Presence, precipitated into your Life and use of whatever you wish.

Our outer common sense, so-called, must tell us, that unless we expect, accept, and rejoice in the "Presence" of the thing we want, how in the name of God can we expect to have it? The poor, insignificant, outer-self struts itself about saying: "I AM too important to give attention to these childlike fairy-stories." Well let me say to you, that one day the individuals, who say this, will be only too glad to listen to those fairy stories, and fill their minds with those ideas that they may come forth.

In every instance in the outer contact of the world of business, whenever there is a negative condition, that seems to touch your world in any way, instantly take your firm stand: "I AM the precipitation and Visible Presence of whatever I desire, and no man can interfere with it."

This is a Mighty Truth. When I speak of precipitation in this manner, I do not only mean through the invisible but through any channel, for all is a precipitation; it is only a little difference in activity.

When I recognize, who I AM, then I have entered into the "Great Silence," wherein is God's greatest activity. This recognition should bring great revelations to the individual, if he holds to it with joyous acceptance.

In your outer experience, the use of any activity, develops your strength to greater and greater efficiency, does it not? If one can apply this in the outer activity, do you not see how much more important it is to the Inner Activity? The more you put it into use the greater the power you put into it. Know you can do it with the Inner Spiritual things far greater and quicker than in the outer things, for with Spirit, the power acts instantly. There is no waiting when the "I AM" acts.

The fact that we give credence to development of the muscular system by use, should make us realize that the same effort given to the exercise and recognition of the Inner Power, would naturally produce far greater results. For instance, man is supposed to perform certain physical exercises in order to develop his muscles. I have in my students, many, many times enabled them to produce powerful muscles in a symmetrical, beautiful body without having taken a single exercise to do it. It is the same with the exercise of your Inner Faculties in bringing forth the Inner Power.

In all development either of the Inner or the outer, the first part of the exercise is mental. Here, we must know that there is only one power and energy to use, and that is from the "I AM God Presence" in you. Therefore, the exercise of your Inner Faculties is necessarily mental—called mental—but I say to you it is *God in action,* because you cannot form a thought without the Intelligence and Energy of God to do it. Therefore, your mental activity is the Energy of *God in action.* Now you see how easy and possible it is, to make a strong physical body without lifting your hand in physical exercise to do it.

Most scientific, medical, and men of physical culture, will deny this, but I assure you it is only because they have not become aware of, or thought deeply upon, the energy or power that is acting, because no kind of activity can take place except by the use of this Inner energy and power.

Individuals allow the impingement of doubts and fears to rush in and overwhelm them, when it comes to the recognition of these great faculties, which are free for their use at any time. You see they are but submerged, as it were by the outer, like a cork that has been pushed beneath the water, which, when released by a little effort pops up to the surface into use.

I must say it is positively pitiful, when earnest students spend so many years, straining at intervals to gain the use of these faculties and then, because they do not operate immediately, relapse into a state of inactivity, until something spurs them on and then relapse again. Persistent, determined recognition of this "I AM Presence," will take you through anything to absolute certain accomplishment, unless you lay down on the job.

I see, and especially at this time, a goodly number of individuals who with a little encouragement and description of the simple use of these faculties, will quickly leap into their freedom and especially those, who have this verbal instruction and the radiation that goes with it.

Is it not appalling, that Sons and Daughters of God will submit to the binding claims of limitation, when with persistent effort and determination, they would open the door and step through into this great Inner Chamber, filled with such Dazzling Light, jewels, gold, and substance from which every kind of food in the Universe can be precipitated? Then, with this Truth plainly before them, these individuals still hesitate, through unbelief, to step through, take this scepter and be free.

Beloved Ones, again I say to you: "*Sing* the great melody of the 'I AM' conquering Presence." Sing it in your hearts *continuously*. *Feel* it with all your ability, determined to use it. Hold fast to that determination and the knowledge and the way will steadily open to give you that Mastery, which is your Eternal Freedom. Just keep joyously knowing that you are through the veil now.

Whatever Mastery the individual has gained over himself, his affairs or his world, is always and should be a Sacred Chamber, an Inner Sanctuary upon which no other inquiring individual may intrude. No one may attain Mastery through the desire of the outer to find the Mastery within another.

To seek, find, and apply the Law of one's own Being is the student's sure road to Mastery, and only when the individual has attained it himself, may he really understand what True Mastery is. There is only one Mastery to be sought and that is over one's own outer-self.

One might walk beside a Master for years and not discover it until his own Inner Faculties revealed the fact. One might live in the same house with a Master for years and not know it, until some crisis arose to be handled, and thus the real power be revealed.

For a Master to discuss or disclose his own attainment of Mastery, would be to dissipate his own forces, and may not be done at any time.

If a student be fortunate enough to have a beautiful experience, and then discuss it with others, there is usually so much doubt poured at him, that he soon begins to doubt himself. It is really funny how convincing someone else's argument can be. If a student will listen to the argument of someone else, why not be at least as fair to his own God-Self, and listen to

Its power and good as expressed through the Inner Experience?

The moment doubt begins to enter, more doubt rushes in. The same with the "I AM." If you put your attention upon It, It rushes forth more and more. Where the conscious attention is fixed, there the energy pours. Dear Ones, do you not see, when you want something revealed or to be inspired in some way, do you not see: "I AM that?" The moment you say, "I AM," you set in motion this power that has inherent within It all these faculties. It has all substance, and must take on whatsoever form the attention of the mind is fixed upon.

The "I AM" is the Fathomless Mind of God. In reaching for understanding, the average student is but contacting the recurring memory of that, which has been, instead of going into the Heart of God and bringing forth that, which never has been.

Individuals and students many times do not and will not realize, that there have been many civilizations of vast attainments, which are entirely unknown to the outer world to-day. Atlantis and Lemuria, or the Land of Mu, as credited by a few to-day are but fragments of the great civilizations that have been.

To do unusual things: The students who wish to do this, take the determined stand: *"I AM the Heart of God, and I now bring forth ideas and accomplishments that have never been brought forth before."*

Consider only: "I AM that, which I wish to bring forth." The "I AM Presence" is the Heart of God. You are immediately in the "Great Silence," the moment you say—"I AM." If you recognize, that you are the "I AM," then whatever you declare is manifest that moment.

To believe, is to have faith it is true. There is an interlocking of belief and faith. In the beginning, a thing is belief, and if held to, it becomes faith. If you do not believe a thing is true, you cannot bring it into manifestation. If you do not believe, "I AM a thing," how can it act for you?

The old saying: "There is nothing good or bad, but thinking makes it so," is an absolute truth.

When you know that God's energy comes forth into the individual, absolutely pure and Perfect, then you must realize, that it is the individual, who qualifies that energy and imposes his own impure quality upon it. This Pure God-Energy is projected forth by the conscious effort of the individual, and he must impose some kind of a quality upon it, for that is his privilege as a Creator.

Every one is constantly qualifying this energy, which is pouring forth continually. Each one is continually pouring his color into it, through his own consciousness.

Every activity of the outer, that qualifies, carries with it the inherent faculty of sound and color. No activity of any kind can take place, that has not sound and color inherent within it. God's Perfection, naturally has no discoloration within it. Within the outer faculty, which gives quality to a thing, is where the discoloration takes place. Every student *must* take the responsibility of his own activity in qualifying the energy he sends forth.

The mind cannot act upon anything, that has not Intelligence inherent within it. Do not allow yourself, in the human sense, to consider the element of time in anything you do, but enter into a thing joyously, and stick to it until it does manifest.

Be like a blow torch. If you will hold steady on the Mighty God Presence, as the Actor doing the thing, you will enter into the fulness and Perfection of everything, ready for your use now. All permanent accomplishment must be by the Self-conscious effort of the individual.

Q. What is sympathy?

A. It is but agreement with imperfection. Whatever you do, be adamant before human sympathy. Watch, that you do not allow yourself to be dragged down into quicksand, when you can use wings to lift yourself above its destruction. Judge not, but keep joyously entering into the "I AM Presence" and all things will manifest Perfectly.

For any imperfect condition, especially old age, use: "I AM the Perfection of that individual."

No matter what is said in the outer world, you must be unaffected by it, for you are coming to this Perfection, and you must bring it about consciously.

If you do not watch, you can let in an expression in a moment, that can follow you for years, if you do not erase it. When you are consciously using the Great Law *know* that the active power of God's thought, knows its direction, goes, and performs Perfectly. Consciously charge the "I AM Intelligence" to use whatever is necessary. Say: "I AM Intelligence, qualify this with whatever is required."

For Healing: I had one student, who so qualified the Electronic Circle about him with the power of healing that he was called, the "Healing Shadow." Of course it was not the shadow that healed, but the moment people contacted his Electronic Circle they were healed, instantly.

Q. Understanding God as Love, why did God individualize Himself?

A. In order to have something to love.

Q. Why were the Rays divided?

A. In order to express Love.

Love is the "Active Principle of God." When you are loving, you are enfolding what you are loving in that "Robe of God," that Radiant Presence and activity.

Never condemn. Try always to understand whenever there seems to be a wrong sex activity, and lift the consciousness of the individual, by focusing the attention upon a high ideal of some kind, in order to control the thought so the sex activity can come under conscious control of the individual, through the use of his own will.

The proper clean use of the sex is for the expansion and expression of Love in the pro-creation of a form that the incoming soul may have an harmonious and loving disposition and temperament. The thought and feeling of the parents are the influencing molding activity. The nature of the Life Principle of the individual is to love.

BENEDICTION: Infinite God of Love! we give thanks for Thy Gracious Out-Pouring to-day, for Thy Mighty Radiance filling all things everywhere. We give praise and thanks that we have entered into Thy World, where everything is so fair, where Thy Radiance, creative with every thought, brings into Perfection all things held within our thought.

NOTES

Raising the body: Nada raised her body 2,700 years ago. In the case of three raising the body at one time; they might ascend at the same moment, or within a few weeks or months.

Controlling an Animal: Use: "I AM here and I AM there, and I command silence there." Also, look the animal in the eye, and know that the Love of God controls it.

The difference between Divine Compassion and human sympathy is as great as that between Light and darkness. Divine compassion holds the student's attention anchored to the "Mighty I AM Presence," calling it forth to produce Perfection. Human sympathy is a rushing forth of energy, qualified by a feeling of imperfection, and but intensifies the imperfection already manifesting.

DISCOURSE VII

October 24, 1932

SAINT GERMAIN

INVOCATION: Thou Mighty, Silent Watcher! even as Thou hast before thee the Cosmic Crystal, send forth Thy Rays, anchoring them in the hearts of God's Children. Teach them obedience to the Great, Cosmic Laws. Teach them obedience to the Light. Fill their hearts and minds with Thy Peace, with Thy Silence, with Thy Poise. Let the rejoicing of Thy Heart fill their hearts every one even to overflowing, with Thy Substance and Pure Electronic Force that brings with It Thy Immeasurable, Infinite Blessings.

Let each one *feel* Thy Omnipresent, Watchful Care, Thy Sustaining Love, Wisdom, and Power.

THE DISCOURSE

I bring you greetings from the Great Host of Light who watch attentively the outpouring of divine radiance, whose great Love, peace, and Light always enfold you, as Messengers of the Light, giving always strict obedience to the Great Light.

Obedience of all manifestation is the first demand of the Great Host. When the command went forth: "Let there be Light!" obedience was the first activity,

76

consequently Limitless Light was at hand. It is so with all outer activity of the One Active Principle, God. The first activity of the outer should be to give perfect obedience to that Inner Presence. Thus, is it enabled to receive harmoniously the unadulterated Pure Essence, and so it should be with friends, with relatives, with associates, and with all outer contact of individuals.

There should always be this wondrous grace of Love, Light and obedience. It matters not the age of the individual. Still the outer expression often, for its need is obedience to the Great Inner Light. When the impulse surges forth to argue, criticize, or feel a resistance, it is your signal that the outer is intruding itself to demand attention. Then is the time, by the power of your free will, to command the outer to be silent and obey the "I AM Presence."

It is useless to argue any point. Silence the outer, and then in loving obedience, give the instruction. In this way, it can come forth unobstructed.

When students have entered the conscious path, the slightest intimation of disturbance or resistance of any kind should be followed *instantly* by silencing all outer activity, and declaring: "I AM the obedient, intelligent activity in this mind and body, I AM the governing power and do govern it harmoniously."

It matters not upon what plane or in what sphere of activity the Son of God—that is, the Son or

Daughter of God—acts, obedience to its Laws or the Divine Laws of the sphere in which he is acting, is always imperative to his steady onward progress.

Some day, I hope in the near future, we shall take up for consideration the elements of outer activity which are most disturbing, and the effect of their activity upon the body. I do not wish to do this, however, until the students are strong enough to hear the truth of this activity without a single twinge of resistance or self-condemnation, because to start an activity within the individual of either condition would be a mistake upon my part.

I spoke sometime ago about the student keeping on guard to watch that in an unguarded moment, he did not find himself unknowingly entertaining some feeling of resistance, criticism, or some activity which he later discovered had been acting.

Every student should constantly use many times a day—for it only requires a minute—and silently declare: "I AM the invincible guard established, sustained, and maintained over my mind, my body, my home, my world, and my affairs." Keep conscious that this guard, being the "I AM Presence," naturally has Infinite Intelligence. This will establish an intelligent guard and activity about you that does not have to be constantly repeated.

Again, we come to the point where every time we use the expression "I" or "I AM," we know that It is

the full power of Love, Wisdom and Intelligence acting. Use frequently: "I AM the full liberation of Divine Love acting."

Now as a preparatory activity for the day, I would
suggest that the students with great joy and firmness,
after having refreshed themselves in the morning,
would silently declare—knowing that the power of the
declaration is Self-sustained: "I AM the governing
Love, Wisdom and Power with its attendant intelligent activity that is acting to-day in every single thing
that I think or do. I command this Infinite Activity to
take place every moment, and be the sustaining guard
about me, and that I move, speak, and act only in
divine order." Then during the day whenever you
think of it, take the firm consciousness: "I AM the
commanding, governing Presence moving everywhere before me during the day, commanding perfect
peace and harmony in all activity."

In this manner, you will lock the door open, for
the continuous outpouring of this Inner Intelligent
Presence which will transform your world, and keep
you from contacting inharmony of any kind, enabling
you to have that steady flow of Inner peace and
harmony in all outer contact.

It matters not what the manifestation may be
within the body or without, the student must take his
firm stand that his body is the "Temple of the Most
High Living God." This is an unquestionable Truth,

and this attitude consciously maintained will more rapidly bring the body into the Perfect Activity which was intended from the beginning. I say to the students in all sincerity, there is no possible way of attaining a quality or a desired attribute without claiming it. The outer has drifted into a limited consciousness of declaring it did not have the desired quality and of course it could not manifest it under those conditions. The thought of the student often is: "Well I have been holding this idea for a long time, but it doesn't manifest, it doesn't work." This is positive proof that somewhere in the consciousness there was lurking a doubt, possibly unknown to the individual.

I tell you that no matter what appears on the surface, if you will continually with firm determination claim the quality, condition, or things you desire, and go right on claiming them with that firm determination, they will find expression in your use, just as certain as you do this; but I cannot urge you too strongly always to keep on guard in this matter, for the outer, when you have tried a thing for a few hours, days, or months and it seems not to have appeared, immediately begins to say: "It's no use, if it were going to have acted, it would have by this time." Such a thing as failure is absolutely impossible when you have set the power of the "I AM"—God in you—in action to accomplish a given purpose, if you hold unwaveringly to it with determination.

Many times, I have seen students nearing wonderful achievement, wonderful victory and freedom, and this outer attitude of, "not yet being accomplished," would rush in, get their attention, to such an extent that it would either retard greatly their progress or shut the door indefinitely.

The student should compel himself or herself to hold before the mind this truth—that when the "I AM" Power and Presence is set in motion, It can no more fail in its accomplishment than the Universe stop its activity. For this "Mighty I AM Presence" to fail in its accomplishment would mean that the Universe would instantly be thrown into chaos. Such is the certainty and power of the I AM accomplishment. It simply cannot fail unless the outer obstructs the way.

Every student should guard with great watchfulness that he does not use the "I AM" in negative expression for when you say: "I AM sick, I have failed, I AM not accomplishing this thing as I should"— you are throwing this mighty energy into action to destroy the thing you wish to accomplish. This always happens whenever you use the word "I" for that is the release of the Universal Power.

Knowing that the "I AM" is you, then when you say: "My head aches, my stomach is out of order, my intestional tract is disturbed," you are throwing the energy into those parts to act according to the thing you have decreed, for when you say "MY," it is the same energy acting, because there is only one person who can say, "I" or "MY," and that is you decreeing for your world.

Any expression which can only be used for yourself is including the energy and activity of the "I AM Presence." The correct attitude to take, if some organ seems to be rebellious, is to instantly declare and hold fast to it: "I AM the only and Perfect Energy acting there. Therefore, every appearance of disturbance is instantly corrected." This is the important point to keep before the student. If through habit, you have thought that certain remedial agencies gave assistance, then use these sparingly, until you gain sufficient Mastery to govern entirely by your "I AM Presence."

I assure you, that even though you think that this remedial agent has given you relief, it is still the same "I AM Presence" that has given the remedial agency the power to give you relief. For instance, I have watched the medical world for many centuries, and when one individual of so-called authority, says that a certain remedy is no longer of use, it is but a short time, until it disappears entirely.

The question within the mind of all thinking individuals is that certain herbs or remedial agencies have a certain natural chemical action corresponding to the element within the body. I say to you:

What gives or makes the chemical affinity? The power of your "I AM" which enables you to think.

Thus, when you come to go round the circle of activity, you will find that there is only One Intelligence and Presence acting and that is the "I AM"— God in you.

Now, why not look this Truth square in the face? Take your stand unwaveringly with the "I AM Presence," *God in Action,* in you, and know that, It is the only Life in you and all things or remedies, to which you alone give power.

Is it not much better to go directly to this "Great I AM Presence" and receive Its all-powerful, limitless assistance which cannot fail, than to give power to something that leads you around Robin Hood's barn to get assistance from something in the outer to which you have given the power?

I know it is not easy for students to turn away from old, old habits or dependence upon certain remedial agencies, but a little thought and meditation upon this fact, will simply compel the outer reason and dependence upon these outer things to give way completely before the "Great I AM Presence."

There is no way of convincing the student upon this most vital of questions, except he apply the wisdom and knowledge with unwavering determination, until he proves for himself the active truth of these simple things and there is no one who can tell to what degree the student can apply this, for only he alone by trying may know. Many times the Inner accumulated energy is such that the student is amazed with the results when he begins to apply this.

The Oriental phrase for "I AM" is "OM." That means the same thing that "I AM" is beginning to mean to the Western World. For myself, I like very much the use of the "I AM" because Its very expression indicates *"God in Action in the individual."* "OM," as understood by the Orientals, is a Universal Presence, and not nearly so apt to give the student the consciousness of the "I AM Presence" *acting in the individual,* as the use of "I AM." This largely explains the reason for the condition in India to-day. Hundreds of thousands in India, through the confusion of many castes, have fallen into the error that the intonation of "OM" was all that was required in their lives. While this brings a certain activity in hundreds of thousands of cases, it does not bring the energy of that activity into the individual's action, and so is of little benefit.

The method of the Ascended Masters throughout the ages, from time immemorial, has been the conscious use of the "I AM Presence," the recognition and full acceptance of *God in Action, in the individual,* which more and more brings into the individual the Full Intelligent Activity of the God Presence—The Godhead.

Those Orientals who have reached great attainment, which many of them have, have become aware of this True Activity through their sincere meditation. Perhaps the simplest, most powerful, single thing that the individual can keep himself reminded of, is that, when he says: "I AM," he is knowingly or unknowingly setting into action within himself the Full Unadulterated Energy of God.

Energy becomes power through conscious use. The fact that individuals are in human embodiment is the command to raise the world of the individual into Perfect Activity. When the consciousness of the individual is raised, everything in the world of that individual is raised into the Inner Activity.

"O Mani Padme Hum" really means God in Action in the individual. Use the "I AM" instead of OM at all times, because many of you have been embodied in an Indian embodiment. At one time you knew that use, and to prevent it calling forth a lesser use, use the "I AM" now to take you to the Full Height.

Whenever you say "I AM," you are setting the Pure Energy of God into motion uncolored by human concepts. This is the only way of keeping the pure energy of God uncontaminated by human qualification. Enormous results can be had in a short time by the determined use of these affirmations:

"I AM this pure inspiration."

"I AM this pure 'Light' right here in action" (Visualize this through the body now.)

"I AM this pure revelation of everything I want to know."

Hold the reins of power forever within yourself. People are afraid of just embracing the Great God power and letting it operate. What is there to fear in God? Its operation is Pure and Perfect and if you do not reach out to embrace the Great Pure God-power, how can you expect to use It and have Perfection? You must claim It for your own. To say: "I AM the Ascended Being, I wish to be now," immediately enfolds the outer in That Raising Presence. "I AM my Eternal Liberation now from all human imperfection." Realize who "I AM" is.

You have to use terms of explanation up to a certain point. Know: "This body is the Temple of the Living God and is ascended now." The human side is such a doubting, criticizing Thomas. All instruction is but to give the individual student a chance to prove it within himself, by applying and using the explanation of the "Law" given. Say often: "I AM the governing power of this activity and therefore, it is always normal." There is no human being in the Universe who can recognize this "I AM Presence" for another. In your recognition of this "I AM Presence" as who you are, every step you gain is a permanent accomplishment, and there can be no retrogression.

BENEDICTION: Thou Infinite All-pervading Presence whose Active Intelligence governs all who look unto Thee, fill each one who seeks the Light with Thy Mighty Inner Light. Hold each one closer and closer in the "Great I AM Presence" that It fill the world of everyone with Thy Great, Great Perfection, and that the consciousness of each individual desires only that Great, Great Presence and Perfection.

NOTES

All jewels are a high activity of God's Substance. The more intense the fire, the greater the purifying power. Gold does not long for or adhere to anything else, all other metals or alloys cling to it. Gold is this way, because it is of a pure element.

In all kinds of fuel activity there is at some point a golden flame. All consuming of outer substance at some point is always red for the red color is the throwing off of the imperfection and impurity. If the impurity were not there the substance would go from the outer immediately into the golden flame.

DISCOURSE VIII

October 27, 1932

Saint Germain

INVOCATION: Thou Mighty All-pervading Presence—Thou All-pervading I AM! we give praise and thanks for the happiness pervading those under this radiation. We give praise and thanks that the Simple Key to Perfect Happiness may be given to bless and to anchor these Children of God into their own firm dominion. We give praise for the harmony maintained within each student and that they feel the necessity to continue it. We give praise that "I AM" everywhere present controlling every outer activity and bringing it into Perfection.

I bring Greetings to you always.

THE DISCOURSE

That, which everyone seeks is happiness, sometimes called bliss, and yet many, who have sought so earnestly, have unknowingly continued to pass by the key to this happiness.

The simple key to Perfect Happiness and its inherent sustaining power, is self-control and self-correction. This is so easy to accomplish, when one has learned, he is the "I AM Presence," and Intelligence, controlling and commanding all things.

Surrounding each individual is a thought-world, created by him or her. Within this thought-world is the seed, the "Divine Presence," the "I AM," which is the only acting Presence there is in the Universe, and which directs all energy. *This energy can be intensified beyond any limit through the conscious activity of the individual.*

The "Divine Presence" within, is likened unto the pit or seed of a peach, the thought-world around It unto the pulp of the peach. The pulp represents, not only the thought world created by the individual, but also the Universal Electronic Substance, ever present waiting to be acted upon by the conscious determination of the individual, to be precipitated into his visible use, as the form of whatsoever he may desire.

The sure pathway, to the understanding and use of this conscious power, comes through self-control. What do I mean by self-control? First: The recognition of the "I AM Intelligence" as the only Acting Presence. Second: That knowing this, we know there is no limit to the power of Its use. Third: That individuals, having been given free will and choice, do create in the world about them, whatsoever their thought, through their attention, is held firmly upon.

The time has arrived, when all must understand, that thought and *feeling* are the only and Mightiest Creative Power in Life or in the Universe. Thus, the only way to the definite use of the full power of one's thought and feeling, which is *God in Action,* is through Self-control—self-correction—by which one may quickly reach the attainment, the understanding, whereby he may direct and use this creative thought-power without any limit whatsoever.

When sufficient Self-control is attained, it enables the individual to hold the thought steady upon a given desire, likened unto the flame of an acetylene torch—held immovable. Thus, thought and *feeling* held upon a given desire unwaveringly, with the consciousness, that it is the "I AM Presence and Intelligence" thinking, that it is *God in Action,* then will they understand that they may bring into visibility— precipitate into visibility—whatsoever they desire.

It has been proved in a thousand ways, that the effect of a thing cannot bring happiness. Only by the understanding of the cause operating, may the individual become Master of his world. Each individual, knowing that he is the Creator of his own world and what he wishes to have manifest in it, will understand that he has at no time any right to create anything discordant in another's world. Thus, is each individual left free to meet the effect of his own creative cause.

I rejoice exceedingly, to see the success with which each student under this radiation, is coming into the Mastery and control of the outer-self. Here I must say to them: "Beloved Students! could you but understand, and see the magnificent splendor of achievement before you, through asserting Self-control over the outer activity, you would bend every effort, every moment to attaining Control and Mastery over all outer expression."

Thus, will you be enabled to maintain the needed harmony, through which the Inner Mighty Power of the "I AM Presence" is liberated into your conscious and visible use. Let use disabuse the minds of these beloved students of the sense of time, distance, and space.

The key, which opens the entrance to all higher spheres above you, lies in the simplicity and firmness of this Self-control. All students should dwell earnestly upon the great truth, that: "Where your consciousness is, there you are, for I AM everywhere."

Long dwelling in consciousness, that there was space, great distance, or that there is time, is all but the outer creation of man. Therefore, to step through this gossamer veil, that separates your outer consciousness from its Full Inner Power and Activity, *is but a state of thought and feeling*.

Those who are reaching to the "Light" so earnestly, desiring to live in and be "Children of the Light," are dwelling constantly in these higher spheres. The beauty of these spheres, surpasses the fondest imagination of the outer consciousness. When you enter them consciously and at will, you will find all creation there just as tangible as your physical buildings are here.

To take your firm stand: "I AM the power of my complete Self-control—forever sustained," will make it easier for you to gain this Mastery. Students must be conscious, that when they recognize the "I AM Presence" acting, it is impossible for It to be interrupted or interfered with in any way. Know there is no time nor space, then the knowing of the vastness of eternity is within your grasp. To enter a higher sphere than your physical world, in full consciousness, is but an adjusting or changing of your consciousness. How do we do this?

A. By knowing we are consciously there.

Affirm Often: "Through the power of the Electronic Circle, which I have created, I AM no longer touched by any doubts or fears. I joyously grasp the scepter, which I AM and step boldly forth into any of these higher spheres, that I wish, retaining perfectly clear conscious memory of my activity there."

In this way, one may quickly find himself enjoying Limitless Freedom and the Perfect Happiness of being active in any sphere he chooses.

To be aware of what is a thousand years in advance is as easily and readily attained, in fact more so, as going to your library in search of a book.

The great delusion, the outer consciousness of mankind has built up, creating time and space in its belief, has been the great stumbling block to humanity's freedom.

Those, who have reached the great disillusionment, that wealth or the outer effect of things cannot bring happiness, will understand with great blessing, that within their own creative thought, power, and *feeling,* are held Perfect Happiness, Perfect Freedom and Perfect Dominion.

When the student once understands, that whatsoever he connects himself with through his attention, he becomes a part of to the degree of the intensity with which his attention is fixed, he will see the importance of keeping his attention off the seeming destructive angles of human experience, no matter what they are.

To discuss the seeming inability, shortcomings, or faults of your friends and associates, but builds that element, upon which your discussion rests, within your own consciousness, and also adds to that appearance, which seems to be in the other individual.

Because there are black magicians in the world, certain of God's Children, who are misdirecting and contaminating the Pure Electronic Energy of the "I AM Presence," is no reason why we should let our attention rest upon that fact, just because we are aware of it. Our business is to hold the attention free to rest within our own Self-control, compelling it by the conscious action, to rest on whatsoever we choose.

Few understand, that when their attention is called to some destructive thing, how much and how often, they allow the attention to revert back to it, or if another has displeased them in some way, how much and how often the attention returns to that incident, when they have the full power to control their attention, and make it obey their command.

Few, even among earnest students, yet understand what a mighty power their faculty of attention becomes under their *controlled* use.

I wish so much to impress upon the students, how foolish it is to be affected, displeased, or disturbed by the imaginary activities of the ignorance of the outer-self. When they once know: "I AM the only All-powerful acting Presence in my mind, my body, and my world," they cannot possibly be affected or disturbed by any of their associations in the outer world. They must know then, that they are entirely immune from hurt or disturbance of the outer mind, of other individuals, no matter what they try to do.

With this understanding, or by giving willing attention to this Great Truth, they will soon find a peace, happiness, and Self-control operating about them to such an extent, that no outer condition, disgruntled comment, or disturbance of their associates could in any wise disturb them, their world, or their affairs. As soon as the individual becomes aware that he really has control of his own creative thought, power and *feeling,* then he knows positively, that he can precipitate into his visible use, or bring into his use from the outer, where it is already created *anything whatsoever* that he will hold his creative thought and feeling firmly upon.

The moment, that he is truly aware of this, he will know he is forever free from the need of the wealth of the outer world, or anything that the outer world can give. Thus has he entered into the Mastery and Dominion of his own world, the only world, that is ever existent to him, and which is his God-given Birthright.

I assure you there is no such thing as a supernatural world. As we step from this sphere of activity into another higher, that one becomes just as real as this is. It is simply a different state of consciousness, we have entered into.

To the joy, glorification and blessing of the mothers, sisters, wives and daughters, I will say, that within 100 years, there will be hundreds, who will be able to use the Cosmic Rays to cleanse their homes and keep them so: to weave their seamless garments when they will have no desire to follow the freakish styles, created by some commercialized idea.

I find so many of the students wondering, how it is that Ascended Beings, or Masters, with all their creative power often choose to live in humble quarters. I assure you the explanation is very easy. The far greater part of their Life and activity is spent in the higher spheres, in which they are directing Mighty Rays of Light to the blessing of humanity, from homes and Temples of Light and Wisdom, so beautiful, so transcendent, as almost to stagger the imagination of the outer consciousness. Those Homes and Temples are Eternal, ever becoming more and more beautiful, so they only spend a few hours in the visible world, which causes them to lower the density of their transcendent forms, that they may become visible to those yet occupying the physical body. If the students will understand this, it will save them much questioning and confusion in the outer expression, which time they can use in the activity of the "Mighty I AM Presence."

This will bring them into that transcendent state and consume the longing for the wealth of the outer world, which is but rubbish in comparison to the transcendent, creative power, inherent in every individual. They can bring this transcendent power into their use, through their own Self-control and Mastery. I say to you: "Beloved students, Children of the One God, is it not worth your sincerest effort, when you know you cannot fail? Take your Scepter of the Mighty Creative Power and be forever free of all past binding limitations, which have beset mankind through the ages." I assure you, that everyone, who enters in to attain this Scepter and Mastery, will be given every needed assistance, if each one will try with all his ability.

The one having the understanding of his Creative Ability, must know that he can create whatsoever he will, in whatever rate of vibration he desires to hold it, whether it be Light or any other condensation he may choose, to maintain it.

You know you have the ability to change your thought from Chicago to New York in the same instant, and you know you can change your thought from a condition of Light to one of very dense condensation, such as iron. Then one cannot help but see, that this which he does every moment consciously and at will, he can bring into a more powerful use by consciously fixing the attention, and holding it upon what he desires.

The attention is the channel by which God's Mighty Energy through thought and *feeling,* flows to its directed accomplishment. Because one has not yet precipitated something from the invisible, there is that lurking doubt, until some simple manifestation has occurred. Then his courage and confidence leap into dominion and in the future he has no trouble in precipitating whatsoever he desires.

The precipitation of gold or jewels from the invisible to the visible is as simple as breathing, *when*

*once that foolish questioning doubt accumulated by
the outer is consumed or pushed aside.*

Mankind, through the centuries, has built up these
walls of limitation. Now they must be broken up,
shattered, and consumed in any way that we can do
it. At first, it does take determination to do it, but
when you know it is the "I AM Power" acting, you
know It cannot fail. The outer only has to hold the
attention fixed on the object to be made visible. Dwell
on this and all of a sudden, you will find yourself
into the activity and you will be amazed that you
dwelt so long without using it.

The length of the Ray from a precipitated substance or condensation of "Light" is controlled by
the consciousness of the wearer. If the wearer's consciousness is raised very high, the scintillation is very
great.

The "Jewel of Light" is yet in its Transcendent
State of Perfection. The jewel in a condensed substance, such as a diamond, emerald or ruby, naturally,
will take on the condition of its wearer, and, if the
rate of thought vibration in the person wearing it
be low, the jewel will become lusterless, while if the
thought be transcendent, it will become very luminous.

When one has become a sincere student, reaching
to the Light, he must qualify everything in his environment with the quality of the "I AM Presence,"

no matter what the appearance seems to be. You see there cannot be a quality or an appearance in your world except what you give to it.

If fear causes you to believe in a disturbing presence, you are responsible for it, for if there were to be a disturbing presence and you qualified it by the "I AM Presence," you see how impossible it would be for it to disturb you. There is only one energy acting and the moment you acknowledge "The I AM Presence" you have requalified that activity with Perfection.

Expectation is a very powerful qualifying consciousness to maintain. Intense expectation is a splendid thing. It manifests always. Man through the centuries has created a veil through which he has shut out these transcendent spheres. Now if he has created it, which he has, then common sense and reason will tell one, that he can uncreate it.

A powerful radiation has gone forth to yourselves and students, with a powerful conviction that will be sustained, until they have this work, which is given to-day. *To convey the simplicity, the ease, and certainty with which the idea, through creative thought and feeling, can be brought into visibility, is a thing the students should dwell upon.* This will dissolve that feeling of "can I," and in its place put the "I can" and "I know."

If the students will keep themselves harmonious,

from time to time, they will have flashes that will give them all needed confidence. Add to all commands on going out of the body, that you retain the conscious memory of whatever you experience. Stick right to a thing from the start and *know, that whatever knowledge you need, will be forthcoming instantly.*

When you allow the attention to become fixed upon a thing, you that moment give it power to act in your world.

BENEDICTION: Thou Great Happiness—the Mighty Presence and Power which "I AM"! I qualify Thee to go forth in the hearts of mankind, anchoring there and filling their minds, bodies, and homes, filling them with Thy Great Happiness.

Open the door of their consciousness, so that the Mighty Power which "I AM" can come forth in Full Perfection. Oh Mighty Presence! hold the Children of Light, the Individualities of God, hold them close in Thy Embrace, letting Thy Quality flow forth in their command, filling them with Thy Great Peace. Oh Mighty Presence of Justice! Enter in and reign in all official places. Let the destructive intent of mankind be revealed, that it may be cast out and be consumed. Let the Fulness and Power of Thy Radiant Light enfold all, and Thy Glorious Transcendent Light fill all places.

DISCOURSE IX

October 30, 1932

SAINT GERMAIN

INVOCATION: Thou Mighty, All-powerful, Active Presence—God! we ever grow in deeper praise, thanks, and gratitude to Thee for Thy Life, Thy Light, and Thy Intelligent Power manifest everywhere in the Universe; for Thy Active Presence manifest in the mind, body, home, world and affairs of everyone.

Enable us to understand and feel Thy Radiant Power, always active in our world, affairs, and business—knowing no single activity can go wrong; for Thou dost govern all action in Thy Love and Justice, guiding and regulating all.

Thou Mighty Supreme Ruler of the Universe! whose Law is justice, whose power is invincible—protect America in Thy Great Blazing, Loving Presence. Reveal to the authorities of the United States of America any wrong activities.

I AM the Mighty Channel of Justice, claiming all now and for all time, that they serve only the cause of America and the Light of God. No human thought shall enter in. No human hand shall be raised against her, for she is sealed within the Love of the "Great Ascended Host of Light" forever.

Mighty God of the Universe! Thy Love, Light, Wisdom, Intelligence and Justice shall fill every office in the land; all political graft shall be wiped out forever, and Thou shalt reign through Thy Creation —through Thy Children in Perfect Justice to all.

I bring you greetings from the Great Host ever watching over and ministering through their divine radiation to heal, bless, enlighten, and prosper all who will accept.

THE DISCOURSE

One of the great needs of individuals, and even of sincere students to-day, is to feel the necessity of giving time, morning and evening, to sincere meditation: to the stilling of the outer activity that the Inner Presence may come forth unobstructed.

Meditation really means—*feeling*—the Active Presence of God. Therefore, when one attempts to enter meditation, he cannot drag all the disturbance, that has beset him during the day, along with him. Therefore, consciously remove from the *feeling* and *attention* every disturbing thing and enter into your meditation to *feel* the "Presence of God," and do not revolve your troubles. When the statement was given: "Know the Truth and the Truth shall make you free," it meant the recognition, acceptance, and activity of the "Mighty I AM Presence."

First: Know "I AM" is the First Principle and absolute certainty of freedom now. Second: Know "I AM" the active Presence governing all manifestation in my Life and world perfectly. Then I have entered into the Truth which shall bring all freedom.

I must relate a thing that would be most laughable, if it were not really serious: You would chastise it and rebel considerably, if your little pet dog continued to carry bones from the alley into your living room. You would think he were doing that which is very much out of place.

Do you know, beloved students of Truth, that when you allow your minds to dwell upon disturbing things, or experiences, you are doing a great deal worse than bringing bones into the living room. The unfortunate thing with students and individuals, which seems so difficult for them to understand, is, never under any circumstances, try to hold the water that has gone over the wheel.

In other words, the unpleasant experiences, losses, or any imperfection that has passed over your wheel of experience to the present time, should never be held close to you. They have gone over the wheel— forgive and forget them. To give and forgive is God-like indeed. For illustration: If an individual or group of individuals has gone into a business undertaking, and through lack of understanding, it has failed or gone to pieces, it is always because of inharmony in the mental attitude and *feelings*.

If every individual in such an association would take his stand and hold it that there was only *God in Action,* only the most perfect success would come out of it. Since the individual has free will, if he will not control his own thought and feeling, he will wreck things for himself and others. Such is the Great Law, unless every individual corrects thought and feeling, and keeps it so.

Everyone, who manifests in the physical form to-day, has made plenty of mistakes—sometime, somewhere—so let no one take the attitude: "I AM more holy than thou," but each one's first attitude should be to call on the Law of Forgiveness, and if he be feeling or sending criticism, condemnation, or hate to another of God's children, a brother or sister, he can never have enlightenment or success, until he calls on the Law of Forgiveness. Further than this, he must say to that person, to whom he was feeling disturbed in any way—silently: "I send to you the fulness of the Divine Love of my Being to bless and prosper you." This attitude is the only release and freedom from the seeming failures of the outer activity.

For individuals to continually revolve, in their minds and discussion, a business or project that has disintegrated, will surely in the end destroy themselves, if they do not face about, and through calling on the Law of Forgiveness, find complete conscious release from the entire situation.

For an individual to hold an attitude of revenge for any seeming wrong, imaginary or otherwise, can only bring upon himself incapacity of mind and body. The old, yet wondrous statement brought down to us through the ages: "Unless you are willing to forgive, how can you be forgiven?" is one of the Mightiest Laws for use in human experience. Oh that individuals and many students could only see, how they hold to themselves the things they do not want, by allowing the mind to revolve upon the discordant things that have passed, and cannot be helped through the outer senses.

The greatest thing that all mankind is seeking— in reality, is peace and freedom, which is always the doorway to happiness. There is only one possible way to receive this, which is to know God—the "I AM Presence," and that, This Presence is the only acting Intelligence in your Life and world at all times. Then stand by this, and live it.

One of the most amazing things that it has been my experience to witness—since coming into the Arisen State—is the distorted idea of freedom, financially and otherwise. There is but one, sure, certain rock upon which to build your eternal, financial freedom, and that is to know and feel with every fiber of your Being: "I AM the wealth, the opulence, the substance, already perfected in my world, of every constructive thing that I can possibly conceive of or desire." This is true financial freedom, and will bring it as surely as it is maintained, and it will not get away, I assure you.

On the other hand, man may use—knowingly or unknowingly—enough of this "God I AM Presence," or God-Energy, to accumulate through the outer activity millions of dollars; but wherein is his certainty of keeping it? I assure you, it is impossible for any being in the physical world to keep wealth that is accumulated, without his being aware that: "God is the power producing and sustaining it." You see before you constant illustrations of great wealth taking wings over night, as it were. Thousands within the past four years have met this experience. Even after the seeming loss had occurred, had they been able to take their firm conscious stand: "I AM the wealth—*God in Action*—now manifest in my Life, my world," the way, the door, would have immediately opened for them to have again received abundance.

Why do I say: "Again to have received abundance"? Because, they had built the momentum, and had attained great confidence. Therefore, all requirements were at hand ready for further use, but in most instances, they allowed great discouragement—often hatred and condemnation—to enter in, which shut and locked the door to further progress.

Now let me assure you, Beloved Children of God, there is no outer condition ever existed in this world so bad, so disastrous, but that there is the "I AM," active Presence of God, with the eternal strength and courage of the Universe, to again rebuild you into freedom and independence financially and every way.

I especially want the students who come under this radiation to understand this, because in this day of falling thrones and governments, individual fortunes and otherwise, they need to know and understand that, if their wealth has flown away through ignorance of understanding, then the "I AM Presence" in them, *God in Action,* is the sure rebuilder of their faith, confidence, wealth, or whatever they wish to direct their conscious attention upon. Thus, they allow this Mighty Inner Energy to flow into their desire which is the only power that ever accomplished anything.

Every individual who has seemingly expressed a loss of wealth to any degree should immediately use the marvelous statement of Jesus: " 'I AM the resurrection and the Life' of my business, my understanding, or whatever I wish to focus my attention upon."

I tell you frankly, beloved students and individuals, there is not the slightest hope for you in heaven or earth, so long as you persist in holding within your consciousness, thoughts and feelings of criticism, condemnation, or hate of any description, *and that includes mild dislike.*

This leads us to the very vital point that you are concerned only with your own activity and your world. It is not your province to judge another, for you do not know the forces playing upon another or the conditions. You know only the angle that you see of it, and I tell you that, if an individual should be entirely innocent of any intent to wrong another, the individuals who send criticism, condemnation, or hate to such an one, are doing worse than committing physical murder. Why is this so? Because, thought and feeling are the only creative power, and while such thoughts and feelings may not touch or harm their objective, they must return and bring with them the conditions sent out by the individual, who sent them forth, and always with accumulated energy.

So after all, the one who holds vicious thoughts to another is in reality but destroying himself, his business, and his affairs. There is no possible way of averting it, except for the individual to awaken and consciously reverse the currents.

Let us go one step further. Throughout all ages, there have been business associations, in which there were one or possibly two with the deliberate intent to do wrong, and through this association, a number of individuals, absolutely innocent of any wrong intent, have been imprisoned. I now tell you, as an Un-failing Law that cannot be changed, that the indi-vidual or individuals, who cause innocent persons to be incarcerated, thus depriving them of their free-dom of action as God intended, will bring that exact experience which they have desired for another into their own experience—*even unto the third and fourth embodiment following*.

For myself, I would rather a thousand times be deliberately shot down, than to be the instrument of depriving any of God's Children of their liberty. There is no greater crime reigning in human experi-ence to-day, than the prevailing use of circumstantial evidence, for in ninety-nine cases out of a hundred, it is afterwards found to be entirely wrong. Some-times the truth is never known to the outer senses.

So beloved students, let no one seeking the "Light" ever set himself up in judgment on another of God's Children.

Again, supposing someone we love very much seems to be going all awry. What is the first thing the outer would do? As a rule, to begin sitting in judg-ment and criticism. The most powerful thing that can and should be done for such an individual by every-one, who knows anything of the circumstances, is to pour out all their Love and to silently know that: "I AM, *God in Action,* is the only controlling Intel-ligence and Activity within this brother or sister."

To keep silently speaking to that one's consciousness is the greatest help possible to be given.

Many times to remonstrate verbally with an individual, sets up a condition of antagonism, intensifying rather than erasing the activity, which the silent work would be absolutely certain to accomplish.

No one in the outer consciousness can possibly know what the "I AM God-Presence" in the other individual wishes to do. These are vital truths that, if maintained, would bring very great peace into the lives of individuals. Many lives with their attendant business efforts, are ruined, because there is lurking, within the consciousness of the individual, judgment, condemnation, or a feeling of some degree of hatred toward another.

The student or individual, who wants to leap ahead in the progress of the Light, should never enter sleep, until he has consciously sent Love to every individual that he feels has harmed him at any time. This thought of Love will go straight as an arrow into the consciousness of the other individual, because it cannot be stopped, generating its quality and power there, which will as surely come back to you, as you send it out.

There is perhaps no single element responsible for so many diseased conditions of body and mind as the feeling of hate sent out to another individual. There is no telling how this will react upon the mind and body of the sender. In one, it will produce one effect; in another, still a different effect. *Let it be here understood, that resentment is but another form of hate, but of a milder degree.*

A very wonderful thought to live in always is: "I AM the Perfect Creative Thought and Feeling everywhere present in the minds and hearts of individuals." It is a most marvelous thing. It not only brings rest and peace to yourself, but releases limitless gifts from the "Presence."

Another is: "I AM the Mighty Law of Divine Justice and Protection acting in the minds and hearts of individuals everywhere." You can apply and use this with enormous force and power in every way. Another is: "I AM Divine Love, filling the minds and hearts of individuals everywhere."

As you think on this, you will understand what was done, when this home was made a radiating center of the "Active Presence of God." You will suddenly come into a realization of the gigantic application of this. Everything in the Life experience of humanity can be governed by the "I AM Presence." The use of the "I AM Presence" is the highest activity that can be given.

When you say "I AM," you set God into action; *but there is a lot more to it which you will come to realize, when you feel and know the enormity of the use of this expression.* Realize the enormous power of the "I AM" to act in things of this kind. "I AM the God power Almighty." There is no other power that can act. When you say and feel this, then you liberate and loose the Full Activity of God.

Another statement: "I AM the conscious memory of these things." Also: "I AM the conscious memory, use and understanding in the use of these things."

When you say: "The Presence that 'I AM' clothes me in my Eternal Transcendent Garment of Light," it actually does take place that moment.

"The Secret Place of the Most High" is this "I AM Presence." The sacred things that are revealed to you are not to be cast forth, for they are as pearls. Know always: "I AM the perfect poise of speech and action at all times." Then the guard is always up for, "I AM the Protecting Presence."

God's Energy is always waiting to be directed. Inherent within the expression of the "I AM" is the Self-sustaining activity. Then you know there is no time. This brings you to the instantaneous action, and your precipitation will soon take place. Always preceding a manifestation, you will feel that absolute stillness.

BENEDICTION: We give thanks "O Mighty I AM Presence" for having entered into Thy Secret Place. Let Thy Wisdom govern at all times, the dispensation of Thy Light. Let Thy Wisdom guard and direct our minds and bodies at all times, that they always act in perfect accord with Thee. As Thou art called forth into action—"O Mighty I AM Presence" —we know we are always charged at all times with Thy Mighty Energy, and that it accomplishes all perfectly wherever it is sent.

NOTES

Legal affirmations: For the one not in the midst of the case, take this statement:

"I AM the law:"

"I AM the justice:"

"I AM the judge:"

"I AM the jury:"

Knowing that "I AM All-powerful," then I know that only Divine justice can be done here.

DISCOURSE X

November 3, 1932

SAINT GERMAIN

INVOCATION: Mighty Luminous Presence! I AM the Conquering Power. I AM the Radiant Splendor filling everything in manifestation. I AM the Life flowing through all manifestation. I AM the Intelligence governing all activity, Inner and outer, making it one Perfect Activity. Out of Thy Light, "Mighty Presence which I AM," all things are precipitated into form. I AM the exhaustless energy governed by Thy Wondrous, Infinite Intelligence. Light the illumining center within these bodies, who come under this radiation. Expand that Light into the Full Illumination of the body and mind, raising it into Thy Active, Perfect Eternal Garment.

Mighty Light! send forth Thy Rays into the hearts of mankind, into all official places, commanding Justice, Illumination and Perfection of Thy Self to express, bringing relief, release and Light unto humanity, and by Thy Governing Principle, command all things in the outer human activity to give obedience. I bring you greetings from the Great Host of Loved Ones, who always watch and minister to those, whose devotion reaches unto them.

From out the centuries of activity, we have arrived at the focal point, where the experiences of ages come into instantaneous action, where all time and space become the "One Presence," *God in Action* now.

Knowing that It is the "Presence of God, I AM" that beats your heart, then you know that your heart is the Voice of God speaking, and as you come to meditate upon the Great Truth: "I AM the Supreme Intelligent Activity through my mind and *heart,*" you will bring the True Dependable Divine Feeling into the heart.

So long mankind has been loving on the periphery of the circle. Once the student becomes really aware that, "God is Love," and Love's True Activity comes through the heart, he will understand that to focus his attention on the desire *to project Love forth, for any given purpose, is the supreme privilege of the outer activity of the consciousness, which can gener-ate Love to a boundless degree.* Mankind has not pre-viously understood, that Divine Love is a Power, a Presence, an Intelligence, a Light, that can be fanned into a Boundless Flame or Fire, and it is within the conscious intelligence of every individual, especially students of the Light, to so create and generate this "Presence of Love," that it becomes an invincible, ex-haustless, peace-commanding "Presence" wherever the conscious individual desires to direct it.

Somewhere it has been said, that Love may not be commanded. I say to you: *"Love is the First Principle of Life and may be generated to any degree or without any limit whatsoever for infinite use."* Such is the majestic privilege of the conscious use and direction of Love.

When I say, "generate" I mean the opening of the door through conscious devotion, to the outpouring of this exhaustless Fountain of Love, which is the Heart of your Being—the Heart of the Universe.

Students, by contemplating this Infinite Power of Love, become such a fountain of Its outpouring, that *Its conscious direction may be infinite in the student's use.*

When my beloved students wish to hasten their liberation from certain events or outer activity, I can but say: "I AM the commanding 'Presence,' the exhaustless energy, the Divine Wisdom, causing my desire to be fulfilled." This will bring the quickest release from any undesirable condition, that the very Law of your Being will permit. Knowing this you may further know: "The 'Presence that I AM' I now remain, untouched by disturbing outer conditions. Serene I fold my wings and abide the Perfect Action of the Divine Law and Justice of my Being, commanding all things within my Circle to appear in Perfect Divine Order."

This is the greatest privilege of the student, and

should be the command at all times. Here I shall say something that should be very encouraging and I trust it will. "Each student, who is earnestly striving for the Light, is being toughened, as you make the toughest steel, that wears the longest, holds the best, and is the strongest. Such is what the Life of experience brings to the individual. When one craves to be released and still there appear trying experiences, it is the toughening of the steel of character and the strengthening of the individual, that gives him at last the Perfect and Eternal Mastery over all outer things."

One may, with the right understanding of this, easily rejoice in the experience, that is enabling him to turn to and bask in the Glorious, Wondrous, "I AM Presence." Thus, beloved students, you should never grow weary of well-doing, or meeting the experiences that sometimes seem to weigh heavily upon you, but rejoice, that every step forward leads to that Eternal Goal, which does not have to be repeated.

This is what methinks the student often forgets to use: "I AM the strength, the courage, the power to move forward steadily, through all experiences, whatever they may be, and remain joyous and uplifted, filled with peace and harmony at all times, by the Glorious Presence, which I AM."

To the athlete on the race track, the beginning of

the race is glorious anticipation, but as he reaches the goal and his adversary draws near, he puts forth every effort, his breath becomes short, and with one last leap, he crosses the line to victory. So it is with students on the path. They know in the use of the "I AM Presence," they cannot fail. Therefore, all that is necessary is to tighten your belt, gird yourself for whatever is required, and with a wave of the hand to your adversary, bid him farewell.

More fortunate than the athlete, the student knows from the beginning, that he cannot fail, because: "I AM the Exhaustless Energy and Intelligence sustaining him or her."

The power of precipitation, the student should understand and remember at all times, is within the "I AM Presence." "I AM here, the Life Principle and Intelligence in this body. I AM everywhere, even unto the Heart of God, the Governing Intelligence of the Universe. Therefore, when I wish to precipitate *anything whatsoever,* I know that: 'I AM the power acting, I AM the Intelligence directing, I AM the substance being acted upon, and I now bring it into visible form and my use.'"

The contemplation of this phrase just expressed, will enable the student to enter into this activity without strain or anxiety.

The question that so often confronts the students in the power of precipitation, is that of money. The first question is: "How is it that money may be precipitated without interfering with the government allotment?" Since the creation of money, as a standard of exchange, gold being its standard and heart, so to speak, and the security of all issue, it will be remembered, that there have been almost a countless number of disasters in one form or another, through which gold and the issue of money have been to the outer sense destroyed. Billions of dollars in this manner have disappeared. Therefore, with any money, and it is usually gold that is precipitated, there is no danger of passing the limit set by a government for its use. Again, there have been billions of Spanish gold and denominations of other countries, that have been burned, lost, submerged at sea, etc., to the extent, that precipitation would have to run into great numbers before there would be any question as to its legality. More often, however, gold is precipitated in its natural state, therefore, always legal in its use.

As the world has recently offered a premium for more gold production, why not precipitate it and bless the world by its use? But, I shall not hold myself responsible for the questions that will be asked, when you do precipitate it, unless you have a mine from which you can supposedly have brought it forth, for you have no idea what the curiosity of the outer mind is, until you call its attention to gold. I assure you the outer is immediately set on fire. However: "I AM the Presence governing it."

The supposed demand to know the source of gold, is but a subtle form of inquiry, that someone else may discover your source. My idea would be to answer their inquiry, that it is none of their business. Simply say: "Here is the gold. Test it. If it is not 100 per cent, you may refuse it. If it is, you are compelled to receive it by the laws of your government."

You will understand, beloved students, that it is only in the outer activity of the physical world, that you require a medium of exchange, for the moment one rises into the power of precipitation, he has little use for gold or money, or any kind of exchange, except as incidents may require.

As one by one you come into the Ascended State, you will have many a hearty laugh over the seeming importance of these outer problems of the physical or outer world, for they are all but the "Maya," which means but constant change. Remember, that there is only One Thing in the Universe, that is Permanent, Real, Eternal, and That is the "I AM Presence," God in you, which is the Owner, the Creator, the Intelligence governing all manifested form. Then to know that you are that "Presence," that "I AM" Presence, places you, beloved student, independent of all outer manifestation.

Do not misunderstand me. I know you have to come into this understanding sufficiently, but if you are sincere, have dauntless determination in your recognition of the "I AM Presence," *God in Action* in you, you will find yourself, even to the outer sense, quickly rising into that Dominion and Independence, in which you can say to all outer things: "Is it possible thou didst once disturb me?" Some of you have had an inkling of how gross and coarse all outer form seems, when once you are liberated from it. To that finer, higher sense, it seems incredible, that you could have inhabited and still are inhabiting and using a form so gross and imperfect. Had you long ago recognized, claimed, and rejoiced in the "I AM Presence," as you are doing to-day, these outer forms would have become so refined, that you could have come back to them with very great grace. However, one has but to rejoice at every step of attainment, and every step he hopes to attain, because *hope becomes faith, and faith becomes Reality.*

Now, beloved students, under no circumstance allow the experience of the outer to pall upon you, but in this recognition, rejoice every day, every hour, every minute that brings you nearer to that goal of freedom and release from limitation, that freedom you have so longed for, and so much desired.

The Light is growing very bright within some of you. Continue on with that calm, dauntless, determination to scale the heights, for: "I AM That Great Presence sustaining you and you cannot fail." You know the old phrase, used to spur one on and especially among soldiers, was to tell them they were cowards and yellow. Now beloved students, I say to you: "That you are not cowards, but that you are yellow with the Golden Light of Truth, of Dominion, of Mastery over all outer things, that have bound you, and with one mighty surge, of the 'I AM Presence,' you break every binding chain, shatter all sense of limitation, and stand forth in your freedom, the Glorious, Radiant, Majestic Being, that you really are."

I like very much to use the statement: "I AM here and I AM there," and if you will contemplate it, you cannot help but overcome the sense of separation.

The student is more or less uncertain, and that always brings anxiety, and anxiety makes tension. As you come into the higher activity, you will become more and more relaxed.

Always take the attitude of calm poise, when anything should manifest. Always be happy and rejoice in the Presence, but there is always the balance to be maintained: it is the Middle Way. Hold yourself within this Center Poise. One can rejoice as deeply in a calm poise as he can in overexuberance. The calm poise conveys a certain something to others that they need, for every human being needs poise, and the conscious realization of the necessity of calm and poise, for it never leaves one off guard. Poise has within it a certain power of Self-control and guard, which is very essential.

You will be not only delighted, but amazed at times at the marvelous things, that will come with it. Use: "I AM that Perfect Poise that controls everything." When you use the "I AM Presence," be sure to keep it as a permanent thing.

Each one try this, and if you do not feel results at first, just go on, for you certainly will as you use it more and more: "I AM the Presence charging this water with the Life-giving Essence, which I absorb and which renews my body in perfect health and eternal youth." Affirm often: "I AM here and I AM there. I AM the conscious action everywhere." To discordant activities say: "I AM the Presence preventing this. I AM the positive, peaceful control of this whole situation."

In the "I AM Consciousness" is the wisdom that knows what is required. Know always that: "I AM the controlling, governing Presence of this meeting or situation."

There is nothing comes into physical form, that is not first perfected on the invisible or higher planes.

The students should not discuss this instruction, but just rejoice in living it themselves. If they will do this, they will receive so much more from it, because there will be no conflicting vibrations to disturb them.

BENEDICTION: Wondrous Presence of the God, "I AM"! we give praise and thanks for this feeling of the certainty of Thy Presence, that is growing within the consciousness of these students under this radiation. We rejoice in the Great Light of Thy Presence enfolding each one, which goes forth unto all humanity, and that is changing all discord into Love and Peace. We thank Thee.

DISCOURSE XI

November 7, 1932

SAINT GERMAIN

INVOCATION: From out the Great Silence, Oh Thou Luminous Brother! we welcome Thee and Thy Ministry unto America, and as Thou hast put forth Thy opening wedge this day, so shall those under this radiation become aware of Thy Presence, O Thou Great Light, that illumines all earthly minds, making them aware of the One Eternal Presence, the One Intelligence governing all the activity that I AM —individualized everywhere.

We give praise and thanks, that there is but One Intelligence governing everywhere and the duty of the student *always* no matter what the appearance, is to accept only this fact and that he becomes a radiant channel to pour out this truth, like a gushing stream pouring itself forth to the Great Ocean of Life. We give praise and thanks, that out of the Silence has come another Presence, who will bless, lift, and enlighten humanity. By the Power which I AM and the accumulated wisdom and energy of the centuries, I project forth into the minds of humanity this day, that intelligent activity, which will guide them aright, and control them to act accordingly.

By the "I AM," the "Universal I AM," the Great One, I command this power to act in all mankind.

I bring you greetings from the Great Host and the Great Master, Himalaya.

THE MASTER HIMALAYA

This is the first time that the Presence of this Luminous Brother has been brought to the knowledge of the outer world. It is He from whom the Himalayan Mountains receive their name. Thus, ever since these have been raised into prominence, have they been a Sacred Unchanging Stream of Life—held unwaveringly. Hence, those souls, who came within their embrace, were caught up and lifted into that Luminous Radiant Form, where they have long sent forth Their Rays of activity to heal and bless mankind.

THE DISCOURSE

As the destiny of India and America are entwined, as two vines encircling the "Tree of Life," so again this day has the radiant help come forth to try and blend in harmony the minds of America, that its progress proceed unhampered and uninterrupted.

To-day there are in America thousands, who have been reborn from India, and there are being reborn in India, thousands from America, each to bring its interblending, balancing process required in both sections of the earth.

This Great Being, who has been introduced to you, has after many centuries in the "Great Silence," again stepped forth to exert that conscious blending process of Spirit and manifestation, to hold forth the Chalice, that its Heart be filled with the Liquid Fire of Spirit, pouring forth into the hearts of mankind, creating that fulness of desire within them for greater and greater Light, looking to and depending upon the One Great Source of Light, "I AM," *God in Action everywhere.*

The entrance of this Great Presence again into the activity of mankind, will spread like a thread of Light through all the activity of America and expand Its Luminous Presence, like a Mantle of softly falling Golden Snow, that will be absorbed by the minds of humanity, the majority being entirely unaware, although there will be some, who will sense the Inner Penetrating Presence.

If those under this radiation, continue in their present harmonious, beautiful progress, it will be possible shortly to bring to their attention certain activities of the nerve fluid, which will hasten their Mastery over the outer form, which means the Mastery over all conditions that seem to bind or limit.

I shall be surprised, if your students do not feel the strength, if they do not feel the Presence of this Great Being to-day. Even as I speak, His Rays go out to them touching the heart, and I feel their thrill of joy, they not knowing just what it means.

Watch carefully, each of you and your students, to be on guard to reverse all negative conditions that appear to the senses. On the lesser things for practice, if the senses report you cold, reverse your consciousness and assert your warmth. If the senses report too much heat, reverse it with a sense of perfect normal coolness. If the senses report to you ecstatic joy over certain enlightenment, say: "Peace, be still," and assert your calm poise and assurance. The ideal in all sense reports is to move in the middle way, the balance, always asserting the Calm Mastery of control which I AM.

This will enable the establishing of a steady, flowing stream of creative ideas and energy from the Heart of the Great Central Sun, from out which has come this Great Being, the Master Himalaya. This will enable you to receive and use immensely more of That Radiant Energy, which He pours forth. The reason for drawing your conscious attention to Him, has been that, if you understand what it means, you may receive without limit from That Energy besides what you draw forth by your own conscious effort.

The students must at all times understand, that the Masters do not come to them of the students' choice, but that they have been chosen to receive the Radi-

ance, a privilege for which words are entirely inadequate to convey the true meaning, that can truly only
be felt or visioned. Again, they should understand,
that the Master's province is not to assume their responsibility by solving their problems for them, but
to convey intelligent understanding, which they may
apply in their own lives to solve their own problems.
Thus, they gain the needed strength, courage, and
confidence to continue to reach up step by step, gaining their own Conscious Mastery over the outer-self
and the outer-world.

Always at certain points of growth (expansion),
we hear students call out many times with great sincerity: "Great Masters, help us to solve our problems." For encouragement and strength, I wish to
say, that far more than one has any conception, is
the Radiating Presence of the Master pouring out
strength, courage, confidence, and Light, which in
most instances the students are quite unaware of in
the outer sense consciousness. There is only one way
in which anyone with wisdom can be of permanent
help, and that is to consciously instruct his brother or
sister in the simple laws by which one may wield the
scepter, gain the victory, and attain to Full Dominion
over the outer-self and his world.

To do the thing, that the student requires in solving his problems, would not only retard his progress,
but weaken him immensely. Only by asserting one's

conscious strength, winning victories, and thereby attaining confidence, which comes in no other way, does the student enter into the fulness of his own powers. With the powerful, masterful use of the consciousness of the "I AM Presence," the student goes forward with absolutely no uncertainty to his goal of victory.

The reason, we have not and do not say more to the student, concerning the assistance that we may be giving, is to prevent his leaning upon an outside source. To say or do that, which would cause the student to lean upon us, because he knows of our Presence, would be the greatest mistake we could make, but the student need never fear, and he should know, that every assistance possible is always given according to the point of attainment he has reached.

The "I AM Presence," the Host of Ascended Masters, the Ascended Jesus Christ, are one and the same thing. Through the recognition and use of the "I AM Presence," *I tell you, you can positively bring forth any quality you wish into the outer conscious manifestation, if you will but do it.*

The need of everyone is to keep reminding the outer consciousness that, when one says: "I AM this or I AM that," he is setting *God in Action*, which is his Life individualized, the Life of the Universe, the Energy of the Universe, the Intelligence at the Heart of the Universe, governing all. It is necessary, it is vital, to keep the outer reminded of this fact. With this consciousness the joyous enthusiasm of the student should increase, continuously. There should at no time be a pall in the joy of its use, because it is positively the road to Full Mastery.

The student must become firmly aware, that he or she is the Conscious Controlling Power, in his Life, in his world, and that he can fill it with any quality that is needed or that he may choose.

The students, who have intermittent physical disturbance in the body, should take the consciousness often: "I AM the perfectly controlled breath of my body," and should in connection with this feel themselves, as often as they can, breathing in that rhythmic breath. This will bring about a certain balance of breathing, that is immensely helpful in the control of the thought.

Sincere students should, whenever possible, avoid listening to things that are disturbing, for in doing this they often let in unknowingly, elements they do not desire. Where they cannot with discretion avoid listening to things of this kind, they should use the following: "I AM the Presence on guard here, and consume instantly, everything that seeks to disturb." Thus, you will not only protect yourself, but help the other person as well. While the student should at no time fear anything, it certainly is necessary to keep up the conscious guard, until he has attained sufficient

Mastery to control his thought, feeling, and receptivity.

From the Golden City, comes this limitless charge of energy, for the blessing of the students of this radiation as well as those of mankind, who are looking to the Light.

Try to keep as much as possible into the joyous enthusiasm of the "I AM Presence." Give It all power and do not hold any questioning in the mind. Throw everything to the winds, and give everything to that "Glorious I AM Presence," and receive its Magic Revelation. It is the Mighty Miracle-Working Presence, that can and does solve all things, not only problems, but questions whose answers need revealing. A remarkable statement, that would be enormously helpful to the students would be to say: "I AM the Miracle-Working Presence in everything I require to have done."

For students to keep meditating and contemplating what it means to say, "I" or "I AM," brings results, revelations, and blessings that cannot be overestimated. I am sure your students will soon begin to show and feel the remarkable activity of this use. To-day I feel the Presence of the understanding and use of this much more powerfully, than at any time hitherto.

On the higher planes there is a constant meeting and exchange of help while the bodies are asleep, far beyond anything the outer-self is conscious of.

Knowing that: "I AM the quality of whatever I wish to use," then you know you can produce in visible, tangible form whatever you have within the consciousness. The moment the questioning of the outer-mind can be put under control and made to subside, the greatest revelations pour forth almost tumbling over each other.

Owing to the need, the Master Himalaya chose to come forth. He brings a special blending of America and India and that is why it is possible for him to come here. As the Inner Presence comes into action, all outer activity subsides. It must necessarily, because it obeys the "I AM Presence."

The Golden Snow is what the Great Presence spreads over America to be absorbed by individuals and the very particles of the atmosphere itself. This will enable the students especially to be greatly assisted and blest, because they have become the focus for this outpouring.

It may be well for the students to understand, that in national requirements, as in individuals, there are qualities needed for certain definite purposes at certain times. That is the reason for Special Great Beings coming forth, These Individuals having predominant the quality that the nation needs at a given moment. The students, who can take this understanding with great sincerity, will find a new element entering into their lives, which will benefit them greatly.

The activity of expectation is quite a vital one in receiving from the Inner Presence. It is a faculty that can be used with a great deal of benefit by the student, who cultivates it. For instance, if we have planned something from which we expect great joy, we feel all buoyed up with expectancy. We can acquire and use this same expectancy in elements we wish to acquire and use, for it is very helpful in enabling them to come forth. If one calls on the 'phone and you are to meet that one in the city, you expect to meet him. If you desire to meet the Masters, one requirement is to expect to meet them. That is very helpful. Why not expect to meet them *now?*

People have become so abnormal in their habits, that naturally they have interfered with their breathing as well as other things. To use the statement: "I AM the balancing-breath," will do a great deal more for them than the use of many breath exercises without the aid of an Ascended Master. The coming, amazing activity will be done by the use of the "I AM Presence," because with its use anything can be accomplished. Take the consciousness often: "I AM the balancing-breath." This sets in motion the *Inner Activity* that maintains the outer Perfection. In whatever you do, always take the "I AM Consciousness," and then you immediately set It into motion.

Take the attitude of calm certainty in your mind and keep on keeping on.

BENEDICTION: Thou Mighty Presence, whom we in great joy have welcomed, we thank Thee for Thy Great Wondrous Radiance and Light, Thy Great Radiance and Conquering Power, and we trust that Thou mayest decree justice now and for all time to mankind.

NOTES

St. G. "I shall have to journey on."
Q. "Where are you going"?
A. "Home."
Q. "Which one"?
A. "The Golden City."

It is clothed in the Electronic Substance, and is just as tangible to you as the physical. Within the Light of the Golden City are Lights that are as much brighter than the surrounding radiance, as these physical lights are in this atmosphere.

Within all Light at certain points is consciousness focused. At those points it becomes illumination. Suppose this room were the Great Sun. It has an atmosphere. The individuals moving within it would have their own radiance about them, the same as the lights in this room.

DISCOURSE XII

November 10, 1932

SAINT GERMAIN

INVOCATION: Thou Mighty Infinite Presence, Thou All-Pervading Intelligence, Thy Love, Wisdom, and Power governs all things. Thy Divine Justice is ever operating in the lives, in the worlds of those who look to Thee with unfailing determination.

We give praise and thanks that Thou art the ruling Power and Governing Intelligence ruling all things.

We give praise and thanks that in our world, Thou art the Ever-sustaining, Invincible Power. We thank Thee.

God always finds a way to help those whose hearts reach out to him.

THE DISCOURSE

The seeming mysteries of Life, with their attendant experiences, are, when rightly understood, blessings in disguise. For any experience that causes us to turn more firmly to the One Active Presence, "I AM," *God in Action,* has served us a wonderful purpose and blessing.

The unfortunate situation, that personalities find

themselves in, exist because they are eternally looking to outside sources for sustenance, directing Intelligence, and for the Love that is the Supreme
Presence and Power of the Universe.

It matters not what the conditions are that we
face, at no time must we lose track of or allow ourselves to be drawn from the Great Truth, that:
"Love is the Hub of the Universe upon which everything revolves." This does not mean that we shall
love inharmony or discord or anything unlike the
Christ, but instead we can love *God in Action,* the
"I AM Presence" everywhere present, for the opposite of hate is Love, and *one cannot hate in any sense
without having loved deeply*. The admonition that
Jesus gave was truly this idea.

Each human being is a power and is intended to
be the governing principle of his Life and world.
In the recognition, that within each human being is
the "I AM Presence of God" ever acting, then everyone knows that he holds within his outer hands, the
Scepter of Dominion, and should use his conscious
determination in knowing that the Invincible Presence of God is, every moment, the intelligent activity in his world and affairs. This keeps the attention from becoming fixed on the outer appearance,
which is never the Truth unless illumined by the "I
AM Presence."

No matter what the problem is to be solved in the

individual's Life, there is only One Power, Presence, and Intelligence that can solve it, and that is the individual's recognition of the All-powerful Presence of God, with whom no outer activity may interfere, unless the individual's attention is knowingly or unknowingly drawn from his central recognition and acceptance of the Supreme God Power.

The Principle of Life, always active, is ever striving to pour Itself forth into expression, thereby producing Its Natural Perfection, but human beings having free will, consciously or unconsciously qualify It with all kinds of distortion. The individual, who stands with his attention fixed firmly on the "I AM Presence," on God, and with God, becomes an Invincible Power which no outer manifestation of mankind can interfere with.

In the recognition of: "I AM here and I AM there," friends, wherever needful, will be raised up to one's assistance, for: "I AM the friends brought forward whenever and wherever it is necessary." The release from all outer dominion or interference can only come through this recognition of the "I AM Presence," *God in Action,* in the individual's Life and world. Many times this requires strong determination to hold unwaveringly in this Presence when appearances seem to be dominating. However, such is never really the case.

The old saying: "An individual is never licked

until he gives up," is quite true, for as long as an individual looks with full determination to *God in himself,* as the Governing Intelligence, there is no human activity that can long interfere. The Mighty Outpouring flowing about each individual, by the activity of the vision, and knowing Its Presence, can be made as invincible, in fact more so, as a wall of steel about one.

Ever down through the centuries, have the majority of mankind given their attention to the outer appearances, thereby inviting all kinds of discord and distress, but to-day there are thousands who are coming to understand the *God Presence within them* as Absolutely Invincible, to the extent, that they are steadily being raised above the injustice, discord, and inharmony of the outer creation.

Until mankind or individuals hold their attention on the "I AM Presence," God within, long enough and with sufficient determination, they will find themselves surrounded by the undesirable, but through this "I AM Presence" each one has the power to raise himself above the discord and disturbance of the outer creation.

At first, it does take determination to hold fast when the seeming storm-clouds hang low, and the outer appearance seems overwhelming, but with a dynamic conscious attitude and the attention fixed upon the *Presence of God within,* it is like the lightning flashing forth from within the storm-clouds, penetrating and dissolving the storm that seems so threatening.

As one advances, he finds himself becoming more and more invincible to this outer creation of mankind that brings such great distress.

The statement of Jesus: "Know the Truth and the Truth shall make you free," was perhaps one of the simplest and greatest truths to ever be uttered, for the first fundamental of knowing this Great Truth, to which he referred, was to know that you have within you this Invincible Presence of God. If you know that and are certain of It within your own consciousness, I mean by that—standing with firm determination in the face of everything—then you know that you do have that Presence within.

Then your next step is to take your stand: "I AM the illumining, revealing Presence from which no outer activity, that I need to know can be withheld from me, because I AM the wisdom, I AM the perception, I AM the revealing power, bringing everything before me, that I may see and understand, and be able to act accordingly."

It is so easy, when you once understand that: "I AM the Only Intelligence and Presence acting," to see how you have the Scepter within your own hands and through this "I AM Presence," you can compel everything you need to know to be revealed to you, and I assure you, this is not in any way interfering with the free will of any other individual.

It is time, that the Children of God, who are looking to the Light, awaken to this Dominion. I assure you, it is no wrong or mistake to claim and demand your own. In doing this, you are not in any way interfering with any other individual.

If at any time, there are those, through their outer activity, attempting to take from us, that which belongs to us, then it is our right to command through the "I AM Presence," that the whole condition be adjusted and our own brought to us. In this we must be very careful, that when we have set the Divine Law into motion, and Divine Justice begins to take place, that we do not become oversympathetic and thereby interrupt the action of the Law.

When human beings are governed entirely by the outer-self, and when they have no consideration for the Power of God, that gives them Life, they are easily led to commit any kind of injustice, but does that mean in any sense that we shall allow them to do it in our world? Not when we know that we have the Mighty Power of God within, to command and demand right and justice from everywhere.

I want to cite you an instance: One of my students was going through a very trying experience, and the nature being very spiritual, I told her to demand right and justice. She did as advised, and presently things began to happen to those who wished to do her injustice. Through kindness of heart she began to relent and wish that she had not demanded justice. She came to me and said: "What am I to do?" I said with no uncertainty: "Stand by the decree that you have issued. You are not responsible for the lessons these individuals have to learn, who have wronged you, so let them get their lessons, and be undisturbed by it."

When individuals start to do wrong, that moment they set in motion the Great Universal or Cosmic Law of retribution, and they can no more avoid retribution striking them sometime, somewhere, than they can stop the action of the planets. To the innocent victim, retribution sometimes seems a long time coming, but the longer its arrival is delayed, the more powerful it acts, when it does arrive. There is no human being in existence that can avoid this Law.

Many times students and individuals have thought that something could be wished upon them. Such I assure you is not the case. The only way one can open himself to undesirable thought is by entering into condemnation and hate. Then, if he has done this, he has generated the thing in which he believed. The student, who knows the Power of God within himself, need never fear anything from anyone. The individual may, if he or she choose, experience the

Fulness of the Activity of God in his Life and world. It is simply a matter of choosing what you shall have. If you want peace and harmony, know: "I AM the Power producing it." If you want adjustment in your affairs and world, know: "I AM the Mighty Intelligence and Power producing it and no outer-activity can interfere with it."

From out the seeming mystery of Life's ceaseless activity, is the Illumining Presence of the "Mighty I AM Within," that stands ever ready to bless you with untold inconceivable blessings, if you only *let* It. How do you let it? By the joyous acceptance of the Mighty Presence, that you have this Mighty Power within you, and then do not hesitate in every detail of your activity, no matter how small it seems, to call It into action, for there is no energy in the Universe, but God to act through your consciousness, your mind, your body, your world.

Say often: "I AM the Presence" in everything you wish to have done. This opens the way for the Power of God to act and bring you justice. *Have no sympathy for the outer, that in its ignorance does the wrong thing.* (Whether in yourself or someone else.)

Keep calm and serene, knowing: "God is the only Intelligence and Power acting in your world and affairs." "I AM" in you, is the Self-sustaining strength and healing, manifesting in your mind and body. This keeps you in greater attunement. Face God:

and the Energy always surges forth to command every situation. Individuals who understand this Law, are not subject to injustice and the conditions, which the outer selves of other beings try to impose upon them.

Keep the outer reminded of this often. Be sure always within yourselves that there is only the Presence and Power of God acting in you and your affairs. Keep using the statement at all times that: "There is nothing hidden that is not revealed to me." This is always necessary. However, no matter what individuals want to do, your safeguard is always to pour out the Love of God to them.

When individuals try to enjoy something, through injustice, without question they never enjoy it, for they always lose some faculty by which they could enjoy it.

Other personalities always have the same privilege to stand with God that you do, and if they do not choose, that is not your business.

God is the All-knowing Presence and Power, knows and discovers all things. You may say for another:

"Mighty Master Self, the 'I AM Presence' within this individual, come forth in Thy Conscious Power, with Thy Mighty insight and foresight, with Thy Wisdom and Directing Intelligence, and see that all things are adjusted for her and that she is given the peace and rest, she so much deserves. I AM the

Commanding Presence directing and commanding this to be done and it is done now. Lift the consciousness into the Full Dazzling Light, where she may see and know the repose, rest and beauty that is hers by her own creation and service."

It is a mistake to let sympathy draw you into conditions that are very destructive. Take the stand: "I AM the only Presence acting there." For helping those who have passed on through so-called death:

"I AM the Presence holding that individual in the sphere where he belongs, teaching and enlightening him."

If the student can get the correct idea of pouring out the Love to his own Divine Self, *he will receive complete relief from every discord.* To perfect conditions say:

"I AM the Presence there governing and healing the situation."

Mankind in general and the doctors have distorted things pitifully. The individual, who wants to rise into the "God Presence" and live there, needs the energy he wastes. The very energy individuals waste is the force and strength, by which, they are enabled to hold fast to the "God Presence." This Energy is the Life they need to enable them to turn and hold steadfast to the "God Presence." When the outer-self has for centuries used That Energy to create wrong conditions, that waste of the energy becomes a wide open drain upon the consciousness of individuals.

Doctors are responsible for much of this terrible condition for they teach the gratification of the sex appetite, and that is the greatest avenue of waste that human beings have to contend with. This is what makes it impossible to hold fast to the "God Presence" long enough to attain the Mastery. This is ninety-five per cent of the cause for old age and the loss of sight, hearing, and memory, as these faculties only cease to function when there is no longer a stream of this Life Energy flowing into the cellular structure of the brain. You cannot tell this to individuals, until they have had such hard knocks, that they are almost desperate with the misery of their own creation before they will listen to you. The will is absolutely nothing without this Life Energy.

There is only one possible way to change anything that has been created and directed into a wrong channel. The attention is what holds it fast to the wrong use or expression of it. Instantly direct the thought to the Higher Self. Many people get the idea that they can control it by sheer force of will, through compulsion. This cannot be done, for you but dam it up, and it only breaks out somewhere else.

The only permanent way to overcome it is to change the attention and rise out of it. Use the statement: "I AM the Governing Presence of this Energy and the only power that can raise it. I AM the Presence raising and transcending it, and that action is forever Self-sustained." Know: "I AM the Presence doing this and therefore it is done now, for God's Activity is always instantaneous."

In any wrong condition, the first thing to do is to call on the Law of Forgiveness. Remember, that when a thing has been set in motion, or energized, it simply acts.

The physical body is the vehicle for contact with the sense world. When nearing the point of precipitation, continue on using the physical vehicle for doing the ordinary physical service. There is the Inner, the mental, and the physical world. The physical body has been created to act in the lower rate of vibration and is the natural vehicle provided.

To direct and handle physical objects by the mind alone needs an accumulation of Electronic Force in the Electronic Circle of the individual. When using the Energy below the Ascended State, this Consciously Generated Energy is held within the Electronic Circle, that surrounds every individual to a more or less degree. This accounts for some individuals seeming to have a limitless amount of energy, for that which is accumulated in one lifetime is carried over into the succeeding lives.

Perhaps one of the most unfortunate things in which human beings live is the man's so-called legal right to bind another individual in the sex activity, when the other wishes to rise out of it.

Even in the ignorance of the outer mind, some natures have a powerful development of the Love Activity. The Pure Love of God never goes below the heart. True Love never requires sex contact of any kind. The Great Ascended Host of Light are ever with those, who want to do right. Send your thought out to them, and you shall always receive help.

You have an Invulnerable, Invincible Power, when you know you have the recognition of the "I AM Presence."

The Law of Forgiveness is the wide-open door to reach the Heart of God. It is the Keynote and Hub on which the Universe turns.

BENEDICTION: Thou Mighty Infinite Presence of God! we give praise and thanks for Thy ceaseless ministry. We call Thy Blessings, Thy Wisdom, Thy Intelligence to act through each one, giving peace of mind, peace of body, and joy of heart, to go forth the Ruling, Conquering, Victorious Presence over all things. We give praise and thanks that the "Mighty Presence I AM," *God in Action,* governs all official places, causing Thy Perfection to be ever-operative and Self-sustained in Thy Name and through Thy Presence.

DISCOURSE XIII

November 14, 1932

SAINT GERMAIN

INVOCATION: Thou Majestic Presence, Infinite Creator of all there is, the "Great I AM," visible and invisible, manifest and unmanifest! We rejoice in Thy Great and Mighty Presence, that Thou hast made us aware of Thy Limitless Power, Thy Infinite Intelligence, Thy Eternal Youth and Beauty. We give praise and thanks that we have become so aware of Thy Great Opulence, Thy Great Abundance, that we feel It like a mighty river in our hands and use, Thou Mighty Endless Source! Thou Ceaseless Stream! that Thou hast made us aware, that: "I AM the Mighty Power of Precipitation." We bow before Thee in adoration and full acceptance of Thy Mighty Presence and Power.

I bring you greetings from the Great Host, and the Great Light of the Illumined Ones is growing rapidly stronger.

THE DISCOURSE

"I AM the Resurrection and the Life."

"I AM the Energy you use in every action."

"I AM the Light, illumining every cell of your Being."

"I AM the Intelligence, the Wisdom directing your every effort."

"I AM the Substance, omnipresent, without limit, which you may use and bring into form without any limit.

"I AM Thy Strength,—Thy Perfect Understanding."

"I AM Thy Ability to apply it constantly."

"I AM the Truth that gives you now Perfect Freedom."

"I AM the open doorway into the 'Light of God that never fails.' "

"I give praise, I have entered into this 'Light' fully, using that Perfect Understanding."

"I AM Thy Sight, that sees all things visible and invisible."

"I AM Thy Hearing, listening to the bells of freedom, which I have now."

"I AM Thy Ability sensing the most ravishing fragrance at will."

"I AM the Completeness of all Perfection you ever wish to manifest."

"I AM the Full Understanding, Power, and Use of all this Perfection."

"I AM the Full Revelation and use of all the powers of my Being which I AM."

"I AM the Love, the Mighty Motive Power back of all action."

I wish to give the most kindly warning to the students under this radiation, *to watch every feeling,* that at no time anyone accept a feeling of jealousy at the progress of another. Each student must always remember, that he has no concern whatsoever, with the other students, except to know that: "I AM the God Presence, there in action." For one student to wonder and question, in his own mind about the progress of another, is most retarding and it is never admissible.

Each student must understand that his only concern is the harmonizing, quickening, and expansion of his own mind and world. The sooner students understand, that the one imperative demand of *the Great Law of their Being is harmony of the mind and feelings,* the quicker will Perfection manifest. Without this being maintained, they cannot go beyond a certain state of progress.

As soon as the students realize this, and begin to use the "I AM Presence," commanding the harmony and silence of the outer-activity, they will find that they can see, feel, and be that Perfection, which they so much desire. When students and friends have a deep, sincere Love for each other, that is not inquisitiveness, that Love is the greatest blessing and uplifting power. Here is one criterion by which a student may gauge himself, at all times, determining what is the power acting.

If one *feels* critical, inquisitive, or out of harmony toward a person, condition, place, or thing, it is a sure signal that the outer-self is acting, and the right attitude is to correct it immediately. Everyone, especially students, must realize, that they have only one thing to do and that is to feel, see, and be Perfection in their own world.

This is so very important is the reason I am stressing it so much at this time, because as students begin to experience unusual manifestation through their efforts, there is always that presence at first, which will say to the individual: "I AM able to use the Law better than the other person." This you know, without my saying it, is a mistake.

One cannot long use the statement "I AM" even intellectually, until he begins to feel a deeper and deeper conviction that: "I AM all things." Think often, what these marvelous two words mean, and *always couple with the use of these two words the statement that: "When I say, 'I AM,' I AM setting in motion the Limitless Power of God in whatever I couple the expression 'I AM' with."* In the Scriptural statement: "Before Abraham, was 'I AM.'" Abraham represents the outer expression of Life and "I AM" represents the Principle of Life, which was expressing through Abraham. Thus, was the Perfection of Life, before any manifestation ever occurred, and thus is Life without beginning and without end.

My beloved students! my heart rejoices exceedingly in the nearness with which some of you are feeling the conviction of this Majestic Presence, "I AM," which you are. Do your utmost to feel calmly, serenely, and if you cannot see it otherwise, shut your eyes and see Perfection everywhere. More and more there will come to you proof of the marvelous Presence of this Truth. You will hear, feel, see, and experience that marvel of all marvels which as children you have lived in,—miracles performed.

There have been written for your benefit, descriptions and explanations of the use of this "Mighty I AM Presence." You, who hold fast to the Truth will come into the three-fold action, seeing, hearing, and experiencing these so-called miracles, miracles until you understand their operation, and then majestic simple truths, which you may forever apply, when once understood.

With all my centuries of experience, I cannot help but say to you as encouragement, that my heart leaps with joy at the nearness with which some of you are grasping the Scepter of Dominion. Go forward, my brave ones. Do not hesitate. Grasp your Scepter of Dominion! Raise it! for: *"I AM the Scepter, the Quenchless Flame, the Dazzling Light, the Perfection, which you once knew."* Come! let me hold you in my strong embrace, that where there have been so long two, there will only be one, "I AM." I AM the

Knower, the Doer, the Perfection expressed now.

I again speak to the individuals, wanting so much to have their problems solved. There is only One Presence in the Universe that can or ever does solve any problem, and that is the "I AM Presence," everywhere present. Beloved ones, let me say in all kindness: "There is no use just seeking to have a problem solved, because where one was, a dozen may appear, but when you know the Perfect Attitude is to enter into the 'I AM Presence,' knowing It is the Unquestionable Solver of every problem, you will as surely as I AM telling you, cause all problems to disappear; for where you live constantly, calmly, and with sufficient determination, in the 'I AM Presence,' instead of having many appear, where one has been solved, you will have entered into the State where there are none."

I command the power in these words to-day to carry to everyone, who hears or reads them, the True Conviction and Understanding back of them.

For the Brain: "I AM the quickening of the cells of this (my or your) brain structure, causing it to expand and receive the Intelligent Direction of the Mighty Inner Presence."

You must know that you have the power, through the "I AM Presence" to consciously qualify your thought in whatever way you will. There is naught to say what you shall do, for you are a Free Being of

Free Will. If you could be conscious of every thought that passed through your mind for six weeks, and keep it qualified with Perfection, you would see the most amazing results. Say often: "I AM the Master Within governing and controlling all my thought processes in full Christ Perfection as I wish them to be."

Blessing and holding others in the Light: When you bless others or visualize them in the Light, there is a double activity of the quality you send out. In doing this, there is a certain amount of protection that is the automatic result, but the thought and quality in the Light and blessing registers principally within one's own consciousness and at the same time intensifies that quality in the one to whom it is sent.

Take the eternal stand that: "I AM what I want to be." You must use the "I AM Presence" consciously always. Rarely, even among students, have they realized deeply what the "I AM Presence" meant. Only occasionally has any real comprehension of the "I AM" come forth, except in the retreats. Jesus was the first to stress it to the outer world. I urge you earnestly, do not give any consideration to the element of time. Manifestation must come instantly when you give the "I AM Presence" freedom enough. Go on, apply, and know, and let the "I AM Presence" take care of the element of time.

When you make a declaration of Truth and stick to it, you must receive. The outer has no power of itself at all. Its duty is simply to know that the "I AM Presence" is acting. Sometimes without being aware of it, the outer-self is looking for the time of manifestation.

I can convey to you the conviction and the feeling that when you command as the "I AM Presence" Almighty God moves into action.

Remember at all times, that when you are dealing with personalities, you are dealing with the outer human creation, and have all right and power to command its silence and obedience, whether it is in your own outer-self or someone's else.

If you will count ten before you speak, you can control all sudden impulse, and back of this is a Mighty Law, which can help the student immensely. When there is a sudden impulse, there is a release or rushing forward of accumulated energy. If there be anger, then the energy is instantly qualified with it, or with destruction of some kind.

The power of Self-control would say: "Only God's Perfection goes forth." This will handle any condition of uncontrolled impulses with which the individual is contending. When the student has already let something go forth, that is undesirable, then the thing to do is to consciously consume it—instantly.

The constant use of "God bless this," directed to

inanimate things, brings amazing accomplishment. *The easy way to see and feel Perfection is to qualify every thought and feeling going forth with Perfection.* When an impulse comes to do anything, instantly qualify it with Perfection.

Story of the engine in a small town: The whistle is the warning, the "I AM" is the control of the engine.

The ordinary human being would not think of running over children and killing them, yet he releases wrongly qualified energy, in thought, feeling, and words, that kill the higher impulses in others. If your personality is not controlled and governed, it has the same qualities as all other outer selves, or personalities, but your "I AM Presence" is the Perfect Control of it.

There is nothing more tragic in the world, than for one person to hold the thought of limitation over another human being. A thought, of imperfection driven at a sensitive person, sometimes limits that one for years and many times the results are very tragic. We must all give everyone his complete freedom mentally. If you speak of freedom for yourself, be sure and give it first to everyone else. When there is a condition in another that we wish to help, use the following: "I AM the Perfect Manifestation there."

The principle within both energy and substance is the same. Substance holds energy within it naturally.

The heart center of substance is Intelligent Action. Vibration in its natural state is pure, always. Vibration is energy in action and must be qualified.

The pulsation in all substance is the "Breath of God" acting. Think when breathing: "I AM the Perfect Energy of every breath I breathe. I AM the pure atmosphere of my world."

Form the habit of constantly qualifying your world with Perfection. The old habit of thinking imperfection has filled your world in the past. Now the important thing is to be Self-conscious that you are filling your world with Perfection all the time. Stand on your feet the first thing in the morning, and say with feeling: "I AM the Presence filling my world with Perfection this day."

Do not be concerned about personalities.

To take the stand: "I AM Perfection acting through any official," would impel the "I AM Power and Action" there.

The first thing in the morning say: "I qualify everything in my world this day with Perfection, because 'I AM Perfection.' I qualify this mind and body with Absolute Perfection and refuse acceptance of anything else."

"I AM" the miracle and "I AM" the Presence compelling its manifestation through Divine Love, Wisdom and Power.

When individuals come and ask about certain use

of the "Law," always preface your statement with,—
"You are an individual of free will, but this is the
way I feel about it."

What is required for the growth of one person may
be entirely different from that for someone else. You
cannot expand so long as you have an opinion about
anyone else. It is stifling to your own progress. There
is a time comes with everyone, when he must stand up
and face himself, his outer creation, then say this:
"Whatever there is of imperfection left in me, has
to get out."

Your constructive desire is, *God in action,* doing
the thing.

Your desire holds the power or energy of the "I
AM" through the attention on the thing you desire
to do.

"I AM the Full Revelation and the Perfect Application, for precipitating what I desire, and I do
know what is the Perfect Thing to do in the outer-
self, while precipitating. Say often:

"I AM the precipitating 'Presence' of this thing."
Do not be anxious, just know it with calm certainty.
When you are conscious of the "I AM" acting, you
know it is moving forward. Do not let in the sense of
disappointment.

"I AM the Perfect Harmony of my thought, feeling, and action."

BENEDICTION: Out of Thy Pure Essence, we

receive now and forever Thy Strength, Thy Wisdom, Thy Understanding application of Thy Great and Marvelous Laws that we may produce and maintain Thy Perfection in each Life, mind, body, home, and world.

NOTES

In a recent news-reel, there have been pictured certain chemical activities and how to use this chemical action upon flowers to qualify them with the desired fragrance. Instead of raising them in the earth, they are growing them in water with excelsior over the top. This shows how near the chemists and scientists are coming to bringing things forth direct from the Universal. This shows the "Inner Activity" coming into conscious, definite use, or the activity held in Consciously Directed Rays.

"I AM the only acting Presence in this deal."

"I AM the intelligent activity in their minds."

"I AM the protection in myself and my property."

"I AM the Intelligence and Presence acting everywhere."

"I AM the visible opulence I desire."

"I AM the 'Presence' producing abundance wherever I choose to use it."

DISCOURSE XIV

November 17, 1932

FAITH—HOPE—CHARITY

Saint Germain

INVOCATION: I AM the Joy, the Courage, the Confidence pervading all the earth,—filling the hearts of mankind,—consuming all generated thought of depression or lack in the minds of mankind, and that which has been sent forth through lack of confidence shall be wiped from the earth.

I AM the Presence, the Perfect Christ Activity, in the minds of all humanity, filling all official places, causing It to sustain all personalities, causing them to turn with quick certainty to the Source of their Being, the Perfect Life manifest in all outer expression. I AM the Presence proclaiming the Conscious Active Divinity in manifestation everywhere.

This shall be! for: "I AM the Supreme Conquering Presence. I AM here and I AM there. I go everywhere touching the brains of mankind as with a streak of Lightning, not with consuming power, but with the 'I AM Presence' that will no longer be gainsaid."

I bring you greetings, joy and Love from the Great Host.

It is so wonderful, beloved ones, to have such perfect peace and calmness in your minds these mornings. Oh! could you understand the value of maintaining that peace of mind. There is nothing that warrants it being disturbed.

Your melodies were beautiful and wonderful words shall come forth to bless through the melodies. There is that Great Joy and Advancing Conquering Presence that will bless your home, world, and students with its Glorifying Presence, with its Presence of opulence streaming forth like a mighty river to all who make themselves worthy, by the peace and harmony of mind.

THE DISCOURSE

I wish to call your attention this morning to the Active Presence of Faith, Hope, and Charity. In this consideration, we will think of Faith as the Conquering, Emanating Power; Hope, the open doorway through the veil, acting in the Pure Presence; Charity, as the determination to think no evil, to speak no evil, see no evil, hear no evil, feel no evil.

Students should always watch the Inner Activity of the outer-mind and not let themselves be fooled by its action. This may sound like a paradox, but it is not. This is more important than it seems at first. If there is lurking back in the consciousness any feeling of resistance—of any kind whatsoever—or that something, which is always ready to bristle when something displeases, pluck it out by the roots. You know it is of the outer, and it will stand in the way of your attainment to prevent it, until you do pluck it out.

To maintain a tranquil, sweet disposition in the face of all things is the certain road to Self-control and Absolute Mastery. This is much more important than any of you can possibly understand at this time, for your attainment of all that you desire.

The Cosmic Masters, Faith, Hope, and Charity: In calling your attention to these three principles, always active in the Life of mankind, I want to assure you that they are not only qualities within yourselves, but there are Beings of Great Light and advancement, who are also known as Faith, Hope, and Charity. The individuals and students, who make the conscious effort to cultivate these qualities and consciously expand them in their worlds, will find themselves receiving great assistance from these Conscious Mighty Beings, from whose names come these qualities in individualization. These are Cosmic, Self-conscious, Intelligent Beings, whose special action with mankind is to encourage and expand these qualities. Therefore, let all the students understand that this is far more than a scriptural phrase or expression. At this time, these Great Ones have come from out the "Cosmic Silence" because of the need of faith, hope, and charity in the minds and hearts of mankind.

The sinister force, that would have destroyed the confidence, the hope, and the charity in the minds of the American People, is doomed to fail utterly. Even now, hundreds, who voted for a wet administration, are finding their own uncontrolled thought recoiled upon them, and are regretting the unwisdom of the action. So out of seeming wrong activity will still come great good. Since the hypnotic force, that was generated, has spent itself, many of mankind are wondering what caused them to do certain things, and their very rebellion will generate the force, that will be used to correct conditions after all.

God, which is Progress, knows no defeat in anything. Let students always remember this, which will enable them to maintain the so much needed peace and poise of mind.

The Majestic Being, "Charity," has a natural consuming force for dissolving and annihilating hate, criticism, and condemnation, and uses the Cosmic Rays as a balancing force in the ethers from which human beings are drawing their very breath and sustenance. So in spite of themselves, they are breathing in the Fire of these Rays.

This reminds me of an illustration. You know, when a person is fainting, many times you hold the smelling salts or ammonia under that one's nose. This is what is acutally taking place under the nose of humanity. It is now breathing in this Consuming Presence. (Ask your students not to discuss this fact with unbelievers, but it is vital that the students understand this.)

Here I want to stress something earnestly. To the earnest, sincere student, there are innumerable means of assistance available to him, much of which is and will remain entirely unknown to him, but from which he nevertheless draws, when his desire for the Light is sincere.

To throw everything to the winds, and stand joyously and determinedly in that "One Mighty Presence, which I AM," enables us to have a continuous stream of victories marked down to our benefit. No effort ever made in the "Name and Presence, which I AM," can ever fail, but must go forward from one victory to another, until one attains and is able to use the Scepter of his Full Dominion.

I wish to encourage and strengthen the very important advancing consciousness concerning the Law of Forgiveness. The correct way to call into action the Law of Forgiveness, is to say: "I AM the Law of Forgiveness and Consuming Flame of all inharmonious action and human consciousness." This sets into motion the completed action.

When we use the statement: "I call on the Law of Forgiveness," we are not always completing the action, because we need to be conscious of who and where that Intelligence is that enables it to be done.

As I look among the students, I find that it is important to keep touching frequently upon the use of the "I AM Presence," for it is doing remarkable things for them already. My very Being lifts up, when I see among the students, those whose attention is held with determination upon the "I AM Presence," how the student becomes a powerful magnet for the Light, and how it rushes to envelop each one, as a mother enfolds her loving child. Could they see and realize this for one moment, their determination would surge into a Conquering Flame, from which there could be no receding.

The time is apropos to-day, and I send forth to each of you and the students, a Conscious Ball of Light, enveloping the heart and brain of each one, that they may receive more continuously the conscious blessing of the "Mighty I AM Presence." I believe that most of them will feel this. Whether they do or not, nothing can interfere with its action to bless them.

To those blessed ones, who find disturbance in the home at times, I would suggest that they use this statement and feel it deeply: "I AM the Conquering Presence commanding peace, Love and harmony in my home and environment." Anyone, who will use this with determination, can have a peaceful, loving, harmonious atmosphere in the home. Some may need to build a momentum to experience its continuous action. Many times, they will have immediate results. To build this into the consciousness is recognizing the "I AM Presence" as the Ruling Power in their homes, for it is *naturally* the Ruling Presence.

If students and individuals, who have difficulty in maintaining Self-control, will sit quietly for five minutes, feeling deeply and thinking to themselves: "I AM Loving Charity," they will find a sense of great relief.

For fainting: You know, speaking of fainting, the individual never faints, only the personality does that. Therefore, if one, who is in the habit of fainting, will take this determined stand: "I AM the Commanding Presence forbidding this nonsense, and I forever maintain control of my mind and body," they will forever control it.

When one first feels the least disturbance, quickly take the consciousness: "I AM the Commanding Presence, and I maintain my consciousness here." One must realize that in the command of the "I AM Presence" he has Absolute Control of this body. The more anyone uses this, the more quickly does manifestation take place.

Q. If the Great Central Sun is the Heart Center of the Infinite, where is that which is the brain center?

A. *"In the pure state, whether in the Infinite or the finite, when there is no imperfection, the brain*

*and heart activity become One, for the motive power
of all activity sent forth is 'Love from the Heart.' "*
Therefore, in the Pure State, the heart and brain are
synonymous, for within Divine Love is contained
Love, Wisdom, and Power.

The Infinite Energy is always present awaiting
use, but does not act except under Conscious Command, in the Life of an individual. There does come
a time in the progress of the individual, when things
act so instantaneously that it seems to be automatic,
but it really never is.

There is absolutely but one road to Self-conscious
Mastery and that is the *Conscious Direction* of the
Eternal Energy into whatever you desire. Now this
brings us to another quite vital point.

Desire is an indirect action of the *attention,* but
desire, sustained by the *determined use of the attention,* causes the desire to become an invincible manifestation. This will give you a slight idea of how
important it is that conscious direction be coupled
with the desire. Conscious use of the "I AM Presence" or the consciously directed use of this Eternal
Energy to a given accomplishment should at no time
be anything but a most joyous effort. It should never
seem like work or tension in any way, because when
you declare: "I AM the Presence, the Intelligence,
directing this energy to a given purpose," you set the
Law in motion in a perfect, easy, calm manner, and it

does not require any "tearing the hair" effort. There-fore, it should always be a calm, serene, determined procedure.

The student should at all times understand that the student never chooses the Master, but the Master chooses the student. Did the student understand what consciousness he was to maintain, it would come about very much sooner. For contacting the Ascended Masters, use: "I AM the Presence preparing the way and bringing visible contact with the Beloved Arisen Masters."

With the use of the "I AM Presence," you have Full Command and Limitless Control over all dis-turbing conditions. When you speak in the "I AM Presence," you are speaking in the "Presence" which the Arisen Being is. You must realize deeply that when you say, "I AM" it is the Full God-Power *acting* and knows no failure of any kind.

BENEDICTION: We give praise and thanks for Thy Infinite Outpouring, "Great I AM Presence." We give praise and thanks that at last, we know Who Thou art and that within Thee are all possibilities. We give praise and thanks that Thy Mighty Pres-ence is always the Governing Intelligence, the Love enfolding, the Light illumining everything on the way.

DISCOURSE XV

November 21, 1932

SAINT GERMAIN

INVOCATION: Thou Mighty Conquering Presence, the Majesty of "I AM" everywhere! we give praise and thanks for Thy Mighty Presence everywhere, Thy All-pervading Energy and Power ever stands at the door of our consciousness for use—that we may consciously direct it to manifest Thy Wondrous Perfection. Forever, we give praise and thanks to Thee for Thy Mighty Presence.

I bring you greetings from the Great Ascended Host, always giving their assistance that you may manifest Perfection.

THE DISCOURSE

Out of the glorious fulness of God's Omnipresent Light and Substance, comes the fullness of all things.

The student, who is strong enough—firm enough—to stand alone with his or her "Mighty I AM Presence," never dividing for a single hour the Presence and power of God, will find himself or herself steadily rising into that Mighty Perfection, forever free from all sense or recognition of any limitation.

The student is fortunate indeed who can hold himself or herself within this Mighty Presence undivided.

For the benefit of some of the students who are so sincere, and yet are unknowingly allowing their attention to be withheld from that Undivided Presence, I wish to state certain facts with no intent to intrude upon the free will of the individual.

These records, which I shall quote, we have within our possession, and they cover the past one hundred years. That of which I wish to speak to-day is the delusion of astrology.

No one living can give his attention to astrology and enter into the "Presence of the I AM" and remain there. Underlying the present use of astrology is the human desire and opportunity to justify and gratify the outer desires. Here let me state an appalling fact, which is within the records we have: "There is no one thing or phase of study which has caused more failure or more indirect murder, than the present delusion of astrology."

In your City of Chicago, within very recent years, was a splendid student of metaphysics, who, consciously accepting the delusion of his horoscope, was driven to commit suicide.

The one thing humanity needs most, and students above all else, is the firm rock and consciousness of the "Mighty I AM Presence," upon which to stand safely and free from the pit-falls of outer concoctions. It is not the negative statements of prospective death and the so-called ill-fated star force to be overcome, that students need to know, but the "Unconquerable, all-pervading I AM Presence" that is the only and all Life of their Beings, to which their attention needs to be drawn and held there with a firm grasp.

In the "I AM Presence" there is no height the student may not reach, but by allowing his attention to be held by astrology, numerology, the many isms of to-day, there is no depth he may not reach.

The present use of astrology has no semblance of the use to which it was put centuries ago. Then, it conveyed no negative statements of any kind. The great harm of the attention fixed upon it is that students accept the negative statements far more than they are willing to admit. The sinister negative force generated by mankind in the world, always takes advantage of such things as this to get and hold the attention, especially of the student who is progressing, and thus, keep it upon that which will pull him down instead of raising him up.

Where there is a horoscope that indicates the death of someone, various minds become fixed upon that idea, and actual indirect murder is committed, so subtle, that individuals would be shocked to be reminded that they had any part in it, but I assure you it is none the less the Truth for all of their surprise.

Could the students of astrology see for one day, from the Great Inner Standpoint, the destructive force generated and used, through the present use of

astrology, they would turn from it as from a poison-
ous serpent, waiting to strike death into their veins.

I say to you, beloved students, in the name of your
Light and progress, and of all progress, stand within
your own "Mighty I AM Presence," let not your
attention be held or divided by any outer thing, if
you wish to avoid the wheel of birth and rebirth
indefinitely.

From the Great Love of my heart—seeing and
knowing from the Inner Standpoint, as you do not
and cannot possibly as yet—I urge you to avoid
everything that savors of a negative expression or condition. Then, you shall rise on the Wings of your
"Mighty I AM Presence" into that Ever-lasting Freedom and Blessing of the Perfect, Eternal, Limitless
Light.

As I said, I do not wish in any manner to intrude
upon your free will, but the gates of Eternal Freedom are open before you, if you will but believe the
Truth I have uttered, which will enable you to enter
within these gates, and receive the Eternal Blessing of
the Light, waiting there to enfold you.

If there are conditions in your Life, home, or environment that you wish to be rid of, command—
through the "I AM Presence"—that they be dissolved
and consumed before its Mighty Light and Power.

Beloved students, who have come under this radiation, with you we shall not touch upon this subject

again. May the "I AM Presence" within you enable you to see the Light and Truth of which I have spoken. I have seen within you the Glorious Light that can be quickened into a Dazzling Radiance, enabling you to express Perfection. Hence, of my own volition have I offered my humble assistance, but if the personality persists in allowing the attention to be held on *anything* but the "Mighty I AM Presence"—which I know is the Mightiest and Only Raising Presence and Solver of all problems—then my humble efforts must necessarily be in vain.

I assure you, dear ones, you have reached a point where you must go up or down. With your determined attention and acknowledgment, constantly held on the "Mighty I AM Presence," there is no condition, force, or Presence in earth or heaven that can prevent your wondrous, glorious attainment into Ever lasting Freedom and Perfection.

If you have not That within you, which causes you to feel and tells you of the Great Divine Love that enables me to voice this Truth to you for your protection, then we must but wait such time as the Truth of It does appear within you.

When students and individuals have once learned of and acknowledged the "Mighty I AM Presence" and then allow their attention to longer be held by or upon outer things, whether it be consciously or unconsciously, makes little difference, for they are deliberately turning their backs to the "Presence" which is the Source of their Being and the Life within them that enables them to move their bodies about. I declare, with all the Love of my Being that: "I AM the Presence" enabling you to see and feel this Truth and stand by and within It, for the sake of your own wondrous progress.

Those, who will hold steadfast enough to That Mighty Presence, will find abundant proof coming into their experience of Its Limitless Power and Intelligence.

Beloved Students! many hands of the Arisen Host are extended to you to give Their assistance, when you can hold your undivided attention on the Active Presence of God in you, and stand there unyielding to the pull of all outer appearance.

"Truth is Mighty and does prevail." May you feel Its Majestic Presence at all times. It is a mistake on the part of the student to feel disappointment, because a certain thing he has worked on does not manifest instantly, when as yet, he has not generated great enough power and activity to produce it that quickly. The attention must always be on the "I AM" only.

Suppose, I were to declare: "I AM the Mighty 'I AM Presence' in Action," and then an hour later, I allowed my attention to be fixed on a star in a so-called adverse aspect to me or an outer condition that indicates disaster of some kind. Do you not see how that would annul the statement I had made that would liberate the power of freedom?

Jesus said: "Ye cannot serve two masters." This means that you cannot divide the attention—for we must stop, look, and listen. I tell you, you cannot make steady progress, if you give power to anything but your "Mighty I AM Presence." The unfortunate thing with so many students is that they do not hold long and steadily enough to the Mighty truth of their Being to gain momentum and strength enough to stand against the pull of suggestion and outer appearance.

The strange thing to me is, that when the student's attention has been once drawn to the All Power of the "I AM Presence"—which is the Only Active Principle of Life they have, *God in Action,* within and about them—they cannot or do not see that they are dividing the power, when the attention is fixed on outer things; and but delaying the magnificent activity and accomplishment which the "I AM Presence" would otherwise bring forth. However, having gone through the mill, so to speak, we have Infinite Patience to wait until the beloved student can grasp his Scepter of Dominion of this "Mighty I AM Presence" and hold it.

I could bring you records of the most appalling things done through the suggestion of astrology. Crimes are committed every week of the year by the suggestions given out through it. *The suggestion given sets the Law into action to accomplish it*. When your attention is on a thing, the power within your-self goes instantly into it.

If the astrologers do not stop holding the thought of death against——, she will pass out. It is criminal. —— is a child of God and is entitled to live here as long, as is decreed. I shall do what I am permitted to protect ——. There are crimes so much worse than physical murder that there is no comparison: because they are committed deliberately by people who know better than to do them. There is one certain, unfailing action of the Law and that is that those who do these things must pay the penalty of a like experience.

To negative suggestions from others say: " 'I AM the Presence,' annulling all this, so it cannot affect me or my home or world." It is the easiest thing in the world to consciously dissipate something that is voiced in your Presence. Simply say: "I AM the only Presence acting here."

To anything you do not wish to continue say: "Through the Presence that I AM this thing shall cease now and forever." Go after it like you were going to knock over a wall. When you really *feel* and *mean* a thing, *you loose the power that does the thing*. Try to realize the Limitless Power at your command.

In the feeling is both sight and hearing, because

we can both hear and see without using the faculties of sight and hearing.

When one becomes instantly angry, he punctures other spheres of that quality and the accumulation rides in. Jealousy is the wide-open channel upon which every other destructive activity rides in. When things are done consciously they have much more power. When the energy is released, it acts because the individual has set it into motion, and it makes no difference whether he be king or chimney-sweep.

When the feelings are excited, they are accepting that instant. You can sit and listen to destructive conversation unaffected, so long as you control the feeling at the solar plexus. There cannot a thing enter your world, unless it be invited.

No good ever came of gambling. —— at one time had a most wonderful power and influence about her. She began to play the market and not only lost the power, but her money as well. Is it not better to stand with your "I AM Presence" than with a gambling channel? *Anything* that gets your *attention* is a subtle activity of the outer to pull you away from your freedom.

For financial freedom: "I AM the riches of God flowing into my hands and use that nothing can stop."

Say Often: " 'The Presence I AM' governs every existing channel in manifestation. It governs all."

A student's Experience: The student had heard and seen an explosion of Light, while the physical body was asleep. If she had consciously said, when she heard the explosion: "I draw into my mind and body the strength of the Light Explosion," she would have received its benefit. The Light was the liberating of certain powers for her use. In such experiences, the important thing for the student to do is *to be alert* and in every manifestation be conscious of the indrawing of Its power. Rejoice that it is the Mighty Power of the "I AM Presence" acting, giving Its strength and power to you.

Command the outer memory to retain and bring into the outer consciousness everything you desire to know. When you use the "I AM Presence" you have set the Law into action and it cannot fail.

God does not act, except through the consciousness of individuals, else he would not have them here. God can only act in the physical world through his individualizations, and even all nature is governed by Individual Intelligence, the ground, the plants, and all.

There is omnipresent all the force and energy needed for a given purpose when loosed by the "I AM Presence." Thus, through the use of the "I AM Presence" you can release power of which as yet, you have no conception.

During the war, when Foch said: "They shall not

pass," he loosed the power by which that decree was fulfilled. He had been in prayer for more than an hour, and when he came out, he was so charged with that energy that as he uttered the command, it became the Governing Presence in the atmospheric condition about him and God acted. The words—"They shall not pass" form a decree. It is dynamic, powerful, real, and looses tremendous power. There is only One Power that acts. Give it full freedom.

Stand with IT and let IT act. Stand in IT and by IT. There is no other power to act. This makes a steady progress, like a glacier coming down the mountain. You are steadily moving forward and gaining a momentum against which nothing else can stand. It is an Infallible momentum, power, and means of achievement of all good things. There is no permanent dominion except in this way.

For Cleanliness, use frequently: "I AM the Presence here keeping my clothes and home perfectly spotless." After a time, the force becomes so powerful, that it instantly consumes or repels anything not wanted. The more you consciously act upon a thing the more concentrated it becomes.

When you say: "The Presence that I am, charge this —— with ——," you can charge the water so powerfully, that it boils with the power of the energy there. Do not let anything question in your mind as to whether your command worked or not.

Whenever commanding say: "I know it is acting with full power."

Know—What the "I AM" means;

Know—What It is to you;

Know—What It can do;

Get this and hold fast with unyielding determination.

Within these students there is the strength, and power to do this, and if they will stand with this "Mighty I AM Presence," great assistance can and will be given.

BENEDICTION: Mighty All-pervading Intelligence! we *invoke* Thy Mighty Wisdom, governing our every activity. We *invoke* Thy Mighty Light illumining each one in the fulness of Its Dazzling Presence. We *invoke* Thy Mighty Love to enfold all in Its mantle of peace. We *invoke* Thy Mighty Power that Love, Wisdom, and Power may act in Perfect Unity, that It perfect all things upon which our attention has become fixed.

DISCOURSE XVI

November 24, 1932

THANKSGIVING DAY
THE PERSONAL RAY OF JESUS AND THE OTHER
CREATED RAYS

SAINT GERMAIN

INVOCATION: Thou Mighty Wondrous Presence! we give praise and thanks for Jesus Christ's Presence to-day. We rejoice in the Fulness of the Christ Activity, the Active Presence of God.

Out of the Fulness of This Presence comes pouring, like a mighty stream, gushing forth from the mountains, the energy of illumination. This Great and Mighty Stream of Life with all its attributes of Perfection surging into the hearts of mankind, is anchoring in everyone peace, Love, harmony, faith, and charity to all.

Thou Mighty Presence, Infinite Love, enfolding all mankind! Give special notice to these earnest students, who have come under this radiation. Give every assistance that is permissible. Strengthen them to stand unwaveringly in the Light and face the Truth, joyously willing to pluck out of their lives and creation all undesirable things.

Fill all official places with Mighty Messengers of Light! Sustain them by Thy Mighty Arisen Host, that they may be strong enough to stand unwavering and successful before any sinister force.

We give praise and thanks for this day, as an uplifting and wonderful memory established in the consciousness of mankind. May that rapidly approaching time come when every day may be a thanksgiving in the hearts of mankind, for Thy Light ever enfolding all, who wish it.

I bring you greetings from the Ascended Host and Jesus himself.

THE DISCOURSE

The first principle of activity from the Godhead is projection or precipitation. Therefore, Its nature is to project or precipitate Itself.

The first activity is the divided Rays going forth into individualization, into visible expression. When I speak of individual or visible expression, I use that term because of the physical activity, not that it is not always visible, because it is; but to those in the physical form, I speak of it as visibility.

Thus, you will see the nature of your Being, as Rays of Light, who you are, as the Natural Quality of Life, which you so much desire at this time. The day is rapidly approaching, when many, many students will begin to use the Light Rays of which they are a part, especially the Ray of Vision and Sound.

Even in your physical world to-day, there are being discovered means and uses of these Rays. These are strange activities, I say strange to the visible activity, but natural always to the Inner Presence. The manner of the use of these Rays at present is crude, it is true; but it will require only another step to take them through the veil.

The power of the "I AM Presence and Intelligence" to use these Rays will always remain infinitely more powerful than any mechanical contrivance by which they are used. However, to the student who has not yet found his ability to use these Rays, the scientist's experience will be of wondrous encouragement to know the amazing truth of the individual's ability to use them.

Here it is important to know, that there are Natural Rays penetrating through all the atmosphere or etheric belt within the earth's atmosphere. When I say natural, I mean those Rays projected from the Godhead or Great Central Sun, which in recent years, shall I say within a few years, have been made permanent.

Then, there are the Created Rays, created and projected by the Ascended Host, by those who have raised the body. The latter are the most potent of all Rays, because they are consciously manipulated.

The Rays the scientists are contacting are the Natural Rays having a certain natural potency.

The great need, as stated in the "Magic Presence," is the preparation of earnest students, who can be raised, and taught the use of these Rays. There are those among you who can do this and, as they are prepared with a determined steadfastness to the Light, they will have more and more of the law revealed to them, concerning the use of these potent forces.

I feel a very great joy in the possibilities before you and your students. I trust, they can find within themselves that strength and steadfast determination to hold fast to the outer and Inner work that is being done for them, with that joyous feeling of sureness of the limitless powers, which true freedom brings.

I have from time to time endeavored to give a word of encouragement, and through that, enfold them in the radiation of strength that is fearless and dauntless in the Light. The loving, joyous stillness in the attitude of the students is wonderfully encouraging, for the expectant attitude is the right attitude to be maintained.

I would suggest that those, who have been having unpleasant experiences, would consciously withdraw from those conditions all power they have been giving them, mostly unknowingly. When it is necessary to discuss some condition to understand it, immediately follow by withdrawing any power that has been given it, and then know: "I AM the Harmonious Presence ever-pervading, whatever the condition may be."

As I have intimated before, and it has only partially reached through, I will repeat it again: "Anyone, especially the student, who has experienced inharmony or limitation in his mind, home or world, can with persistent, tensionless effort—by holding with determination to the following statement—keep his home clear of anything undesirable: 'I AM the Governing Presence, governing in Perfect Divine Order, commanding harmony, happiness, and the Presence of God's Opulence in my mind, my home, and my world.'"

When I say: "I AM the Governing Presence," I AM fully, consciously aware, that I have set in motion the Full Power and Intelligence of God, producing the desired conditions, and that they are thus Self-sustained.

It seems to me that it has not been clearly understood, that when you use the expression: "I AM the Presence, in my mind, home, and world," you are not only commanding the Conquering Presence of this activity through your own consciousness, but *you are calling forth the assistance of the "I AM or God Presence," into your home and world, of whoever contacts it.*

This is so vital for the student to understand. Do not be discouraged, if you do not see immediate manifestation of this harmony, which you desire, but

go right on *feeling the "Conquering I AM Presence."*
Do you not see, that in This Consciousness, there is
no other Presence to act, except what you are conscious of? All other activity of the outer, that is undesirable, is but a distorted activity and use of this
Mighty Energy. Therefore, when you say: "I AM
the Conquering Presence, I command this I AM Presence to govern perfectly my mind, home, affairs, and
world," you have sent forth the Greatest Decree possible to be given, and you have but to *feel the
sustaining-power of this in the face of every appearance,* and you will find Perfection manifest in your
mind, home and world.

*I wish the students would read this particular part
every day to keep before them the Mighty Truth
underlying these statements.*

Now we come to a vital point, and that is the
Personal Ray or Rays sent forth by Jesus direct. Many
will ask, why especially Jesus? I answer: Because
humanity has been taught to look to the Presence of
Jesus the Christ, few having any knowledge at all of
the Ascended Host of the Great Masters of The
Great White Brotherhood, who wield limitless
power.

Yourselves, and your students will have, for the
next seven weeks, the Personal Ray of Jesus the
Christ. Those, who can put aside any thought of other
personalities, and with open arms, mentally speak-

ing, welcome these Rays into their minds, home, and world, may find almost anything possible.

I assure all of you, that the idea of these Personal Rays of Jesus the Christ is no imaginary thing, and you our beloved Messenger, have the personal thanks of Jesus the Christ, for your fearless stand and use of the Ascended Jesus Christ Presence.

As the Messenger gives forth riches of wisdom and truth, so should students, in their loving sincerity to the teacher, through the "I AM Presence," work for the health and prosperity of the Messengers. This would open doors to the students not otherwise possible.

There are indications at this time, that during the next seven weeks, revelations may be given to some of a certain use of Liquid Light. I wish the students' attention to be fixed on this, so that those who are ready may receive. Here let me say, that the right attitude of the student is always to rejoice at the advancement of his or her brother or sister, for each individual receives that which is most needed at the time, and if one receives one thing, another may receive something else. So the student, should at no time, feel that he should have the same thing that someone else receives. (I mean in regard to revelation.) As no two are alike, or of the same state of advancement, you can see how they could not each receive the same thing at the same time.

The most wonderful attitude of the student is to continually bless, and rejoice at any revelation that comes to his fellow students, thus, keeping the door wide open to that glorious Inner Presence at all times.

For the encouragement of those interested in aerial transport, I wish to say, there is nearing the approach of planes, that will be proof against accident. These will make transportation quick, sure and easy anywhere one wishes to go. The obstructive mental attitude, of those interested in aerial navigation, that has been opposing the coming forth of this much needed knowledge, is rapidly being broken down, until there will come forth a flood, so to speak, of wonderful ideas and Perfection which can and will be used in this wonderful means of transportation. Many of you will not need them, but there are always those who do, for one's own aerial equipment, within him, will always far excel any outward conveyance, for the Higher Body is the most wonderful vehicle of aerial transportation there is.

Some of my argumentative friends may suggest, that this vehicle is not able to carry great loads, but I say to them: "How shall ye judge, until ye are able to use this means?" It is most amusing to watch the activity of so-called practical minds, who feel that there is nothing real, except that they can feel and handle, but unless one believes in the Limitless

Powers and Laws of Intelligence of God Individualized he can in no-wise receive to any great extent from this Mighty Inner Presence.

The practical mind that forever doubts a thing it cannot see, has a long way to go, unless as you lop off the undesirable limb of a tree, this limb of doubt be cut off. You know it is a good idea, after it has been cut off, for you to consume it in the Consuming Flame, that it does not come back again. It seems so difficult for the student to realize, what a *tremendous power the consciousness of this Consuming Presence is*.

To some it is difficult to get away from the thought that It is imaginary, but could you see, from the Inner standpoint you would see that It has a Mighty Presence and Power and is very real.

I wish you for about two minutes to feel this Dazzling Ray of Light penetrating every atom of your Being.

There should be splendid accomplishment during the next seven weeks. The reaching out of humanity, as Christmas time draws near, with the already added impetus of the Christ-Force, enables accomplishments to take place at this time which have not before been possible.

There are certain activities, which must be contacted by the Inner Presence before the outer attention can be drawn to them. This is hard for the student to understand. *The student must first reach out,* and he can only reach out through his Inner Presence.

A simple, but very wonderful thing, is for one to give praise every night and morning for that magnificent Presence of Life, which animates the mind and body. It is a tremendous thing to feel deeply this thanksgiving for the Presence of Life, that holds within Itself all things. Just be grateful to Life for all It is and contains. The very Presence of Life enables us to do the things we are conscious of and desire to do, because we cannot move without this Presence, we cannot even think without it.

If one would take this statement: "I AM the Presence thinking through this mind and body," he would receive some very remarkable ideas.

The brain is the first point where obstruction begins to register, because that is the point of contact with wrong ideas. Wrong ideas register most quickly and intensely in the brain structure, because that is the field of atomic activity. However, the attention held upon the "I AM Presence" so releases the Power of the Perfection, *which is within the electron* at the center of the atom, that the wrong ideas and obstruction to the Light simply dissolve and disappear.

Q. Don—"Where are you going?"

A. Saint Germain—"To the Golden City."

"From this time on, until three weeks after New

Year's Day, it is a time of great rejoicing in the
Golden City, for it gives a great opportunity to convey into the physical world, through the Light and
Sound Rays its own Mighty Radiance. If humanity
could understand and appreciate this fact, remarkable things could take place, but that does not prevent individuals, who can grasp it, from receiving its
remarkable benefit."

*The very simple thing, if students could only
understand and apply it, is to absolutely keep the
mind off every personality,* and know only: "I AM
the only Presence there." It would open the doors—
Oh so wide!

Love and a reaching out to an Arisen Being enable radiation to be given, that would not otherwise
be possible.

One cannot long interfere with the progress or
growth of another. For if the one obstructing does
not release and relax his hold upon the other, who
is ready to go higher, the obstructing one will be
removed by his own action. If one continues to hold
steadfast and sincerely to the Light, personalities will
be swept aside, or harmoniously disconnected from
the individual's world.

At this state of growth, it is necessary to know:
"I AM the Active Presence of all channels of distribution of all things acting for my good." When the
thought comes: "This is all I have," nip it in the bud

and say: "I AM the opulence of God in my hands and use today." This is the time to stamp it right out of your mind and *feelings*.

This must be held as a Sacred Silence within each individual. Take this as a sacred, reverent knowledge to be used. When you take from the "I AM" self, it is impossible for you to take anything from any personality, which rightfully belongs to that one. You are decreeing for your world, so you cannot take from anyone, when knowing your own Law: "I AM the Presence acting everywhere." There is no possibility of division of the "I AM Presence."

If you need money say: "I AM the Active Presence, bringing this money into my hands and use instantly." It is so important to get away from the importance of money. It is but a means of exchange. Do not give it power. Put all your power back with God and then when you command—*no matter what it is you want*—you have all power instantly on hand to bring forth the fulfillment of your decree.

The vibration within any element is always the Breath of God, Eternally Self-sustained. All pulsation is Breath of God. The simple consciousness that: "I AM the Presence of Perfect Health," is this Breath of God acting.

"I AM the Presence of forgiveness, in the mind and heart of every one of God's children." This releases enormous vibratory action after its kind. Hold the following with vividness: "I AM the Pure Mind of God."

BENEDICTION: Thou Infinite Mighty Personal Presence, Jesus Christ! we give praise and thanks for Thy Radiance, for Thy Intelligent Rays, for Thy Qualifying Presence.

We give praise and thanks that we are conscious of that Special Radiance at this time, and that we may through the loving open door of our consciousness, receive of Its Mighty Presence.

DISCOURSE XVII

November 28, 1932

SAINT GERMAIN

INVOCATION: Thou Mighty Infinite Presence, All-pervading Intelligence, All-pervading Substance of Light, Thou Mighty Presence, Thou Ascended Jesus Christ now manifest through His Mighty Radiance! we give praise and thanks unto the Light, unto Thee, O Mighty Brother! we give praise unto the Central Sun to the One from whose Ray we receive to-day.

Out of the fulness of Thy Radiant Life, O God, we bow in adoration before Thy Mighty Presence.

I bring you greetings from the Great Master, or God Meru, whose Messenger is Nada. He is to the one great mountain of this earth, whose mystery shall one day be explained, as the Master Himalaya is to the Himalayan range. Nada is with me in the Golden City upon whose Twin Rays we come forth to-day.

During these next seven weeks, as designated, and as you have felt, our joint Ray, shall come to you each time from the Golden City.

THE DISCOURSE

When the students are strong enough to bear it, we will bring forth in descriptive expression, one of the most stupendous expressions of the right use and wrong use of this "Mighty I AM Presence." This actual experience took place in what is now the Andes Mountains in South America at a remote period, when the children of God first began to forget their Source, and to claim the Mighty Energy of which they were aware, as their own. Only through that authority could such an experience take place.

Students and mankind have but a small conception, even in the distress they have created for themselves, of how mightily this force was used at one time for selfish purposes. A similar condition has never before been known. There still remains to-day the subterranean city, which will be described, and in which this activity took place.

Oh! that the children of God would awaken to the stupendous activity that the Powers of Light use for the good of humanity, when their attention is sincerely focused on That Light.

If the many students, of the various angles of Truth, on the earth to-day, could put away the ignorance of the outer mind, and believe in the seeming miracles all down the ages, how it would break the shell of the outer-self and let in the Light. The faith, to believe in the things not seen, is one of the greatest means to open the door to the conscious activity of the "Light of the I AM Presence."

As you use the automobile and airplane to cover

distance quickly, so does the "Great I AM Presence" use the body. The body represents the airplane, and the mind is the mighty motor, through which the "I AM Presence" propels it.

Students, I am sure, have not understood how subtle a form doubt takes at times. Where there is a questioning in the mind, knowingly or unknowingly, concerning the All-power of the "I AM Presence" it is a subtle form of doubt. Those, who want or attempt to argue the question of the Reality of the Great Truth of Life whether they believe it or not, are admitting doubt into their lives.

In this day, no sincere reasoning mind, once turning its attention and keeping it firmly fixed on the "I AM Presence," can argue, doubt, or question the Omnipotence of that "I AM Presence."

The scarcely recognizable form of doubt that lets into the mind, argument concerning the Source of its Being, is but a lack of strength to stand up against the Law of Resistance, by which growth in the outer can be measured.

There is a vast difference between sincere questioning to know the Truth, and the human propensity to argue against the very Reality they want to believe. We always welcome, most earnestly, sincere questioning for Truth, but we will have nothing to do with that nature, whose dominating propensity is to argue against the Reality of Truth. The more the argument of Truth is admitted into the Life of an individual, the greater the barrier that one sets up to surmount before that distant day, that he does surmount it.

The students, who criticize, condemn, or sit in judgment upon this channel of the Truth's expression, will surely find themselves standing upon the edge of a precipice, into which they may plunge at any time, for no reason in the world except their own creation.

I wish all to understand, This Radiance of the Light has been established for *a certain definite purpose,* and It will go forth doing Its work, regardless of any personality or of all personalities in existence. I say this plainly, that the students of This Radiation may understand, that they are dealing with Mighty forces, which are as Real as reality can be, and those, who cannot stand the test and Radiance of the Light, need never, never blame anyone, but themselves, for they have free will and are given the use of the "Mighty I AM Presence," by which they can maintain absolute Self-control.

I must put plainly before them again, the sure way that they run into deep waters of doubt and questioning, when they are foolish enough to attempt to discuss the Sacred Truth, that is being given them for their own liberation and use, with those who know nothing about it.

This much I may say to you: "In the past, students who were taken into the retreats, for instruction, were never permitted nor do they ever think of discussing the Truth with each other. They silently, earnestly apply the instruction of their teacher, and the results they desire are certain to follow.

Better were the students stoned in the streets than to condemn, criticize, or judge the Light that is given them; for if they will enter into the "I AM Presence," as directed, every question—every problem—in their lives will disappear as the mist before the radiance of the morning sunlight.

I take it that all the students are strong enough to hear the Truth and use the Strength of the "I AM Presence" to govern and control the outer, that they may receive the full Presence, Love, Wisdom, Power and Opulence of the Great and Mighty "I AM Presence," that enables them to think, to feel, to live, and that has given them the desire to reach for the Truth —the Light.

I wish to say plainly and with the "Wand of Fire" placed in the consciousness of the students, that this Brother and Sister, who are giving this forth, are but Messengers of Those, who have known and proved this Law, for many centuries. *These Great Beings, to whom your attention has been drawn are no myth or figment of the imagination of the outer, but Living, Wise, Loving Beings, possessing such*

*power, which They may wield or use at Their own
discretion, that it is not possible for the human mind
to conceive it.*

Always before there has been great, almost limitless, time in which the student could wander about
making his decision—whether he wished to act in the
Light or wander on in ignorance of its Mighty Presence and Power. The Cosmic Cycles have turned
again, again, and again, until the time has come,
when the children of God must make their decision
final—whom they will serve.

Never in the history of the world, has there been
such opportunity or assistance given to the children
of earth, to face the "Sunshine of God's Eternal
Light," and walk steadfastly and fearlessly into its
Radiant Splendor, free, forever free, from all limitation, living in the Abundance of that Light, enfolding them like a mantle of peace and rest.

Again I say, to the beloved students: "If you cannot feel in your hearts the Truth of these instructions, brought to you on a golden platter, then don't
ever, in the name of your "I AM Presence" say or do
that, which would discourage another from the Light,
that he might receive. The plain unadulterated
Truth I give to you in the fulness of the Great Love
of my Being, that its Radiance may cause you to
understand and know what it means *to dare, to do,
and to be silent.*

Any feeling of questioning, in your minds of the Reality or genuineness of the Source of your instruction, but hampers your progress and causes you to require months or years to accomplish what you might easily do in a few weeks with a free, peaceful mind.

As one, who has chosen you, I know and feel your every thought. It is very easy at times for the student to think that his acts or thoughts are under cover and not known, but to the Arisen Host, there is no act or thought that can be hidden from them, because everything you think or *feel* is registered in the etheric world about you, as plain as the nose on your face.

So do not ever make the mistake of feeling that you may think or act in secret. You may readily do this from the outer-self, but never from the "I AM Presence," which the Ascended Host are, *with no obstruction*. This, my dear beloved students, is as far as I am permitted to go in helping to set up the guard for you. In the future, no further reference to this will be made. Remember, that the decision lies within you to go forward or not.

Now, I shall say something very encouraging. The only possible reason why the Personal Ray of Jesus could be given forth to those under this radiation at this time, was because seven of this group of students, were witness to the Ascension of Jesus the Christ, two thousand years ago. He saw and recognized them then, as He sees them and is giving, not only recognition at this time, but great assistance.

As This Radiance goes to you beloved ones, so does it go on reaching into the hearts of those, who can receive the Presence. Because of This Radiation, many, who have a deep Love for Jesus or of Jesus through the orthodox channels, will be awakened to the Presence of the God within. Outside of this, the joint activity, of Jesus with the Ascended Host, is spreading its mantle of Love, Peace, and Light over humanity, this being the time of year, when their attention is most easily gained.

Beloved Ones! does it sound incredible to you, when I say the Masters of Light and Wisdom have passages through the earth in all directions, just the same as you have on the earth, highways for your automobiles in going from coast to coast.

Did you understand the atomic structure of the earth, you would not feel this such an incredible thing; for those Great Ones who have assisted the progress of humanity from the beginning, have but to use certain Rays and they walk through the earth as easily as you would walk through the water; different however, in that they leave the opening behind them, while in your walking through the water, it closes behind you, and the path is not apparent.

Just so with the Great Beings, who have blazed the trails for humanity into the Light. The trail remains, that those children of lesser Light may always find the pathway and follow it. If at times, they should make a mistake and turn on to the by-way, they have the "I AM Presence" to call them back to the main power and carry them forward, until they too may be Torch-Bearers or Trail-Blazers to those still following on.

"I AM the Mighty Presence, who never becomes impatient or discouraged at the long periods, in which the children of earth turn aside from the Light, enjoying the sense activities, until they become so repellent to them, that with almost their last breath, they cry aloud: 'O God! save me.'"

I cannot help but smile to myself, as I wonder how some of you may think me a very crabby old fellow, but if so, one who has the courage to tell you the Truth of your needs, that you may profit by it. When you come to know me better, you will not think me such an old crab after all.

So long as the student has a questioning in the mind, he does not open himself to the Truth of the instruction fully.

If it is seen that it is worth while, determined entirely by the up-reaching of humanity to the Light, then the Natural Rays are made permanent to the earth, and placed within the center. The earth is composed of earth, water, and air. The Rays are the Cosmic Fire interpenetrating all the three other elements. The Rays pass through the earth, and where they interlock, they soften and form this Luminous Radiance, the concentrated activity of the Light.

One Ray enters the crust of the earth at a point just south of the center of the Gobi desert, and the other one enters just east of Lake Titicaca in the Andes Mountains. It is the largest lake in South America, and the largest in the world, and was a point of very great importance centuries ago.

These are the two most intense points of Light in the earth. There is always a Cosmic Activity taking place at certain cycles that may not be interfered with. The Great Cosmic Laws are exact to the minutest detail, and there is no such thing as failure or accident connected with them.

A great change, which takes great quantities of people out of the body, only takes them where they cannot fight for a while. In the world war, both sides hated the men they were sent against, and also the governments that sent them, because of being sent.

Never consider anything in the world, but the "Great I AM Presence." *Watch and govern your feeling, for if not it will lead to a point where it will catch you unawares.*

Many times, the student, who knows the Law, when something comes up and he is disappointed, he should turn to the "I AM Presence" immediately, and ask what is to be done; but instead he so often holds the attention on the disappointment, and then it sometimes almost takes an earthquake to shake him loose from it.

Take the statement: "This resistance must give way, and the sight and hearing must come through."

Take the firm statement: "I AM the Presence of your Perfect sight and hearing," to heal those conditions. Each should take the statement: "I AM my Perfect sight and hearing."

The Arabian Nights' Tales: They originally came from the Masters, who gave them out as a Veiled Truth to help humanity, and those, who did believe them through faith, received marvelous manifestations.

In the beginning of these marvelous experiences, there must be faith to tide over, until we can manifest the Reality, for faith is the sustaining power, and if we can keep it generated, it becomes Reality.

There are always the two activities of the Law, when you get deep enough into the action of it. They are first condensation, and second, etherealization. Go serenely along, and do not let time, place, or things interfere.

The outer mind must be calm and steady, and the outer and Inner will must become one. As the attention is fixed on it with firm determination, more and more of the Inner Operation is revealed, until you can consciously manipulate it.

BENEDICTION: Presence of Meru, Nada, and the Great Arisen Host, we give praise and thanks, for Thy Radiant Splendor, for Thy Wisdom, for Thy Substance, that Thou art generating to make visible. We give praise and thanks, that Thy Great Wisdom and Intelligence is one with the "Great I AM," which "I AM," ever bringing more of Itself forward into conscious action. We give praise and thanks, that in the acknowledgment of the "I AM Presence," we have the Key to all things visible and invisible.

The Ascended Master, Jesus

The Ascended Master, Saint Germain

DISCOURSE XVIII

December 1, 1932

SAINT GERMAIN

INVOCATION: Thou Mighty Illumining Presence which "I AM"! in gratitude and praise we enter into the Fulness of Thy Presence to-day, and forever receive Thy Limitless Blessings, Thy Strength and Courage, Thy Joyous Enthusiasm, all of which is Self-sustained.

We know there is but One Presence, and "I AM that Presence" of all Activity, all Wisdom and Power, and in the Freedom of that Mighty Presence we stand serene, unmoved among all outer things, which seem to point to the contrary.

"I stand serene in Thy Great Forever, I claim Thy Great Dominion in my place. I stand in the Radiance of God Eternal, ever looking Thee full in the face."

I bring you greetings from the Great Host, and with it their blessings for the happy enthusiasm which has been entered into. We shall endeavor to sustain you in that joyous enthusiasm as the Hub of This Radiation, because all the students will feel and act it.

Far more has been accomplished this week than

was anticipated, and we enter with you into the great rejoicing. The loving blessing of each student unto the other is most commendable, and this simple thing will open the door, Oh so wide! to receive the fulness intended for them.

THE DISCOURSE

I would be so pleased to have everyone of the students, just at this time especially, use the statement with all the enthusiasm they can command: "I AM, I AM, I know I AM the use of God's Limitless Opulence."

Here, I wish to explain that when there is a group of students in accord, working from the same principle, that when they use this statement, they not only bring into their own world and use this Great Opulence; but they bless their associate students with the same thing, because "I AM the Presence in each one." This is the mighty power of co-operative action.

The students, who maintain the loving blessing to each other, are really held in the "Embrace of the Great I AM Presence," and when they acknowledge Its action, they are commanding the same blessing and action for the other students, that they are for themselves.

This is the correct attitude to be sustained, and if maintained sincerely, in the heart of each one, no one within this embrace will want for any good thing; but the student, who allows any feeling to remain of unkindness to the others, will shut himself from this Great Radiance and Blessing.

Now let us enter into the keynote of what you touched this morning,—the simple understanding of God's Will and free will. God's Will is the Opulence of Good-Will—the birthright of every one of God's children.

When you are reaching to the Light in the use of the "Mighty I AM Presence" with sincerity, it is not possible for you to do otherwise than God's Will being done. As Children of God the Father, who has given His Children free will that they may choose, they must understand that it is for them alone to decree what shall act in their lives and world.

Having free will, the student must understand that God can only act in his Life and world according to his conscious direction.

God is the Principle of all Life and each child of God is an individualized conscious active part of that One Great Principle of Life, Love, and Power.

God has given into the keeping of every one of His Children This Marvelous Consciousness, which is Omnipresent, eternally elastic—as it were—which can be drawn into a focal point to write with the Pen of Light, or expand to encompass the earth.

Consciousness is always subject to direction through the use of the free will.

The most unfortunate understanding, established by the orthodox idea, that God acts of His own free will in the Life of the individual or a nation, is positively *not true*. God can only act through the mind of his own individualization, which is clothed with the personalities that you see about you. These personalities are but vehicles of use and expression of this Mighty Individuality, which is God's Will and your free will, and it only comes into use by your conscious direction.

I say to you that every function of your body is sustained through conscious action, although you are not aware of it, but as you reach deeper and deeper into the *Consciousness* of the "Mighty I AM Presence," you will come to understand that it is impossible for any outer action to take place without Self-conscious action.

A simple proof of this is what any of you may test at any moment. I wish to do some physical act. Preceding that activity always comes the thought to do it, otherwise the hand or body would not move in action. That, which people have chosen to call involuntary action, is the thing that has mystified their understanding of their own Being.

The students should take this humble explanation, and meditate upon it often, for it will clear the mind of any obstruction. You are Self-conscious, Free will Acting Beings.

This is really of vital importance to these blessed earnest students. I love every one of them, both men and women, even though the ladies' husbands might object.

In both of your classes this week, the "Individualized Presence of Jesus the Christ" stood in your midst. At . . . . in the form of "The Tree of Life," each student being a branch. At . . . . From His "Pillar of Dazzling Radiance" within which was His Visible Personal Form. At . . . . His Form was within the "Tree of Life" but not visible,—not to mention others of the Arisen Host, who were present. There were also Nada, Cha Ara, Lanto, and Myself.

I wish to say to that class of blessed boys with the one pink rose in their midst, that I joyously hold them all in my fond embrace, that they may use and inhale the Radiance of my Being. They have Freedom and Dominion within their grasp, if they will hold fast to these instructions, and apply them.

Further, I wish the students to understand, that the Stream of Life, flowing through the mind and body, always comes into them pure and unadulterated, containing within it all strength, courage, energy and wisdom, that can ever be desired, but in the lack of control of their thought and feeling, they are unknowingly requalifying that Pure Essence with the outer ideas upon which the attention has been fixed.

To form the habit, every moment the mind is not otherwise occupied, of being Self-conscious that: "I AM the only Intelligence acting," will keep that Mighty Wonderful Stream of Life from being discolored, and shall I say disqualified, by the wrong conceptions of the outer activity of the mind. This is the simple secret of really all Perfection, if one can but comprehend it.

This Great Life comes into everyone's use Pure and Perfect, but through lack of understanding, the outer mind is constantly re-qualifying It with discordant conceptions, and thus human beings change its otherwise Perfect Action into that which they find expressed in limitation and discord in their outer activity.

This should make clear to the students, the simple activity that they should Self-consciously maintain, in order to keep this marvelous Perfect Life, that is constantly flowing through their minds and bodies, in its Pure Fragrant State, for I tell you truly, that those who will follow and maintain this idea, will find the emanations from their own bodies becoming rarer than the lily or the rose. Further, in the consciousness of this Perfection, which is constantly flowing into their use, they can know it as perfect health and beauty of face and form, until Its Radiance shines forth like the sun.

O Beloved students, when it is so simple, requiring so little consciously sustained effort, is it not worth all it requires on your part to enter into the Fulness of this Life Stream and receive Its Fulness and Blessing?

In the Oriental activity, there was a secret society, in fact it began in China, maintained gloriously in the Light, until the one then in charge at the head of the order, thought in one of the war ravages, that his daughter, whom he loved so deeply, was killed by an Englishman—which however was not the case— but it brought about the breaking up of the order and the pictures of "Fu Manchu," of which I think there have been four produced, are the picturing of this to the outer world, *showing how the "Light" may be distorted by something starting the feeling of revenge.*

This one known as "Fu Manchu," was at the beginning of that activity a wondrous, beautiful soul, and it shows how sometimes the ravages of war and the lack of control of the thought and feeling in the individual, bring about such distortion in the Life Stream.

In connection with the South American Activity, which the present work has drawn joyously to their attention: Until this focus of Radiation began, it was doubted by most, except Nada and myself, the possibility of establishing such a focus in this busy Western World, but they did not know what I did, it not having been revealed to them, the fact of our long association. So I said on my own responsibility: "I shall try it out."

Now I have the full co-operation of all who might have questioned. The Master from Venus, and Lanto, also stood with us. I said to them: "The time has come when there are those outside of the Retreats, who can be made True Messengers of the Light." Thanks to you, I have been proved right. Now, I of course ask you all to stand with me in the sustaining of this.

This proves that it is possible to establish this Mighty Active Presence in the midst of a hailstorm. I have always maintained this, and most of the time I have stood alone; but the ability of the students to grasp the use of the "I AM Presence" is making tremendous things possible, and I say sincerely for your encouragement, that with this marvelous condition maintained, which has come to this point, it is not impossible to have various ones of these Ascended Beings sit in your midst, as visible as your own physical bodies, and speak to you.

This is not just a matter of the desire of the students for it, but rather the preparation of the students for it. This good Brother, until recently of course has not known it, but for thirty years he has been being prepared for it. Half of that time your preparation was going on in the invisible, and it has been a remarkably beautiful thing to all who have observed it.

Q. The other night while in deep meditation, I heard the words: "Into the City of Delhi."

A. "Which really means into the City of Light."

Q. On Monday, November 29, 1932, I heard in the morning before the discourse, and again to-day before the discourse, the words of Jesus: "Ye have been with me in my sorrows, ye shall now behold me in my Glory and see the reward, which my Father doth give me."

A. "And so shall it be in your outer experience."

The very words which Jesus used from time to time, all may use and will use sometime, somewhere with fulfillment, for the words he used at all times were "Life" and contained within them that Ascended Life or Perfect Life.

Q. How is the political situation?

A. "There will not be nearly so much accomplished by the element that sought entrance as they anticipated. The old saying: 'That if you give a calf rope enough, it will hang itself,' is true with certain forces. Sometimes when they think they have won an easy victory, they have sounded their own death knell."

The accomplishment of the past few days drew the

attention of many in the Golden City, who, as we projected the Vision and Sound Rays to-day, came to look and behold the accomplishment. I say this for the encouragement of the students, and while we are giving forth the work to-day, those in the Golden City are sending forth to the students their Glorious Radiation.

It has been a great joy to me to prove that in the land of America, which I have so long worked for, that there were those, who could receive that, which you are receiving and giving forth at this time. There are those Masters from Venus, who have seen this with me for some time. The Kumara's field of action was in other ways, but They are now observant of this accomplishment.

There is no radiation goes forth anywhere in the Universe except through conscious projection. The radiation projected from the stars, so-called, to our earth do not and cannot come into contact with the earth without the conscious direction of the Cosmic Being, who is the Conscious Directing Presence of that star or planet. This conscious direction is what makes the radiation from one planet to another reach its destination, but the radiation thus directed does not carry any adverse aspect to any individual there.

The Universal, Cosmic Laws of the earth, which impel growth through the law of experience, hold within themselves that, which you know as resistance.

If there were not that, which the individual knows as resistance, he would not make conscious effort, and this would make it impossible for advancement in understanding, or the return to the Father's House, from which the children of earth have strayed.

Resistance has nothing whatever to do with discord. *Resistance is a Natural Law. Discord is a human creation.* There is no discord in the Universe, except that which the personality creates.

Take the dynamic consciousness: "I AM the Pure Mind of God in everyone present here." *This shuts out human desire.*

Take the consciousness: "I AM the governing Presence of this." The desire first comes in the mind, and if you take the consciousness: "I AM the Pure Mind of God," it consumes the thought and keeps the human mind clear from the desire entirely.

When the liquid precipitates in the hand, instantly qualify it as Liquid Light, and it will manifest as That. Give the command for that quality before beginning the precipitation.

One student should not expect to see the same activity as another; the students are not supposed to see or feel alike.

There is not a moment in the day that we do not visualize something, because the power of vision is acting all the time. Keep all out of the mind except the picture you want, for that is all with which you are concerned. Do not let the attention become focused on the seeming emptiness.

BENEDICTION: In great devotion, in the fulness of our hearts of Love, in the fulness of our adoration to the "God Presence, which I AM"—the Ascended Jesus Christ—we pour forth our gratitude and praise for the sustaining Presence, the good of every description held within This Radiance of which we are receiving hourly. Thou Mighty Presence, as we find ourselves held within Thy Mighty Embrace, we become imbued with Thy Radiant Intelligence, Thy Marvelous Strength, Thy Invincible Courage to hold constantly within Thy Mighty Light. We thank Thee.

DISCOURSE XIX

December 5, 1932

SAINT GERMAIN

INVOCATION: Thou Majestic Presence of the Ascended Jesus Christ! Thou Who hast gained Thy Eternal Dominion over all things, Thou Who rests serene in the Heart of the Eternal Father, pouring forth Thy Wondrous Radiance, enfolding all mankind! we give praise and thanks to Thee. Our hearts fill with great rejoicing that the Ascended Host with Thee see and manipulate the dawning, Eternal Light for the blessing of humanity.

Through his own Personal Ray, Jesus will now speak his wish to the students:

JESUS' DISCOURSE

JESUS:—When I said: "I AM the open door which no man may shut," I meant humanity to understand, I referred to the "Great I AM" which is the Life of every individual manifest in form. I did not wish to convey that the personal Jesus was the only one to whom this great privilege was ordained. Each one of you, beloved children of the One Father, has the same Mighty Presence within you, the "Great I AM," that I have, and that I had at that time, by which I achieved the Final and Eternal Victory.

Here, I wish you to understand for encouragement, strength, and certainty in your minds, that the Consciousness I used for this Great Victory was the use of the "I AM Presence" which you are being taught. When I had made search through all the avenues available at that time, and at last, the determination and desire for the Truth led me to the Great Master—whom you shall one day know—who gave to me this Inner Secret and Mighty Acknowledgment, turning me to that "Mighty Presence, the Great I AM." Through His Radiation, I was able to comprehend and at once begin using it. This is the only way by which any individualization of the Ray of God may achieve the Eternal Victory, and build his structure upon a firm foundation from which no outer activity can ever disturb him.

At this time, I wish to convey the simple, all-powerful use of this Presence to you. All, who have achieved the Mighty Victory, and who have been able to raise their bodies, as I did or *who raised them before* have used the conscious activity of that "Mighty Eternal Presence, I AM."

When I said to my disciples and to humanity: "The things that I have done shall ye do also, and even greater things shall ye do," I knew whereof I spoke —knowing that within each individualization or Child of God, there was this "Mighty I AM Presence," by whose use you are impelled forward with no uncertainty. I say, "Impelled," because I mean just that.

The constant use of your "I AM Presence" does impel you forward in spite of any activity of the outer-self. So long as this single idea is held firmly, storms, distress, and disturbance may rage about you, but in the Consciousness of the "I AM Presence," you can and are able to stand serene, unmoved by the seething vortex of human creation, that may or may not be about you.

There is but one way by which you and the Father may become eternally one, and that is through the full acceptance of his "I AM Presence," Energy, Love, Wisdom and Power, which He has given you, golden links, golden steps, by which you climb serenely upward into your final achievement.

Sometime, somewhere every individualization of God, the Father, must find his way back to the Father through his "I AM Presence," fulfilling his cycle or cycles of individualizations in the use of the activity of the outer-self. The earth is the only sphere in which there is the density of the atomic structure that you experience. The conscious recognition and use of the "I AM Presence," which you are, steadily raises the vibratory action of your atomic structure, unclothing and liberating the Electronic Activity which is hid within the atom, enabling you to become Self-luminous Beings.

I wish it here distinctly understood by all who may receive this or ever contact it, that I am not and never was a Special Being created of God different from the rest of humanity. It is true, that I had made previous conscious effort, and had attained much previous to that embodiment in which I won the Eternal Victory. My choice of experience two thousand years ago was to set the example which every individualization of God would and must sooner of later follow.

How I urge you, Beloved Children of God, to look upon me as your Elder Brother—one with you. When I said or left the word that: " 'I AM with you always,' the 'I AM Presence, which I AM' and which you are is one. Therefore, do you not see how, 'I AM with you always'?" *Think deeply on this, and try to feel its reality.*

At the time and after my ascension, I saw the immensity of the Radiation I would be able to pour forth to my beloved brothers and sisters upon the earth from the sphere where I had become fitted to dwell. I wish to say to you in all truth: every individual who will send his conscious thought to me with the desire to be raised above the limitations of earth or of his own creation, and will live accordingly, will receive every assistance from me that is possible to be given according to the steps of growth in consciousness that he attains from time to time.

Do not misunderstand me at this point, when I refer to growth, I am speaking of humanity in general. I do not refer to some who have previous attainment sufficient that in their present use and full acceptance of their "I AM Presence," they may rend the veil of human creation and step forth into the "Embrace of the Ascended Blazing I AM Presence" at any time. There are some in the group of students already drawn together, for whom it is possible to do this. That depends entirely upon themselves, upon the calm, poised intensity by which they become conscious of their "I AM Presence."

These great tidings I bring to you, because I proved them in my own personal experience.

Before I became fully decided in what manner I should leave the example to humanity, I suddenly, from an Inner Impulse, began to use the statement: "I AM the resurrection and the Life." Within forty-eight hours, after I began using that statement with great rejoicing, I saw what was to be done, and I wish to assure you that it was the conscious use of the Mighty Statement: "I AM the resurrection and the Life," which enabled me to make the ascension in the Presence of so many, and *imprint or record upon the etheric records, that example for all humanity, which will stand eternally present.*

It was unfortunate that the veil of the orthodox idea was drawn over the minds of the people, preventing the comprehension that each one had within him the "I AM Presence" the same as I had, by which he could attain, do the same things I did, and win the Eternal Victory.

Such, beloved students, is my personal message I leave with you, spoken through the Light and Sound Ray, into which any of you may enter, see, and hear with sufficient conscious preparation.

Again, I urge you to think of me as your Elder Brother, ready to give you assistance at all times. Do not think of me as a Transcendent Being so far beyond your reach that contact is impossible; for the "I AM Presence" which enabled me to make the ascension is the same "I AM Presence" that will enable you to make the ascension as I did, only to-day, you have the assistance of the Great Arisen Host of Beings who have won the Eternal Victory and joyously stand at your service, as you make yourselves ready.

With my Love I enfold you. I again repeat: "I AM with you always."

Saint Germain: "Did I not have a surprise for you?"

BENEDICTION: Into the fulness of Thy Mighty Silence, O Great Presence, we come to rest, to feel Thy peace, to love Thy harmony pervading all. Oh Mighty Love Presence! that beats the hearts of all mankind, strengthen Thyself within their hearts: draw and hold their conscious attention upon Thee, the "Great Love Star" in the heart of each one. Glorify Thy Presence and Thy Creator in them, bless all mankind with that strength to look only to Thee, and to stand steadfast facing Thee.

DISCOURSE XX

December 8, 1932

SAINT GERMAIN

INVOCATION: Thou Mighty Invincible "I AM Presence"! speak Thyself into the hearts of the children of men: fill their hearts and minds to overflowing with the Magnificence of Thy Presence, with the conscious strength to look to Thee and know Thee as, "The One,"—The Mighty Eternal Source of all things—by which the consciousness of mankind is sustained. Make them to know Thy Great Ownership, that it is Thee alone that is the Owner and Giver of all things and that they may thus manifest unselfishly one to the other. We thank Thee.

I bring you greetings from the Great Host who are ever pouring Their Radiant Presence into your lives.

THE DISCOURSE

It is with great rejoicing, that the many, who have been observant of this accomplishment see how truly the students are entering into the "Mighty I AM Presence," and how the things that have been disturbing are being dissolved, and are dropping away as though they never had been.

Beloved students, can you realize how great our

rejoicing is, who have trod the pathway of attainment into that Great Freedom of Mastery over all limitation, to see you entering into this Presence, which, if maintained, will bring you certainly and surely to that same Freedom? It is only when the outer becomes sufficiently obedient, giving all power to that Great Inner Presence, that one finds peace and rest in this Mighty Acknowledgment.

In that peace and rest flows a Mighty River of Energy, like a mountain stream flowing through a fertile valley lined with flowers and perfect vegetation.

So in that peace that passeth understanding, do you move more and more, finding that Eternal River of Energy flowing into and through your Being, spreading its blessing and opulence into your Life, and experience everywhere you go.

While it is true that the intelligence is the channel through which you must receive, yet as you *feel* with deep sincerity, the "Truth of the I AM Presence" will you find that stillness becoming greater and greater, until one day: "Thou shalt see the door of thy creation open wide before thee, and thou shalt step forth with open arms into that Freedom, inhaling the fragrance of the Pure Atmosphere of the Etheric World, wherein thou wilt be able to mold that plastic substance into the Perfection of everything upon which thy desire is held."

You are making such splendid progress, do not let any fear of persons, places, conditions, or things interrupt or disturb you; for the "Presence of the Light" stands before you, beckoning you on, that you may be held in Its fond embrace, receiving of Its boundless riches of every description which It holds in store for you.

I shall now say something which may seem astonishing, but I assure you it is very true. Last night as the question was asked: "Had you all been together before?"—I wish to say, that it would not have been possible for you to have been drawn into this intensified action of the Great Inner Law, if you had not previously had harmonious association and training. While it may be difficult at first for you to comprehend it, you are receiving intensified training, that heretofore has only been given after a three year probation in the retreat. Some of you have stored up treasures of Energy. I mean by that, energy created by your conscious activity through your "I AM Presence." Others have stored up treasures of Light. Again, others have treasures of Love. Others have gold and jewels, which were placed in keeping to be used in this embodiment. Several of you are on the point of releasing into visibility—into your hands— these stored up treasures. Do not think I have gone into fancy day-dreaming, but I AM calling this to your attention for your benefit and blessing.

I wish each one of you to go by yourselves some-time during the day for at least five minutes, and talk to your "I AM Presence" something like this: "Great Masterful Presence which I AM! I love, I adore Thee. I give back unto Thee the fulness of all Creative Power, all Love, all Wisdom, and through this Power, which Thou art, I give Thee full power to make visible in my hands and use, the fulfillment of my every desire. I no longer claim any power as my own, for I now claim Thee, the Only and All-conquering Presence in my home, my Life, my world, and my experience. I acknowledge Thy Full Supremacy and Command of all things, and as my consciousness is fixed upon an achievement, your Invincible Pres-ence and Intelligence takes command, and brings the fulfillment into my experience quickly—even with the speed of thought.

"I know that Thou art ruler over time, place and space. Therefore, Thou requirest only *now* to bring into the visible activity, Thy Every Perfection. I stand absolutely firm in the full acceptance of this now and forever, and I shall not allow my mind to waver from it for at last, *I know we are One.*"

Beloved students, you may add or weave into this anything else you wish for your requirement, and I assure you, if you can live in this, and I shall endeavor to help you do so, you will experience the opening of the floodgates of God's Abundance.

I think here that I should explain to you: The most important, the most desirable thing that anyone can do, is to fix within his or her mind the one permanent necessity and that is—*to keep at it until one reaches so deeply and firmly into this "Mighty I AM Presence," that all Love, Light, Good and Riches flow into his Life and experience* by an Inner Propelling Power that naught of outer personalities may at any time, anywhere ever interfere with.

This is the object of true training. This is why students were brought into the retreats as they could be found ready or sufficiently progressed because, as I have said before, it is easy enough to solve your problems as they come along, but I ask you, what good does it do to continue to solve problems, unless you have something, somewhere, to which you can anchor that raises you above the consideration of any problem.

To find your "I AM Presence" and anchor to It is the only desirable thing to do. Until you come to this point of firm anchorage to your "Great I AM Presence," of course it is necessary to solve your problems as they come along; but how much better it is to enter in and set free that Mighty Presence, Energy and Action that has already solved the problems before they appear to you. Is this not more acceptable than to awaken every morning, and find these problems coming up—staring you in the face—as though they were something really important, which after all they are not? Yet, I am sure you will agree with me, that some of them, or at least your outer sense about them, is that they are tremendously ponderous.

With your glorious obedience to the Divine Principle of created Beings, we shall move along the pathway with our Armor of Invincible Protection buckled on, until the intensity of the very Light that you enter into will no longer require the armor.

Is this not worth all the effort it takes to accomplish it, that you may ever move in this Glorious Freedom? Then, when you awake in the morning, you will no longer find these visitors appear.

As I have spoken these words, I have held you, each one, in the Searchlight of my Vision, even without your permission, so that when you hear these words, you will feel the Inner Conviction of them with a strength that will delight you.

When critical or disturbing thoughts try to find entrance into your consciousness, slam the door quickly, and command them to be gone forever. Don't give them a chance or time to gain a foot-hold, remembering always, that you have the strength and the sustaining power of the "Mighty I AM Presence" to do this. Should you have difficulty in holding the door shut, talk to your "I AM Presence" and say: "See here! I need help! See that the door to this disturbance is closed, and kept closed *forever*."

I want you to get fixed in your consciousness,· that you can talk to your "I AM Presence" the same as you could talk to me, believing that I had limitless power; because I tell you it is no idle comment when I say: "You can cause this Mighty Presence to handle every condition in your entire experience, and raise you into that Freedom and Dominion of all things."

As some of you have already reached into the activity of the Universal Substance, I want to call the attention of all of you to the fact that: the substance of your bodies and this substance, seeming to be invisible about you, is immensely sensitive to your conscious thought and feeling, by which you can mold it into any form you wish.

The substance of your body can, by your conscious thought and feeling, be molded into the most exquisite beauty of form—your eyes, hair, teeth, and skin made dazzling with radiant beauty. This should be very encouraging to the ladies and I am sure will be to the gentlemen, only they don't like to admit it.

Beloved Brothers and Sisters, when you look into the mirror, say to that which you see there: "Through the Intelligence and Beauty which I AM, I command you to take on Perfect Beauty of form, for I AM that Beauty in every cell of which you are composed, and you shall respond to my command and become radiantly beautiful in every way, in thought, word, feeling, and form. I AM the Fire and Beauty of your eyes and I carry forth the Radiant Energy into everything into which I look." Thus, you can cause to come into appearance the Perfection that will give you all the encouragement you want, to know that, "I AM always the Governing Presence."

I wish to say to you who desire your forms to become more symmetrical: Start your hands at the shoulders and bring them down over the body to the feet, feeling the Perfection or symmetry of the form you wish. Through your hands will go the energy or quality which you desire to manifest. If you will try this with deep earnest feeling, you will be amazed at the results. This is the greatest reducer in the world. This, I assure you will cause the flesh, as it comes into more beautiful symmetry and perfection, to become firm and yet supple in every way, because you are sending the energy of the "I AM Presence" through these cells, causing them to obey your command. This may sound ridiculous, but I tell you, it is one of the best, surest, and most perfect ways to bring about the Perfection of the body. I tell you, anyone who will practice this will bring the body into any condition that one desires.

I want the students to get the fulness of the idea, that they are Masters of their forms, their minds, and their worlds, and can inject into them whatsoever they wish. The Pure and Perfect Life of God is flowing through you every instant; why not switch off the old design and switch on the new? Do you not see how important it is to perfect the body?

What can the Inner Presence do with a body that is sick or out of harmony all the time? When this is the case the attention becomes so fixed upon the body that the "I AM Presence" cannot get the attention but a little part of the time. It is so easy, if you will but do it. With this treatment of the flesh with the energy of the "I AM Presence" it becomes firm and Perfect.

The reason I speak of this with such deep, earnest feeling to-day is because I see the change and improvement in almost every one, and by special conscious attention directed to this, how much more quickly will each be brought into that Perfection which he desires.

When an individual has an abnormal abdomen, *and anything that is more than straight is abnormal,* he should raise the left hand in this position, palm up, move the right hand in a rotary motion over the abdomen, moving from left to right. Each time the hand passes over it, feel deeply the absorbing activity.

The quick charge of energy through the hand goes into the cells contracting and reducing them into a normal condition. I assure you this instruction is no idle fancy, but is of tremendous import, and will accomplish the purpose for which it is used, absolutely without question, if applied with earnest feeling.

The consciousness, of course, should be that: "the energy flowing through the right hand is the All-powerful, Absorbing Presence, consuming the unnecessary cells, and bringing the body into a perfect, normal condition."

This will not only adjust the abnormal size of the abdomen, but will penetrate through the form, charging the intestinal activity with a cleansing, purifying process that will be of inestimable benefit. Those, who have found the activity of those organs lazy, will find them quickened into normal action. I assure you that the ladies will not need to use rolling pins, or roll on the floor; also I assure you the ladies are not the only ones who use rolling pins.

The unfortunate, almost appalling condition is, that individuals, having within them this Mighty God Presence, will give every imaginable power to outside things to produce results within and upon themselves, when whatever remedial agent they use, whether exercise, drugs or anything else, has little effect, if any, except the quality and power they have consciously given these agents. This treatment acts upon the cells wherever they are, be they bones or flesh.

How prone the outer mind is to question the ability of this Inner Self to handle any part of the body. If it will handle one kind of a cell it will handle all. Make the outer accept the full power of the Inner Presence and thus, let it expand into use in all things.

The outer mind, through long habit, has given enormous power to drugs and remedial agents of every kind, but do you not see that the only thing that does it, is the power and authority you give it, to have an effect upon your body? I do not mean for a single instant that individuals, who have not become aware of the "I AM Presence" should cease all remedial agents, but if they will fix in their minds firmly that: "No outer thing has any power in their experience, except what they give it," they will begin to rise out of the limitations into which they have placed themselves. Here let me say that, ninety per cent of the power given to outer things is unconsciously given, and even most students are not aware of it.

Now to turn about and give this Great God Presence within you all power, to do the things you require and wish to do, will accomplish them with a speed and certainty far beyond what any outside remedial agent could do. Some will grasp this idea with tremendous tenacity, while others will require more effort, but it is surely worth while making any effort to accomplish it.

Remember, the "I AM Presence" knows all things for all eternity, in all ways past, present, and future without limit. If the student would think of this Great Presence, contemplate It, and know that It is all Love, Wisdom, and Power, then when he fixes his attention on something to be accomplished, he knows this Presence is the open door, the all-powerful accomplishment, and It cannot fail.

Call on the Law of Forgiveness and direct the energy of the Master Self to correct and adjust the wrong, and in that way obtain freedom from its re-action. You see, my dear people, that *there is so much unnecessary power given to the outer activity and stress of things which the "I AM Presence" cares absolutely nothing about.* It is at no time concerned with the mistakes of the outer-self, and if the individual but understood that, he could turn away from all these discordant activities, and give the "Master I AM Presence" *within* all authority and power to dissolve and dissipate the wrong condition, he could never in any way feel the reactions from his wrong doing.

When the individual allows himself or herself to continue to criticize, condemn, or judge another of his fellow beings, he is not only injuring the other person, but is *unknowingly admitting into his own experience, the very element that he is seeing wrong in the other person.* The true understanding of this will make it easy for individuals to forever cease that undesirable activity, when they know that it is for their own protection.

Let us put it in another way. Whatever the conscious attention is fixed firmly upon, that quality is impelled into the experience of that indivdual. Whatever an individual sees with deep feeling within another individual, *he forces into his own experience.* This is the indisputable proof of, why the only desirable feeling to be sent out from any individual, is the Presence of Divine Love, and I mean by that, Pure, Unselfish Love.

Students ofttimes wonder, why they have so many conditions in their experience to handle, as they become more and more sensitive. It is because they see an appearance, which they have been taught to know is not real, and by allowing their attention to become fixed upon it, they not only invite, but *force* it, into their own worlds, and then have a battle, in order to clean house. This can be avoided, by instantly taking the attention off the appearance, and knowing: "I AM, I AM, I KNOW I AM free from this thing forever"—no matter what it is.

This all comes of course from a lack of Self-control in the individual or an unwillingness to use that Self-control to govern the outer. There are these two distinct conditions with students: one is willing enough to make the effort, but unknowingly allows his attention to become fixed on the undesirable things: the other one, through a quality of stubbornness, is unwilling to make the necessary effort to conquer it.

No teacher should at any time hold a thought of criticism about any student, for if he does, he will invite that same criticism unto himself. If students get the right idea about this, they will stop it for their own protection.

If one keeps silently seeing a discrepancy in another, it is even worse than the spoken word, for it allows the force to accumulate. When discrepancies are forced upon your attention simply say to your "I AM Presence": "There is the 'I AM Presence' within that person, and with the human I am not concerned." *It matters not whether it is a person or inanimate object, the moment you see an imperfection, you are forcing that quality into your own experience.* This is so important, it cannot be stressed enough.

Your first consideration should always be to your own Divine Self—adoration to It always. This gives you the opportunity and strength to rise to the height, where you can give help to thousands where now it can only be to a few.

No amount of service can be of any permanent benefit, unless the individual first accepts and gives adoration to his own Divine Self, "The Mighty I AM Presence." Those, who want to serve the Light, and really do good, should understand this clearly.

When students say: "If I only had the money, what good I could do," it is exactly the reverse thing that they ought to do. If one will enter into the "I AM Presence," he will have all the money he wants, and it cannot be kept away from him.

Take the stand with everyone: "There is only the 'I AM Presence' acting there in that person."

It is much better not to touch upon a thing than to give an insufficient explanation.

All outer experience is but a discipline. For those who are coming into this work, the present training is really a finishing school or experience, and that is why some of them feel it is a little strenuous. All the Arisen Host feel with great joy the Love and gratitude poured out to Them, and of course They respond almost without limit.

"I AM is all there is, everywhere present, visible and invisible."

The consciousness most needed for each individual will come from time to time, as the students continue in the use of this. Do not let yourselves strain after *things*. Just take the calm, certain attitude of the Ascension. Calmly, quickly, lovingly accept it, and just Be: this avoids tension. Nothing is more powerful than this.

BENEDICTION: Thou Mighty, All-pervading, Infinite Presence, "I AM,"! we give forth our gratitude to Thee that we have found Thee, that we acknowledge Thee, the All-powerful Creator, making Thyself fully visible in our every need, in our full illumination, in our full Mastery, and Dominion over all outer things. We thank Thee that Thou art the All-pervading Presence, and that Thou dost with Thy strength and wisdom impel Thy Perfection everywhere.

DISCOURSE XXI

December 12, 1932

SAINT GERMAIN

INVOCATION: Thou Infinite Presence! expressing Thy Perfection everywhere, we welcome and praise Thy Perfect Manifestation in our lives, homes, and worlds, that Thy Radiant Light may forever consume everything unlike Itself, that Thy Wisdom may always direct, Thy Love always enfold, Thy Light always illumine Thy Perfect Pathway, and that Thou dost hold us firmly in Thy Glorious Radiance now and forever.

I bring you greetings from the Great Host, Their Joy and Love for this co-operation, for that which can but bless, illumine, and awaken.

THE DISCOURSE

Oh! that students or any individuals who know of the "I AM Presence," could but realize that there is no greater consciousness, no greater activity, the conscious volition can set into action, than the recognition and acceptance of the "I AM Presence."

No matter what the angles of Truth are from the thousands of avenues, by which mankind reaches out to gain greater and wider understanding, every one leads to this which you now have the gracious privilege of knowing, understanding, and using.

Any kind of knowledge or power is absolutely worthless, unless *used*. Those who will apply and enter into the use of the "I AM Presence" with *deep feeling,* will see and feel within their own Beings, as they again come in contact with other channels of understanding, how transcendent the knowledge of the "I AM Presence" is, in comparison with all other ideas of Truth.

I AM holding fast to this idea for the students' sake, that they grasp fully the Mighty Truth, that when they say: "I AM whatever I wish to be or manifest," they are actually setting into visible, physical activity, the Mightiest Presence and Power of God, which "I AM." This differs from any other statement that was ever put into a group of words.

There is no other statement or group of words in existence that actually set such power into motion to accomplish any given purpose, to which the conscious attention is directed, as does this Mighty Expression. This is why Jesus, The Christ, coupled it with the most important statements that He made. If the students of This Radiation will meditate or contemplate the statements that Jesus made, upon His Own Ray to them, it will help them to grasp the fulness, the stupendousness of this, more readily.

I wish every student of this radiation to fix firmly in his mind, that: concerning these instructions there may at no time be a charge ever made for them. The student is always free to make Love-gifts as his heart directs, but to make a definite charge, under the Law by which these instructions are given, would close the door immediately. Just the reason for this, I may not explain to you at this time. It is not that the laborer is not worthy of his hire, but this work comes under an entirely different activity of the Divine Law, which I will one day explain to the students. Feeling as I do the earnest, most worthy desire of some of the students to come physically within this Inner Circle or Radiance, so to speak, I shall endeavor to explain how it is not possible to be done, beautiful and loving as the desire and radiation of the beloved students are.

This beloved Sister and Brother have gone through thirty years of strenuous, conscious preparation for this work. The Electronic Circle within which this Radiation must focus would have to be entirely re-arranged and re-adjusted. It might require some years to again bring it to this point, lovely and beautiful as the radiation of the others is.

Each individual has his own distinct radiation and vibratory action. While the invisible mechanism, shall I call it, for this work is in one way very powerful, yet in another way it is as delicate as a gossamer veil.

I assure you, beloved students, that either my Personal Presence or my Consciously Directed Ray is always present, whenever either this beloved Sister or Brother is giving forth these instructions. Here let me urge you that at no time is it wise for any student under this Radiation to give forth verbatim these instructions to one who is not yet under this Radiation. Extracts verbal or otherwise may be given forth for the help of others, but we do not wish anyone to be so unfortunate as to say, he is authorized to give this forth, when he has not had permission to do so.

This channel must always be kept clean, pure, and unselfish and these instructions may not be commercialized at any time. The application within the instruction that is given from time to time, if used sincerely with true feeling and confidence in the instruction, will cause the student or the teacher using it to become such an invincible magnet, for the Opulence and Riches of God that there will be no need to commercialize the instruction for the sake of a livelihood. For any individual, whether at first he has the full understanding of its meaning or not, who will be conscious that: "I AM the omnipresent, limitless supply of God's Riches and Opulence in my use," will sooner or later come into the full conviction of this Mighty Truth.

I understand fully how important the financial support of the individual seems to him, but I say to you, beloved students, that financial support is always as the shifting sands, until you begin to consciously apply the use of the "I AM Presence," as your Omnipresent, Limitless Supply, of either money, Love, understanding, Light, or illumination. So try to receive the full conviction of the radiation of this which I give to you, that you may use it with a certain, unwavering consciousness, that will give you *forever* your freedom from all financial strain.

Knowing that the "I AM Presence," which you have set, or are setting in motion, is the same in every other individual on earth as it is in you, and as it is in the Universe, giving you the power and intelligence to make this declaration, then you know that whatever your conscious application implies, it is acting everywhere, just the same as within the present application that you make.

Heretofore, I have hesitated to give you this very definite application, or explanation of this application, but your earnest demand has impelled it forth. I send with this a certain specific radiation which shall enable you to use this with absolute confidence.

The student should *always remember, that it is only by conscious effort that he can keep his mind at peace, that this Inner Power may flow through unhampered,* to the accomplishment of his desire. As a child in school, you were given certain problems to solve, for instance, we will say in mathematics. At the same time, you were given the means by which to accomplish this. If you did not make your application as directed, you of course would not receive your correct answer. Consequently, you kept at it—kept trying and trying, until your answer was proved. If you did not understand how to go about it, you went back to your teacher for instruction, and found what was required. So it is in this, which is now given you. This application never has and never can fail, in the accomplishment of anything upon which your attention is directed, if you will but continue to apply it with determination, and stick to it until results are in your hands, or presence.

Now here, let me call your attention to a most powerful explanation, which Jesus, the Christ, gave you in his own words: That in all the teaching he received through the various avenues, and I assure you some of them were very great, it was only His instruction, conscientiously applied, that finally brought to Him or revealed to him from Within, the many, amazing, magical statements, one of which was: "I AM the Resurrection and the Life." It was this statement which he used, that enabled him to give the example to humanity, which will last throughout the centuries.

Whatever demand you make of the Universal, All-knowing Presence, wherein you use the words, "I AM," it must bring the same, definite, certain results that his statements brought him, when he declared: "I AM the Resurrection and the Life." Try earnestly to *feel* the mighty importance of this.

Here let me caution you, and assure you with great emphasis, that no matter who or what you are, what place you may be in from the growth standpoint, when you make application with the words, "I AM," you positively cannot fail to accomplish that to which you apply it, if you will hold fast with unwavering determination.

Beloved students, I feel the Great Love sent to me, and never fail to respond to it.

Always *first* give your Great Love and Adoration to your own "I AM Presence," the Master-Self, then to those who may be able to assist you. Many of you are making wonderful strides. Go forth with certainty in your hearts, always being aware: "I AM the Conquering, Victorious Presence, in any achievement I desire; that I AM now the Full Dominion of every application that I make; that 'I AM the Presence' always within every demand, supplying, and fulfilling it."

There is no mental state that shuts the door against the very thing you are striving for, like a feeling of distress about it. On the other hand, the proper attitude is to joyously take the stand, that: "I AM the Presence that enables me to see or hear with the Inner Sight and Hearing" and at no time to let one's self become disturbed, because another is using a faculty different from one's own, but rather rejoice in it.

The teacher or student should be quick to realize, that no ignorance of the outer activity of the mind should have any power at any time to disturb him, even though directed at him personally.

At all times, turn to your own "I AM Presence," and demand to know and see clearly, the plan that you should follow.

The Masters' pictures and the instruction should be considered a sacred thing to the students. Adhere always to the time-worn statement: "To know, to dare, to do, and to be silent," because when students begin to discuss these things with unsympathetic individuals, they scatter the force, instead of holding it within, for their own illumination.

I say this with all the vehemence of my Being: "Let the student forever remember that it is impossible to have a selfish desire or intent, when reaching to the "Master I AM Presence" for Love, Wisdom, Power and Illumination. As an illustration, I might say, and I am sure he will not object: that this good Brother is the only student I have ever known, who has completely governed that impelling force, to become a teacher which always asserts itself somewhere along the pathway of the student.

It is not that the desire is an unworthy one, but in

so many, many instances, the students attempting it too soon, before they are sufficiently fortified *mentally* meet with obstruction which they are not able to stand against, and they become permanently discouraged from further effort, defeating the wonderful work that they might have accomplished later.

The most important thing in any student's Life, is the Love and Adoration of his own "Mighty I AM Presence," with patience to the extent, that he becomes so anchored in that Mighty Presence, that he is always fortified by It.

An individual, who is a stirring-stick, can do more damage in one hour than you realize. Anyone whom you can once get to apply earnestly the "I AM Presence," will never backslide. I AM determined to keep the "I AM Presence" before the students, so they realize that they are using a Mighty Intelligence, Power, and Love, and that they are setting It into action.

Jesus came of his own volition, and gave to the students the way he accomplished the overcoming of the last enemy.

It takes enormous strength to stand your ground. *There is nothing can give you permanent success in the outer activity, except the conscious use of the "I AM Presence."* Stand adamant against the thing that would sway you off. Take the stand often: "I know what I am doing, and I am doing it." *You may sometimes have to say very strong things, in order to shut off interference, but do not be susceptible to it.*

Decide what you want to do, and then say: "I AM the Presence doing it." The use of the "I AM" prevents the development of anything out of balance. "I AM" is the All-Balance, because It is the Power and Governing Intelligence of all Perfection. Its very *activity* compels the Balance.

The "I AM" Command is the activity of the thing that is already there, impelling it into the outer activity. There are several in America now, who, if they would take Jesus' stand: "I AM the Resurrection and the Life," and live in it day after day, would raise the body as sure as the world. *You cannot use the words, "I AM," with anything and not couple with it the power to do the thing.*

There are two things retarding to a student's spiritual growth. One is when the husband or wife does not agree with one's efforts, and the other is outside suggestion. *You have your "I AM Presence" which is All Intelligence, so make yourselves adamant against suggestions of any kind—good or bad.*

Sometime, we will devote an entire discourse to the wise handling of the psychic. There is not one out of ten thousand that understands, that the awakening of the sight into the psychic plane is *not* a spiritual thing. When people begin to see on the psychic plane, they are but using the physical sight a little expanded and do not know it.

In the psychic realm, the suggestions given offer just enough Truth to anchor interest, and hold the attention, until psychic forces get a good hold on the person. This always comes through the fascination of the phenomena. When one focuses the attention upon the "I AM Presence," it will draw him into the fulness of the "I AM Presence."

The inhabitants of the elements are used for all activities of Nature, but they do not prevent other forces acting, and they are not the only activities in nature. There are times when these Great Cosmic Beings direct their attention to Nature.

Every thought sent forth by an Ascended or Cosmic Being, contains within it a Perfected Form. If that Being's idea is on the manifestation of snow, or whatever it is, it would take on the Perfection which was within His thought, because all thought carries form.

Say: "I AM the Presence entering into and revealing to my outer consciousness, this activity." Then, the outer mind would get the full Inner Activity, and bring It into your outer activity.

When people enter into the psychic plane, everything is distorted, and they have no definite proof of the Truth. Those beings in the psychic plane who seek to get others under their control, begin to prophesy, and it is one of the first things they do. No one can take a stand against a Messenger of the Light, and not receive the re-action into themselves, because the Light repels all that is unlike Itself.

BENEDICTION: Out of the fulness of Thy Mighty Opulence, Oh! "Mighty I AM," we feel Thy Flowing Energy, we feel Thy Enfolding Love, we feel Thy Qualifying Presence, hastening us into Thy Perfection. We feel Thy Glorious Presence enfolding us in Thy Mighty Mantle of Peace, enabling us to maintain Perfect Self-control, sustaining us in Thy Mighty Perfection, that we may manifest Thy Mighty Presence—now.

DISCOURSE XXII

December 15, 1932

SAINT GERMAIN

INVOCATION: Thou Infinite, Abiding Presence! Thy All-pervading Light, Thy Opulence of Substance is Omnipresent and All-pervading. We open the activity of the outer consciousness into the conscious direction and molding into form of every good thing we desire. We give praise and thanks for Thy Intelligent Action in our minds with Thy Love, Thy Wisdom, and Thy Power, to guide us, to raise us, into all Perfection.

I bring you greetings from those Ascended Ones who ever minister to the Messengers of Light, wrapping their Mantles of Light, Illumination, and Protection about them.

THE DISCOURSE

I had not intended to explain quite yet the undesirability of any thought or condition of the psychic plane, but the demand compels it to come forth.

In the first place, the student must understand that what is called the psychic plane, has nothing whatsoever to do with Spirituality. It is a faculty of the human consciousness, which can be brought into play by human beings who will give sufficient attention to it, but the individual, who wishes to reach into the psychic plane alone, either consciously or unconsciously, had better never been born into that embodiment.

The fascination of the phenomena of the psychic plane, I assure you is most alluring, for those whose attention becomes firmly anchored in the psychic plane do not loosen themselves from it in that embodiment, and it may take several embodiments to free them.

In all strata of consciousness, there is a fragment of truth unrecognized, otherwise it would not be possible for it to be sustained, because you must understand that in all things and in all activities, there is some more or less of the God-Energy acting, misused truly, but nevertheless active.

The sincere student will give no attention to the phenomena of psychic seeing or hearing, but understands that he must push directly through, by the power of the Inner Will through his outer determination, and enter within the Electronic Belt where only the Truth is expressed.

Beloved Students, while it is necessary to explain this, I want you to make up your minds not to have any fear.

Within the psychic stratum of thought and *feeling*, is the principal activity of what we know as the sinister force in this world. Sometimes, souls with splendid Inner Attainment, not understanding the true reality of this of which I speak, have allowed their attention to become drawn to this stratum, because of the premature awakening of this physical faculty, by a semblance of Truth being presented to them and some phenomena—enough to hold their attention. After the attention becomes fixed, everyone without exception will find that semblance of Truth disappearing.

One of these attributes, which is perhaps most fascinating, is the false prophecies which are made, causing the individual to make wild prophecies, and once in a while, one being fulfilled in order to bind the attention more strongly. With this, there is a certain substance which is drawn into the brain. (This I may not yet explain further to you.) This makes it impossible even for the Master to interfere to help the individual, because of his own free will by which he has accepted it. There are a few cases, however, in which the individual realized the mistake before he had gone too far, and by intense calling to be liberated, one of the Brothers was sent to release the individual completely.

There is occasionally a rare nature, who because of its great purity, passes through this psychic stratum without ever knowing it or contacting it. This kind of individual is very fortunate indeed. The forces within this stratum work most directly upon the feeling nature, and this means upon the passion of the individual, because it is most easily reached.

Men and women, who have lost the controlling power over their passion, which may be either sex or anger, have knowingly or unknowingly become entangled in the psychic stratum of thought and feeling, thereby opening the doors of their beautiful and wonderful Temples of God. Through the open door, the forces within the psychic stratum fasten upon them, intensifying their own passion into an uncontrolled condition, which otherwise might be controlled. Far better had such an individual walked into a den of rattlesnakes, for then he would have but thrown off the physical body and been free; but once enmeshed in this psychic sphere, they are often bound for many embodiments. Why is this? Because they make records within their mental worlds from which they do not know how to extricate themselves. Consequently these souls are reborn again with those same tendencies, until after the second or third embodiment, they become the depraved creatures you see about you wherever you go.

Sometimes the influence is cunning enough to hide this from the outer world for a long time, thus carrying on its nefarious work, as it thinks, in secret. Here comes the most heart-rending part of this explanation, I mean to say, it seems so from the outer sense.

On the higher planes of activity, there are great and beautiful souls who volunteer to go into this stratum to help, through their *radiation,* to break its hold upon humanity. These volunteers are both masculine and feminine. More often, however, they are feminine. This explains why beautiful souls, in a feminine embodiment, become united in outer marriage with the masculine soul who has become enmeshed in this psychic condition. Often the individuals thus enmeshed become most cunningly sensitive, and with remarkable accuracy, sense conditions. Thus, many times causing others with whom they come into contact to temporarily think it is real.

If individuals coming to the point of being united in marriage, man-made, would call out to the God Within, the "Mighty I AM Presence," that: "If this marriage is taking place through the desire of passion, then let it never be done," great grief and torture would thus be avoided.

Now we come to the real part.

The individuals, who through their own efforts or through instruction being presented to them, get the true understanding of what the "Mighty I AM Presence" means, and that It is the True and Mighty Self, and hold earnestly to that, never again can they be drawn into those discordant things, unless from their own volunteering from the Higher Planes of activity, where they know exactly what they are doing.

War periods, more readily than any other, open individuals to this psychic plane. Consequently, it has always been observed that after war periods, there is always a greater unleashing of the uncontrolled passion than at any other time.

Knowing this, should in no wise cause anyone to fear this psychic stratum. If students find themselves conscious of passing through it, they should instantly take the consciousness: "I AM the Controlling Master Presence always victorious," and they will instantly find strength to face whatever appears, and go fearlessly and serenely through.

Jesus suggested that this explanation be given while the students were under the triple radiation. (This Triple Radiation means that in His Radiation He always carries with it the Triple Activity of the Father, Son and Holy Spirit, or the "I AM Presence." All who apply the use of the "I AM Presence" are receiving the Triple Activity as long as they maintain It.)

Astrology

One of the saddest things I have to say to you is, that: many of those attempting to cast horoscopes are unknowingly drawing themselves into the psychic net, and are becoming sensitized and voicing the adverse conditions which exist only in this stratum.

This is one of the most unfortunate activities, because the individual is so entirely unaware that he has opened his door, until he has become so enmeshed, that no amount of argument or reasoning will change his belief in astrology. In the past twenty years, the avenue of astrology has been used for this purpose more than any other. Many times through this, the thought or radiation from this stratum says, that certain conditions will manifest for the individual, which he cannot avoid. If it is not said in so many words, it is *felt* through the radiation. This is one of the principal reasons why the last cataclysm of Atlantis occurred, and why the people of Atlantis in the great majority, refused to listen to the Wisdom of the Masters, who prophesied from Reality the destruction of Atlantis.

I understand beloved students, that some of you, who have been so interested in your horoscopes, may think I am severe. However, such is not the case, but my Love for you is great enough that I may speak to you the unadulterated Truth. If you cannot believe the Truth which I speak to you, then you must go on your way, for you are individuals of free will which I have no desire to interfere with, except that I AM privileged to point the way.

Individuals, who will cling tenaciously to the "I AM Presence," need never, anytime, anywhere, ever fear any of these things, because it will correct them, and hold them steady on the True Pathway of Light, up whose Golden Stairway they may climb with definite precision, into their Full Dominion and Perfection.

I assure you, beloved ones, that my heart goes out with all its strength to the individuals whose attention is held by astrology, for they are so unaware of the pathway strewn with thorns, which they have entered upon that will pierce their feet, causing them to cry out in agony, and only when that agony becomes great enough, will they call out with all their Beings and say: "OH GOD! SHOW ME THE TRUE WAY."

Beloved students, you, who so earnestly seek the Light, know there is but the One Presence that is your Invincible Protection, and that is the "Great I AM Presence," God in you. Do not let your attention ever be held by these many outer manifestations—astrology, the power of numbers, spiritualism, on any of the many things that would take your attention away from the "Mighty I AM Presence" which is your Real Self.

If you turn to It at all times, It will lead you in the Pathway of Light, strewn with the rarest flowers, whose very fragrance will enfold you with that strength and, "peace that passeth understanding," with that stillness of the outer that will enable you to enter into the Great Silence wherein you will find the Greatest Invincible Activity of God, the "I AM Presence."

Beloved ones, surely you must understand that you cannot serve two masters and gain any victory ahead. Having free will you must choose. If you choose the outer, forgetting your "Invincible I AM Presence," then my Love goes with you, enfolding you in Its Mighty Mantle of Protection, until such time as you choose to return to the One God.

If you choose your "I AM Presence," and adhere to It, then your struggles are soon over, and you will find yourselves moving in that sphere of peace, harmony, and Perfection wherein you look upon the outer world with great compassion, but never with that human sympathy which would stifle your own growth.

This reminds us of the old time-worn statement: "Seek ye first the Kingdom of Heaven and all the outer things are added or given into your use, under your command." That Kingdom of Heaven is the "Great I AM Presence," the only Reality of you, Who is the Owner and Giver of all created and manifested things.

Is it not strange, beloved students, that one will so long wander about in discord and limitation, when the Master Presence of Light, the "I AM Presence," walks by one's side at all times, waiting one's decision to turn to It and receive Its radiant, glorious blessings of Perfection in all outer manifestation? Such is your privilege, Oh Beloved Ones!

In spite of all outer activity, the atmosphere of the classes is truly divine. While I am sorry that some have not felt the *true* importance of their "I AM Presence," and that they still reach to outer things, I but wait, enfolding them in my Love, for they have free will.

Perhaps I am a little old-fashioned, but when I see individuals that are so good and so fine, I would just like to pick them up and hold them in my embrace, until they could realize the full importance of their own "Mighty I AM Presence;" but this I may not do, for I so well know that all, who have any desire left to reach to the without, must do so, until that desire is no longer apparent.

The students must understand that they cannot divide their attention between the "I AM Presence" and outer things, for it is a house divided against itself, and must sooner or later fall.

All greatness is dependent on the "I AM Presence," and It is the governor of the form or should be. In It is all strength, courage, and power.

Those blessed children! If they could only realize fully what a privilege stands at their doors, and how in a comparatively short time, they could gain freedom from *all* limitation.

THIS DICTATION

The situation is this: When students ask, if they might listen to these dictations themselves, they are entitled to the explanation of what is necessary for work of this kind, for it is most unusual we know.

The fact is that the One God, is always Perfect, always was, is now, and always will be, and the "I AM is that Presence;" but if they have not been aware of this, the body and brain of the student must go through a period of adjustment. That adjustment of the outer-self takes weeks, months, or years to accomplish, according to the requirement of the student.

Never in the history of the preparation of students, has the Master ever allowed them to come within his own Inner Electronic Circle. The students come or are taught the application, but they never come into the Inner Electronic Circle of the Master Himself.

The Electronic Circle prepared here for this work has required thirty years of preparation, and no matter how beautiful the Radiation and Love of an individual are, we do not have the time to prepare and adjust the atomic structure of the brain and body of the students, *at this period of world crisis,* but with their sincere determination and use of the "I AM Presence," they will be *prepared* for the "Presence of the Ascended Host."

The atomic structure is a mechanical machine, and the innumerable parts must work in harmony and perfect cooperation with each other. The students do not understand that when a certain, definite, specific work is to be done, there must be definite preparation for it. For illustration: Take one, who by nature is endowed with an unusual quality, for giving forth lectures in public; if he have the assistance of the Ascended Host, there must be special preparation for it. The individual would be so prepared, that from twenty minutes to half an hour before the lectures, that one would be enclosed in a Tube of Light into which nothing entered, except the Radiation of the Inspiring Master.

BENEDICTION: Out of the fulness of our hearts, Oh Mighty Presence! we give praise and thanks for Thy Love, Wisdom and Power. We give praise and thanks for the Mighty Rays that have gone out to each student to-day. We give thanks for the intensity of this focus that quickens the assurance within the students of the Truth of their "Mighty Presence of the I AM" which is the True Self. Strengthen them, each one, with that firm determination to hold to that One Presence which is all Freedom, all Perfection, Eternal Youth, and Beauty.

NOTES

Q. Is the God, Meru, large of stature?

A. The God, Meru, is about seven feet and of the most wonderful proportion. The God, Himalaya, is about seven feet two inches. The God, Tabor, is about eight feet. He comes from a very, very ancient race of people.

DISCOURSE XXIII

December 19, 1932

CHRISTMAS PREPARATION

SAINT GERMAIN

INVOCATION: Thou Mighty Infinite Intelligence, Thou who dost have power over all things! we welcome Thy All-pervading Presence, Thou All-pervading Life, the animating Principle of every human being. We give thanks that, "I AM the Great and Mighty Presence," that: "I AM anchored in the heart of every one of God's children," fulfilling the Perfect Plan in spite of all resistance of the outer activity of the mind.

We give praise and thanks that the conscious direction of Thy Mighty Energy is sufficient, by those of understanding, to bless and to prevail with Thy Wondrous Light and Intelligence everywhere.

I bring you greetings from the Great Host, and personally from Jesus, who will again speak to you over His Ray to-day.

THE DISCOURSE BY JESUS

In the Fulness of My Love, I come to you again to-day over the Great Light and Sound Ray, this time to direct consciously the Healing Ray to every one of the students. This Ray I will sustain for two weeks every day, that they may have the radiance of the Healing Power.

In my ministry to mankind among the hills of Judea, I stirred the latent memory within the Inner Records of mankind, and its work is still going on to-day. I wish the students to understand, that preceding all conscious healing upon my part, within my own mind I was always conscious that: "I AM the only Healing Presence," and, as that "Unlimited I AM Presence," I had the right, the power, and the ability, through that Presence, to command all outer activity of the mind to be silent, and obey Its command.

Thus, when I spoke to individuals, I spoke with that Authority of the "I AM Presence," which I recognized as the Only Intelligence and Power acting or that could act. I was conscious of the outer activity of the minds of those of humanity about me, but as I said to you before: "It was only when I began using, 'I AM the resurrection and the Life,' that the fulness of my mission, and how it was to be fulfilled, was entirely revealed." This is the particular point I wish to stress with the students to-day that: Within each one of them is that same "Mighty I AM Presence," which I used to accomplish the *Perfection* of that Mighty Presence. This seemed to humanity at that time, the performing of miracles. However, I assure you, it was but consciously setting into action and use, Cosmic Laws, that are ever about you to be set into activity through conscious direction. The mistake that students make, and which delays their achievement, is in feeling that they are acting a falsehood, in declaring the Perfection they do not yet see manifest in their appearance or activity. I tell you sincerely from my own experience, that *we must acknowledge the One Presence, Intelligence and Power, then, claim it as our own in our every thought and activity*. It is the only way this Mighty Perfection can be brought into the outer appearance and the fulness of our use. Because that Perfection has not yet appeared, seemingly, should not deter you from applying and claiming Perfection as your own: for anyone with average intelligence has but to stop and think that the Energy, the Life-Principle that he is using, is God, "The Mighty I AM Presence." Therefore, Its Presence, Power and Energy is always Self-sustaining.

In the claiming of this Mighty Presence and activity, you consciously set It into action in your Life, home, world, and affairs. To-day, as in the time of my attainment, the financial struggle seems to be most weighing, and yet, within the reach of your conscious manipulation and direction of the Mighty Energy, Substance, and Opulence about you, *you have everything* with which to draw to you that Wondrous, Omnipresent Opulence of God.

When you say, "I AM," you are stirring that into action to fulfill your conscious demand. One of the first and mightiest things that became clear in my consciousness was my ability, everyone's ability, to qualify this energy, consciously directed, with whatever the seeming need demanded. Thus, the energy may produce for your use, gold, silver, money, food, clothing, means of conveyance, or whatever the conscious demand is.

All this you must claim with determined conscious effort, which knows, that *in the conscious demand, is the "I AM Presence" speaking and acting.* Therefore, It has All Power and Authority to clothe whatever the demand is, with Its kind.

In the consciousness that: "You are the 'I AM Presence' acting at all times," *you then must know that you are, that moment of recognition, an invincible magnet of attraction, that causes every activity of the Universe to rush to you to fulfill the demand.* The only reason it does not seem to be so, is because somewhere in your consciousness, there is a *feeling* of uncertainty, either of your ability, of your authority, or the omnipresence of It to act; but I assure you, as one having attained, and having gone through the complete process of attaining, that it is a pleasure, the privilege of myself and others to place before you these simple Laws, yet Mighty and Invincible in their activity, that will give you Dominion and Freedom over all the things that seem to be such a mountain of obstruction in your way. As you continue to accept and use these Laws in your activity, you will find that you are attaining Dominion, not only over the one element, but all four elements—earth, water, air, and fire.

When you have become conscious of the *"Flame of your Divinity,"* you are acting from the highest of the four elements, which is Fire, and the True Activity of Spirit.

As the conscious activity is to the unconscious, so is the Conscious Use of the Flame to the recognition of the Light. The natural element of your soul is the "Flame," accounting for the ancient Fire and Sun worship. When one becomes conscious that he has, is, can use, and direct this Consuming Flame, he has entered into Mighty Power.

When one becomes conscious that he has dominion over the four elements, *he has but to practice its use to become conscious that: he may direct the lightning, master the storm, control the waters, and walk in the midst of the fire, unharmed.* Will you kindly tell me how any being can have the use of anything, until he acknowledges it, and knows that he has the ability to make it his servant in use?

Then, by the practice of its use, he becomes absolutely invincible in its direction. I wish so earnestly to make clear to you, that you are being given and taught the exact Laws which I used, and which everyone who has attained the Ascended State must use.

It is all a matter of use, once you know of these Laws and that the "I AM Presence," which you are, has all intelligence, power and authority to consciously direct the energy, through the outer activity of your mind. Then do not fear to use it, to heal, to prosper, to bless, and to enlighten your fellow man.

Erase from your mind forever, that there can be any selfishness in your conscious recognition, that the "I AM Presence" is directing. It matters not what you require for your attainment, wherein it makes you more able, of greater ability and power to bless. Then do you not see that there can be no selfishness in the desire for this greater attainment and Perfection?

For any individual to feel that he must wait upon the attainment of another is a great mistake. Individuals may attain only through their own, conscious effort in this wonderful recognition. No one can grow for another or attain for another, but each may be of immense help to the other, by knowing with intensity, that: "I AM the only Presence and Intelligence acting within that individual," for the one you wish to help. This may be qualified with whatever the person seems to need most.

Every individual's first duty is Adoration and Love to the "One Mighty I AM Presence," which is every-where present.

Do you not see how in this, it is a joyous privilege to love your so-called enemy, because: "I AM the only Real Presence and Activity anywhere"? If the ignorance of the outer activity of the mind seems to have created disorder, pain, and limitation, then you know that the miscreation has no power of its own. There is nothing but the wrong belief of the individual to sustain it, consequently, it has no Self-sustaining power.

If you have been unfortunate enough to create inharmony, disorder, limitation, then can you not see that you alone—through the power of your "I AM Presence," the Consuming Flame—must consciously call on the Law of Forgiveness, consume through that Flame of Life, which you are, everything in your world which you have wrongly created?

This should easily make it clear to you, how you set about to cleanse your world of its disorder and its mistaken creation. Then you stand forth, clothed with the Sun, the Light of Eternal Life, Youth, Beauty, and Opulence, holding within your hand for instant use, the Scepter of Power of the "I AM Presence," which you are.

It is important to know that this One Mighty Energy, does all things according to the quality you give It or the wish you want fulfilled.

One thing students should be intensely conscious of and that is: "I AM the Eternal, Harmonizing Presence and Activity everywhere I move, and of everything to which my thought is directed." This, constantly used with the *feeling* of its invincible power, will keep the atmosphere of your world purified, harmonized, and held in readiness for any conscious direction to go forth with great speed to its accomplishment.

When you wish to speak with authority, silently to, or of another individual, speak his given name and you will find, the help, the energy sent, much more easily received. It is like calling the attention of a person to whom you wished to speak. Naturally, your first impulse is, if you are going to speak to one of the family, you first say Don, Mary, or Dick to get their attention, and then you proceed to give your message. So it is when directing the energy silently.

Within the Inner World, in this recognition and use of the "I AM Presence" knowing that: "I AM everywhere present," you see how you may speak to one across the earth, through the "I AM Presence," as readily as though that one stood in the room in your physical presence.

I warn you, if you attempt to use this knowledge to harm another, then remember that through your own soul and body will pass the bolt or your intent to another. Try always to remember, that you are not human beings so-called, but you are Gods and Goddesses in embryo which, through the conscious effort, you can bring into Full Dominion.

I say to you, beloved students of Light: "Arise! Awaken! to the fulness of your God-Dominion. Fearlessly use the conscious knowledge and direction of this "Mighty I AM Energy" for your freedom, prosperity, blessing, and enlightenment. Each of you is a glittering, dazzling, Jewel of Light, projected into a world of chaos and darkness, that the Radiance of your Light may expand, expand, and again expand, that all darkness of the earth be consumed in this "Mighty Radiance of the I AM Presence," which you are.

Do not hesitate, beloved children! grasp this Scepter of your Power and Dominion, use it to heal, to bless, to prosper, to enlighten, and you will find all earthly things bowing before you, and rushing to fulfill your slightest demand.

Such beloved ones, beloved brothers and sisters, the "One Mighty Presence, which I AM," is the conscious ability I convey to you this day, with its Self-sustaining strength, courage, power, and enlightenment, to go forth attaining your freedom *now* with these Personal Rays, which I project to each of you for these two weeks. I assure you these Rays are no idle fancy, but a tangible current of Energy containing in It all things, and blessing you according to your acceptance.

I clothe you in this Mantle of Light, within it is all power. I hold you close in my Mighty Embrace, "I AM with you every hour."

SAINT GERMAIN:

Again have you been blest by that Electrifying Presence. I need not add to it, unless there are questions.

When you realize that "I AM" is the only Presence, Power, and Ability to think in your brain cells, and you are accepting only the activity of the "I AM Presence," then you make It the All-Power fulfilling every outer desire. Therefore, if you desire something needful in the outer activity, *it is the "I AM Presence" producing it through your conscious demand, which has nothing to do with so-called human desire.*

Say often: "I AM always loving obedience unto the Light."

Everything will become more alert, more quickened, and more powerfully protected as you use the "I AM Presence," more and more.

The Great Central Sun magnet: The more one is conscious of this great magnet working, the more powerfully it acts in his own sphere.

An awakened individual never uses a destructive force. When the Master of Suerne projected the force and the army was killed, he simply projected it for the protection of his people, and the destructive qualities which the others brought with them to slay and kill, qualified the force sent out by the Master, and it destroyed those who sent it out. You can see how easily it would do that, when they came to destroy.

Every individual, if he have understanding, has a right to protect himself. The students should always be taught never to judge the action of a Greater Intelligence than themselves.

When phenomenon is produced by an Ascended Master, the activity so transcends the intelligence witnessing it, that it is most difficult for them to be sustained in the acceptance of the actual Truth of it. It is utterly impossible to satisfy the outer activity of the mind.

Projected vision: The etheric record is reclothed in substance. You cannot reclothe a record of scenes except in their own environment. The individual's record goes with him, wherever he goes and can be reclothed anywhere he is.

BENEDICTION: Thou Mighty, Infinite Presence! Thou Wondrous Brother of Light, Wisdom, Love, and Power! we give thanks for Thy Radiant Presence, glorifying all who look to Thee and in that Glorious Presence, we send to all mankind Thy Enfolding Light, lifting them into Thy Presence always.

DISCOURSE XXIV

December 22, 1932

SAINT GERMAIN

INVOCATION: Thou Infinite, All-Loving Presence! we feel Thy Peace, Thy Love, and Thy Wisdom pervading all—everywhere. Knowing there is but the One Mighty Presence of which we are a part, we know thou art omnipresent, pouring Thyself forth, filling every need on demand, lifting the consciousness of mankind Unto Thee and holding it anchored there, until the "Light of Eternal Life" fills all Beings with Its Radiance, carrying them forward with that Inner Impulse to eternal, permanent recognition of the "Great I AM."

I bring you greetings from the Great Ascended Host and especially from Nada, Cha Ara, Chan, and Diana, Goddess of Fire.

THE DISCOURSE

As the consciousness of the students is raised into the activity from the higher or Fire Element, everything in their Beings begins to act with an intensity that many times they do not understand and, as they begin to work more from the Fire Element standpoint, the more necessary it is to keep up the guard.

The training that we are endeavoring to give forth

277

to bless, protect, and enlighten the students, is to train one's self to be on guard at all times, and while all should understand and with every effort use the "I AM Presence" to maintain Self-control yet, if something happens unexpectedly, to stand serene in spite of it.

Use the statement frequently: "I AM the Presence on guard."

If something unexpected happens, just say: "We will dismiss this," and go on in that joyous happiness. Try not to have any *feeling*, but to know: "I AM the Mighty Presence governing everyone's activity."

Whenever there is a Center of Light of the Intensity of this focus, there is always the element that would seek to enter through someone. If you are working about the house, keep using: "I AM proof against any sudden disturbance." This sets up a certain armor that will keep the atmosphere harmonized.

Use often: "I AM the Presence which nothing can disturb."

Always hold yourselves in a joyous, calm attitude, regardless of anything that takes place.

For one you wish to help say: "Here pal, through the 'I AM Presence,' we give you the strength to control that."

The very marvelous manner and radiation of your

two classes this week was the most remarkable thing I have ever seen in classes of students. The great Love and Harmony, within the hearts of these students maintained a sufficient length of time, makes almost anything possible. It is a rare thing. Here are three classes in which the same Love and Harmony is maintained.

Do you feel the great wave of peace and joy that came like a breath of a spring morning? I will explain, that you may see how far-reaching is that wonderful, loving care.

The Great Master, whom Jesus contacted, who enabled him to gain the victory, is the same One who was my teacher, and it was His Radiation which came just now. He wishes me to tell you that: "As you pass along the Pathway of Light, you will find the easiest way to overcome disturbance is to turn away from a thing and—forget it." You may have this Master's name later.

To wrong activities, say: "That is not correct," and *then quickly pass it off. This avoids a disturbance that builds*.

As we reach into the Light, we are one great family. Knowing that there is but the "One Great I AM Presence" everywhere, you being the individualization of That, there can only be the one great family, Children of the One God.

In the very first place let this be understood: If a

worthy individual is critical, say with very definite certainty: "There is no one who wishes to intrude this upon your free will. We do not mind sincere questioning, but we do not tolerate criticism nor argument."

The Messenger must refuse acceptance to the discordant things by pouring out the Love Element, that the discord may be consumed. The Messenger must be fortified or else the work is left half undone. No class or work of the Messenger can be sustained, if the Messenger allows argument or discordant feeling to generate.

It is very difficult for the average individual to understand, that *the quickest way to stop any kind of disturbance is: to stop discussing it.*

The thing in your own aura is the only thing that needs attention. The thing recorded in your atmosphere can only come through *your feeling.*

The spoken word, unless there is a sense of condemnation or anger back of it, will not record inharmony on your Inner atmosphere.

Of the two undesirable conditions, it is far better that one explode, and get a thing off his mind, than to hold the feeling within, of resentment or of being hurt, for that is what registers on your Inner Atmosphere. From my standpoint, *I see what is registering in your feelings* and therefore on the Inner Atmosphere.

You know how a carbuncle forms. Well! let me tell you, that in your mental world, exactly the same thing takes place as the physical carbuncle expresses on the physical body.

It is most important to do something to keep yourselves from harboring a *feeling* against persons, places, things or conditions, for these build and record on the Inner Atmosphere.

If the desire comes that: "I wish so and so would do this or that," check it immediately, and say: "There is only God in action there."

When a *feeling* is registered in your atmosphere, it is anchored there until you dissolve or consume it. *It is always the feeling that makes the Inner record.*

There is no use consuming a thing, if you do not break the habit of generating the cause. One can easily conquer this by saying: "I AM in command here." *Do not let your feelings run rampant.*

Many times individuals are brought together for the sole purpose of compelling them to correct these subtle activities, that most people pay no attention to, whatsoever. This is a matter of stilling the outer in order that the Truth may be received. This is so vital in the individual's Self-correction.

As you rise in consciousness, the energy is waiting like an avalanche for expression, and *if the energy is not controlled, it will rush in and cause you to do things that you would not have done for the world.*

Whatever energy is given into your use is to be sent out harmoniously. That is the Natural Law of your Being.

If one does not understand that he is to govern the energy flowing through him, and he contacts a discordant element, the energy flowing through becomes qualified by that discord, and he should immediately either check it or requalify it with Love. In my experience, if I met a discordant element, I simply said: "Here! I shut my door, you stay out."

The Universal energy flowing through you is naturally harmonious. Shut your door, and then figure out who's the matter.

People resist persons, places, conditions, and things, *because they have not mastered themselves.* The students must maintain this Self-governed harmony within themselves long enough to let the momentum be created, that becomes the permanent guard.

If one will maintain harmony within himself, I tell you he will draw all good things unto him. The unfailing prompter is, that the moment that one expresses some kind of discord, he is to realize that he is the one to blame. There needs to be no written thing to warn anyone.

The moment there is something discordant, it is the prompter warning you to get busy on yourself.

Each individual is his own guard and prompter at all times.

There is Only One Power in the world that can correct anything, and that is the "I AM Presence" in each one. If we refuse to recognize, that we are the creators of our own disturbance, how can we ever correct it or be free from it?

There is no person, place, condition or thing that warrants our ever being disturbed with the ever-present "I AM Presence," beating our hearts each moment, and Who is ever All-powerful.

If one will correct himself on these discordant feelings, he will let the "Great I AM Presence" flood his world with all Perfection. If the individual will not correct himself, how can he ever gain the Eternal Victory?

The "I AM Presence" is the All-power of the Universe to make this correction. Let the "I AM Presence" flow, until it washes everything clean.

When your attention is fixed firmly upon the "I AM Presence," which you are, it is as though your body were a fine sponge through which this Pure Energy is pouring, cleansing it of all imperfection.

If we will stop the discord, the "Stream of the I AM Presence" automatically cleanses away all impurities. You thus have an unlimited power in your hands to intensify your right commands.

Even from the scientific standpoint, knowing that

the cells of the body are renewed in less than a year, if the discord could be shut off for one year, the mind and form would express Eternal Youth and Perfection.

Either from a sense of false pride or something, humanity will not face the Truth, that: *the cause is within themselves. The habit of always blaming the other fellow for what has happened to us, is the thing that blinds us to the Truth and prevents Self-correction.*

A wonderful illustration of this is in the beautiful child-form. Until the child is old enough to begin to register the discord about it, its body is beautiful and expresses Perfection. This Perfection of form would always be maintained, if there did not enter into the consciousness of the child the discord of the outer world. There are those who would say to me: "What about the child that is born sickly and disturbed?" In most cases that is a condition brought over from the preceding embodiment, or in rare cases, where there is intense discord between the parents, this may be intense enough to register upon the child; but if you will notice in cases of that kind, as the child begins to grow and develop, it will show less and less of that disturbance. That is absolute proof the discord was not of its own creation, but was imposed upon it by the parents, because the soul was strong enough to rise out of it.

In this particular point, one should understand the amazing conditions of suggestion wherein individuals are constantly surrounded.

For instance, let us take the environment and association of individuals who have been in the habit of going together. In that friendly association, each one is susceptible to the suggestion from the other. If it be discordant, then that association will be broken up, sooner or later by one grand row. However, seventy-five per cent of the individuals moving about in the outer world, are not aware that they are taking on suggestion either from association, environment, or conditions out-pictured before them.

The correct attitude of the student who becomes aware of his "I AM Presence," is immediately to take the firm stand that: *"I AM invincibly protected against any imperfect suggestion."* Thus, one can build about himself an atmosphere, that will immediately repel all suggestions that seek to intrude, wherein there is a destructive element.

I think it necessary to call your attention to your old copy books which said that: "If at first you don't succeed, try, try again." There is no way to gain Victory and Dominion over limitation, except to keep at it until you accomplish it. If you question your accomplishment, you are postponing your victory that much longer.

Those students who really begin to understand that

in the recognition and use of their "I AM Presence," they have the Universal Power at their command, then they know it is impossible to fail in their application, because the more they use it, the more of its sustaining power they have.

Every time you feel a Christ manifestation, say: "I praise Thee and accept the Light of Thy Presence, the 'Full I AM Activity.'" Take this attitude always, and then you shut the door to any undesirable creation from those who have passed on.

Always remember that you are the Master of what shall come into your thought world, and unless you realize that you are the Master you are susceptible to all kinds of thoughts and feelings.

For others, know: "I AM the Presence taking —— into —— accomplishment."

If we give attention to a condition of disturbance, we are giving power to something else but our "I AM Presence."

BENEDICTION: Thou Mighty, Infinite "I AM Presence"! we rejoice in Thy Ceaseless Outpouring, Thy Enfolding Presence protecting and governing the Life of these beloved students. Help them to enter into the Fulness of Thy Presence with no uncertainty, that they may bless mankind wherever they may be or go. Intensify Thy wondrous Light within the outer activity that each one may become a great channel to heal, to bless, to prosper, and to enlighten.

DISCOURSE XXV

SAINT GERMAIN

INVOCATION: Infinite "I AM Presence"! from Thy Ancient Sanctuary, we find Thee pouring forth Thyself into manifestation with conscious intelligent expression, that Thy Perfection be manifest in all phases of Life, and that all of earth which has been wrongly qualified by mankind, be raised into that Ascended State—Thy Eternal Perfection.

I bring you greetings and especially from the Retreat in Arabia, that Great Center of training for the use of the Mighty Rays.

I have two surprises for you to-day. I say, I, because we are all one.

I trust that I need no introduction, as I speak to you over the Light and Sound Ray. Nada speaks.

THE DISCOURSE

How beautiful this day always seems to us in the consciousness conveyed to humanity, representing that birth of the Christ Activity, in all mankind, and to the students who have become aware of what the use of the "I AM Presence" means to them, in setting into motion, Love and Intelligence to do their bidding, according to their direction of that Limitless Power.

So long, individuals have wondered how to attain the Christ Consciousness. The first mighty step is in the recognition of the "Great I AM Presence," God dwelling in you. The second step is in the use of that "I AM Presence," for when you say, "I AM," *with the understanding* of what it means, you have then and there entered into the Christ Consciousness.

It does not mean that you immediately express the fulness of that Christ Consciousness, for you must first know where you are going, and what you wish to do, before you can accomplish it.

All the Ascended Ones have gone the same path, and use identically the same application, because all roads lead to the Great Central Sun, the God-Head.

Our Beloved Brother Jesus, performed one of the greatest blessings to mankind, in not only setting the example from his birth, and achieving the Ascension, but in making the Eternal Record that stands radiant, pouring Itself to humanity. Little can the unarisen realize what this means to mankind. It is an Eternal Beacon beckoning them on into the Light and in the example of the Ascension, Jesus stated definitely, not only what could be done, but what *must eventually* be done.

Great as were the wonders he was able to perform,

he gave the marvelous promise, that: "Even greater things than these shall ye do." Many times students wonder what greater things could be performed than Jesus did, but he tells us that he only performed *a few* of the Universal services that can be rendered to our fellow men.

To us, this day always symbolizes the conscious beginning of that most marvelous of all achievements, the Ascension. The *moment* the individual *becomes conscious* of this fact, the process of his own Ascension has started and according to the fulness of his grasp of this Truth, may the individual accomplish it quickly or require time to do it.

My personal experience has been that, when I became aware of what it meant, and began the use of the "I AM Presence," I found that shortly, I was entirely unaware of time or place and that each day, as I entered more fully into this expansion of consciousness, I found that all things of my desire were right within reach, and mark you, *right within my individual, governing power;* and with it came the consciousness that: "Divine Love was the Mighty Cohesive Power, holding all things together and in place—that this Divine Love within me, of which I had begun to learn, made me an invincible magnet for everything upon which my desire rested."

This simple Truth is one of the Mightiest that first comes to the student. At first, It causes one to realize that, really *he can rise above these seeming limitations* about him, and then, he finds one by one, that *he is actually doing it.*

Then comes the Great Inrush and Outpouring of this Mighty Self Within, that holds the substance of everything the heart can wish, within Its Own Embrace, and your ability and authority, mark you, to qualify and mold this substance, is that which causes it to take on the form of your requirement, whether it be peace, Love, gold or enlightenment.

I say to the beloved students: "Awake, O beloved students *to your authority, to your right, to your conscious ability,* to apply this Great Law, to your Perfect health, eternal youth and beauty, the riches of God, the glorifying of your mind and body, and then to ascend into the Arisen Dominion, into your Eternal, Everlasting Freedom."

After you begin to find, step by step, that you *are* accomplishing, then you begin to forget all this outer condition surging about you, in the glorious *feeling* of being held in the Great Embrace of that Mighty Master-Self Within, *that never has and never will give cognizance to time or space.*

You are the Master and have Dominion in your Life, and over your world, *the moment you recognize* that the Energy, Power and Intelligence which you are using, is the "Mighty I AM Presence."

How fortunate indeed are those individualizations

upon earth, who become aware, really aware of this Truth.

Jesus said: "Know the Truth and the Truth shall make you free." This is one of the mightiest phases of that Truth. Apply it, O beloved ones! with full determination, shutting out all uncertainty from your minds, and you will climb steadily that Jeweled Ladder of achievement, and as you look back upon each step gained, more and more will that blazing radiance shine forth, and you will wonder: "How could I have gone so long in the shadow, when above me stood this Mighty Flame of Life, ready to consume instantly all my unfortunate, ignorant creation?"

I tell you beloved ones, that *you do not have to wait indefinitely* in the recognition of this Mighty Presence. *Fold your arms about it* in all the adoration you can command, and It will raise you quickly out of all these seeming limitations, clothing you in that "Seamless Crystal Garment," blazing with Radiant Light and held with a Jeweled Girdle, that it is your right to wear, and in your hand that Blazing Scepter of Dominion, the Searchlight of your Mighty Soul, which you can turn upon anything, upon any place, upon any height, and draw to you the revelation from within it. Such, beloved brothers and sisters, is the picture of achievement which we have used and attained. Such, we know you can do, because we have.

Never grow weary of the consciousness, that: "I AM the Ascended Presence," and when you say that, know: "It is the Self-sustaining, emanating strength by which I reach my full dominion."

It makes me very happy to be home again, for the happiness in your hearts, to see the many rungs of the ladder you are past, and that you have the conscious consciousness that you can achieve the Greatest of God's Gifts, the Fulness of Himself.

Cha Ara

It is with much joy that I too may say a few words over the Light and Sound Ray to you, and to answer in person the many calls of the hearts to Cha Ara.

I do have many a good laugh in moving about among the students, who have so much longing that I make myself visible to them, and yet some of them, upon the slightest movement unusual, catching their breaths lest I do. You know it is most comical, the outer activity of the self wants a thing so much, and at the same time experiences all kinds of prickly sensations about it, but beloved ones, I say this: "I may not appear nearly so frightful as you might think, so trust me at least to have a pleasing form or appearance, and at the same time for the benefit of the dear Sisters, I shall endeavor to bring along some Attar of Roses."

Q. "From Kashmir?"

A. "That would be quite appropriate."

Q. "Why not your own brand?"

A. "You are very alert. I do not need to purchase it as you do, for I am privileged to brew my own."

May I add a word to the beloved students, commending them and urging them to continue that wonderful, glorious "Presence of Love" and goodwill, not only to us, but to each other, because it makes a wonderful condition in which the expansion of consciousness goes on in leaps and bounds.

I must commend them on the feeling of certainty within themselves in the accepting of our "Presence" and the consciousness of their ability to apply the Law of their "I AM Presence," for it is increasing with great speed.

Do not be discouraged in your call for our visible appearance. While our hearing is perfectly good, I assure you, yet in that call is something that you require. In the *call* for a thing is a certain vibratory action that the student needs, which cannot be explained, except as you see it from the Inner Action.

AMERICA

"O America! Precious Jewel in the crown, the diadem of earth, that Flower of Ancient Wisdom and Light! again you shall come into the power of your full bloom in spite of all the seeming obstructions and appearances to the contrary at present.

"Within thy soul, O Mighty America! is the strength to shake thyself free from the barnacles that have attached themselves to thee, the barnacles of selfishness and the creation of the outer activity of the mind of unawakened human beings. So shall you again come into the fulness of that Light which is your birthright."

Beloved students of this radiation, *no matter what the appearance seems to be in the outer activity, do not allow that appearance to find anchorage in your consciousness or the suggestions from others concerning America.*

Stand serene in your God-given Dominion, knowing the Truth, *seeing America free,* governed by Divine Love and Justice.

The net that the sinister force of earth has seemed to draw America into will yet find the *"Sword of Truth and Light" sever the net each way, making of it the Open-Ended Cross of Freedom, of Light, and Justice.*

The most valuable thing in the individual's Life, in the things which he cannot help, is to shut his eyes to the appearance of them, acknowledge, and set forth into action the Mighty Power of the "I AM Presence."

Do you not see, beloved students, how very, very foolish it is to keep accepting the appearance, through suggestion or otherwise, that *you do not want, whether it is national, state, or personal, when you have such an extraordinary privilege of setting into activity, the "Mighty I AM Presence" to correct whatever has the appearance of less than Perfection?*

The *habit* of mankind has been to see imperfection, where we see perfection. Now in the recognition of the "Mighty I AM Presence" *fully accept Its Perfection every hour of the day.* This does not mean that you have to dwell on this by the hour, but *you can at least assert once every hour of the waking state:* "I do accept the full activity of my 'Mighty I AM Presence.'"

Each time you assert this, you are building it more powerfully into your outer activity, for you are already using this energy and why not acknowledge at all times who and what It is you are using, thus giving It the dominion It wishes to convey to you.

In this way you can set into motion for the freedom, protection, and blessing of America, your beloved country, an invincible power. You do as yet, little dream of the mighty potency and power of adjustment it can cause to take place, when consciously set into motion by one or more who recognize Its Invincible Universal Power.

Now let me suggest that instead of listening to the constant lamentation and suggestion of all kinds of destructive activities, *that you know the "I AM Presence" consumes them and requalifies all this energy with Freedom, Protection, and Perfection for America and the world.*

For your encouragement, I want to say, that all those human beings, who started the cause of this present condition, did not foresee that it was going beyond their control, and through it, many of them have lost their outer ability to longer foster it.

So will those, who are attempting to bring back prosperity by the unlimited use of beer, find things going beyond their control and instead of temporary prosperity, things will sweep into actual prosperity.

So now, as at all times of seeming chaos, will come peace on earth, good-will to man, and the Light of the expanding Christ, in the hearts of individuals, permeating the earth, will draw to Itself Its own.

Again for the benefit of the beloved students, I urge them not to discuss discordant things any more than is enough to understand a situation. Then turn completely from it, and never let it hold your attention again, for I assure you what you entertain in your consciousness will find expression in your Life and world. So fill it with the "Great I AM Presence" holding in Its embrace the Mighty fulfillment of your every desire.

See that Perfection, that Full Perfection of Its Activity everywhere in your Life and world. Do not be affected or disturbed by the creation of others where you cannot help, except to see Perfection, knowing that back of the seeming shadow is the Blazing White Light of the "I AM Presence."

This beloved ones, is my greeting of the season I leave with you. In closing, my mother and others of the Ascended Host, some of whom you do not know, but who know you, send their greetings of Love, peace, opulence, and strength to each of you, to bless you on your way to your final victory and achievement.

Saint Germain: Well, very fortunately, the Radio Corporation can't charge us up on overtime on our station. I suppose if they knew of it they would want to charge us.

I want to say a word or two in conclusion, and that is, to urge the students to recognize that when they say, "I AM," for whatever they want to be accomplished, they not only set the "Great I AM Presence" into action for the accomplishment, but *they should be deeply aware that It holds within It the Self-expanding, Self-sustaining, Self-emanating Power*.

While repetition is good and is ofttimes required to produce a deeper conviction, yet in the present advancement of the students, they should become more conscious of its innate, inherent, Self-sustaining power. This would give the outer consciousness a fuller comprehension of the sustaining power, so that, if the outer activity of the mind is occupied with other duties, *it can send forth the charge of the "I AM" into any achievement once an hour, without in any way interfering with the student's work.*

It is such a mistake for the student to let register in his mind the absurd idea that he hasn't time for these things, when it only takes a moment to powerfully realize the Mighty Invincible Activity of his "I AM Presence" in whatever his attention is required to be used.

However, this application might be very helpful: *"I AM the Mighty Presence commanding the time, all the time I require for the realization and application of this Mighty Truth."*

On the other hand, if many times during the day, one will for a few moments take the consciousness that: "I AM the only Intelligence and Presence acting," it will naturally adjust things according to the requirement. It is so easy to set the consciousness into motion, knowing one is not restricted by any sense of limitation.

TEMPLES OF LIGHT

They are located in the Etheric Belt above the earth's atmosphere. The radiation is poured out from this Belt to the earth through its atmosphere. The Etheric Belt around the earth and that around Venus would be vastly different. Venus is within the Etheric Belt, while the earth is below that.

Warning: *Do not give recognition to anyone who is a tool for the sinister force.* Simply know one thing only: "There is only the I AM Presence, Intelligence, Light, and Power acting." *Do not be concerned about any personal activity of any kind whatsoever, at anytime.*

The student's business is to see Perfection, *feel It and be It, no matter what any human appearance seems to be.*

BENEDICTION: From out the Heart of Thy Great Silence, Oh "Mighty I AM Presence"! comes the solution of all things, the Perfection of all things, for Thou art the Only Governing Power, Perfection, and Intelligence in all outer experience, for Thou art the Presence governing all human expression. Only as we see Thy Perfect Manifestation in all things, do we cause Perfection to manifest in all things.

DISCOURSE XXVI

December 29, 1932

SAINT GERMAIN

INVOCATION: Thou Mighty, Infinite Presence! All Enfolding Love, Infinite in Thy Activity, gracious in Thy Loving Power, we salute Thee heart to heart, face to face, pouring forth eternal gratitude for the outpouring of Thy Mighty Energy—for the use of Thy Directing Wisdom, for the Presence of Thy Opulence in our homes and use. We acclaim ourselves that *active part* of Thee, Self-conscious of Thy Divinity, maintaining every hour Thy Supreme Command.

I bring you greetings from the Great Host who minister, and Who watch all activity.

THE DISCOURSE

We all rejoice exceedingly in the wondrous, loving presence of the students, for the great harmony, joy, and accomplishment that has been attained.

How mighty that Miracle-Working Presence, "I AM," can and will manifest Its Dominion if such a wonderful state is maintained, and I tell you with no uncertainty, *it can be maintained,* ever growing greater and greater in the comprehension of that God Presence in Its Supreme Power of Divine Love.

Every student should remember with definite certainty, that in this Quickening Power of the "I AM Presence" within his Being, everything good or otherwise is stirred into action. If there is latent within the consciousness: rebellion, resentment, or the inclination to judge, it means that all this will be stirred and brought to the surface to be consumed, and I tell you with no uncertainty, that unless the student consciously consumes that which is brought forth to the surface, it will consume him. If one finds himself becoming irritated, he should seize the reins and, issuing the command through the "I AM Presence," declare: "That this be governed harmoniously." Here let me again remind the students, that the greatest thing in their progress is Self-correction and there is no person, place, condition, or thing to blame for what they entertain, but themselves. This is most imperative for their future progress.

These beloved students have arrived at a point where these subtle conditions must be made clear and thoroughly understood, otherwise they will find themselves facing conditions they are unable to govern.

I repeat again to the students to be greatly encouraged, because of the strides they are making in Self-control, the fuller and fuller acceptance of these Mighty Laws of Life, and their willingness to apply the mighty whip of Self-correction; for I tell you frankly, and I speak from experience, that the outer activity, which we term the human, has to be flayed with no uncertainty before it is brought under subjection to the Divine Command.

The reason I gave the use of the Ray or Flame through the hand is, because the minds of some are attuning more rapidly than the atomic structure of the body is being raised. This activity of passing the hand over the body will maintain and sustain that equalization of the quickening of the mind, and the raising of the atomic structure to its balancing point.

I am so happy and willing to give every assistance to the students, as are others, but *there are certain bounds beyond which we may not go,* because of the Self-conscious advancement of the students, *which they must do for themselves.*

However, every one of them has everything by which to be encouraged, but again let me urge them that at no time may they divide the attention of the "I AM Presence." To do this means, that you are releasing the stream of energy and giving power to outside things, and simply delaying your progress.

I speak from experience. It is not possible to divide the attention, for it must *all* be given to the "I AM Presence" *in order to go beyond a certain point of attainment.*

I do not wish to bring any shock to the students under this radiation, but I must speak the Truth, that: "If those beloved students who have been brought under this radiation are not able to hold their attention *entirely upon the 'I AM Presence,'* it *will close the door to our assistance to them for a long time.*" This need not be done, if the students will follow the direction, make the sincere effort every time the attention wanders off, bring it back with firm determination, and say: *"I give all power to the I AM Presence, which I AM, and I refuse with determination, acceptance to anything else, ever again."*

I wish to prepare the students, that there will come the time when they may not be sustained by our Messengers, but must rely on their own ability to hold with such a firm grip upon the "I AM Presence," that they will receive Its Mighty, Sustaining Power.

It is useless and a mistake for any student, after months of instruction, to each day or every few days, allow himself to be thrown into a sense of depression or doubt of the Inner-Power or his ability to apply it. This childish attitude of mind will in time shut the door, if it is not discontinued.

Each student should take his *positive stand,* the *moment* discord of any kind attempts to enter into the mind, and assert his Dominion by declaring: "I AM the Almighty Governing Presence of my Life and my world and I AM the peace, harmony, and courage, Self-sustained, that carries me serenely through everything that confronts me."

It is so important that the students have the benefit of the manuscripts, that we must discontinue the instruction until they are completed, for according to their ability to accept that which is illustrated in the manuscripts will the "Great Judge" determine what shall next be given. We may not under any circumstances take the student beyond the point where he is well fortified.

I must say for the protection of the students, that should certain phenomena manifest about them, to be calm, poised, and unmoved by it at all times, and to go serenely along, not allowing their attention to be held by it, for it is not unlikely that in this number of students, that some may have sufficiently generated energy from past understanding, at a certain point to produce certain phenomena. In such a case, they should always take the firm stand: "I AM the Governing Presence of this, utilizing it in its highest expression and use."

You see that in all this amount of instruction that has been given, it is but a fragment which the student must build upon. The student must always watch for ideas from within himself, upon which to build his expansion.

The first premise for every student on earth who wishes to attain permanent achievement, is to first remind himself that: "I AM the Presence and Intelligent activity." This is the first principle, and in It he can never go astray.

I assure the beloved students, that they need not crave or desire phenomena, for the Natural Law of their Being in their sustained progress, will produce abundant phenomenal proof as they are ready for it. In this, mark you, I do not in anywise refer to the appearance of any of the Ascended Ones, for that is an entirely different thing, and is really not to be taken as phenomenon of any kind.

I watched with great interest the Inner Activity of the students, Tuesday and Wednesday, and it was very gratifying to see the expansion of that Inner Light within them, as the Power of Love grew more intense. It should be remembered by the students that, *when they say, "I AM," they are making the outer activity a Mighty Magnet for the Light to reach and expand.*

I think it would be very wise for each student to take the attitude at this time, or in the beginning of the use of both the instruction and the manuscript: "Great I AM Presence, take me within Thyself, there instruct me, and cause me to retain the Full Memory of these Inner instructions."

As Messengers of the Light, this training is very essential, but the idea should not in anywise cause anxiety to go, or tension in the desire to retain, because an attitude of that kind might easily close the outer memory of the Inner experience.

I cannot help but smile to myself at the closeness with which some of the students are coming to most surprising things, but I trust they will always find themselves poised and serene in whatever the experience is, knowing that: "I AM the One, Eternal, Self-sustained Life in action," and to forever remove from their consciousness that there is such a condition, as so-called death, anywhere in the Universe.

The outer activity of the mind and world is a passing maya, shifting as the sands of the desert, and need never cause anyone the slightest concern, for: "I AM the Eternal Life, knowing no beginning and never finding an end."

Out of the heart of that Great Silence comes the Ceaseless, Pouring Stream of Life, of which each one is an individualized part. That Life is you, Eternally, Perfectly, Self-sustained, and the garments it clothes Itself with are of but little consideration, until one comes to the point of recognition, wherein their attainment has prepared them for the "Seamless Garment, Self-sustained, Radiant with every prismatic color."

Then, may one indeed rejoice in that Eternal Garment that is Ever-Radiant and Changeless, which has removed him from the wheel of cause and effect, and has made him a Being of Cause only, and that

Cause is the Radiance of Divine Love, ever pouring and evolving from its Conscious, Self-poised, Radiant, God-Center—the Heart of the "I AM Presence," which is Eternal Youth and Beauty, the All-knowing Presence, containing in Self-conscious action, the past, present, and future, which after all are but the One Eternal Now.

Such is the eternal elimination of all time and space. Then, you find your world peopled with Perfect Beings, your buildings decorated with choicest jewels, you, standing in the center of your creation— the "Jewel in the Heart of the Lotus"—Its petals your Mighty Avenues of Its Perfect Activity.

Such is a humble picture of that which stands before you, beckoning you into your Perfect, Eternal Home and Radiance.

You see, I feel that Glorious Radiance and, if each one, and especially the students, could center themselves in the Presence of Divine Love and hold themselves there firmly, what wonderful experiences would come to them, if they would shut out the interference of the outer activity of the mind.

For one to take the attitude that: *"I AM the Presence of Divine Love at all times,"* would do such wonderful things. To use this statement and feel it, would at all times close the door to the outer activities of the mind.

The solution of every problem is always right at

hand because the *"I AM Presence" always holds everything within it*.

A demand is the *impelling of the solution* into expression. "I AM" is the Intelligent Active Principle within us, the Heart of our Beings, the Heart of the planet and the Heart of the system.

I cannot refrain from reminding the students again, for they should always know, that: "Whenever you say, "I AM," you are releasing the One, Almighty, Intelligent Energy, Power, and Self-sustained Element." Keep at it, and you will come into a condition so supreme, so wonderful.

When you are looking into the physical sun, you are really looking into the Great Central Sun, the very Heart of the "I AM Presence."

You must take the unconditional stand with your body, that: "The I AM Presence governs this physical body completely, and compels it into obedience." *The more attention you give your body, the more it is the master, and the more it will demand and keep demanding from you.*

When the physical body is either chronically ill or continually showing disturbance, *it proves that it has been given attention over a period of years* to one disturbance or another, and it will never improve, until one takes the positive attitude and whips it into obedience.

You can positively produce whatever you want in

your body, if you will fix your attention upon the Perfection of it, but do not let your attention rest on its imperfections.

For the Ascension: "I AM the Commanding Presence." Use this often, for it stills the outer activity, so you become centered in the Activity of Love.

The *instant* you feel something discordant, turn away from it. You have the Scepter of Power in your consciousness—*now use it.*

You are to follow Jesus' command: "See no man after the flesh." *It means exactly what it says: Recognize no human imperfection, in thought, feeling, word, or deed.*

Cha Ara, his Mother, Nada, and Saint Germain were working very intensely on the expanding of the Inner Light within each one who was here. We wished that the students might see from the Inner standpoint. It would be an experience never to be forgotten.

A very powerful thing to use in problems is, to take the simple consciousness: "God in me, the 'I AM Presence,' come forth! govern and solve this situation harmoniously." It would do wonders. The whole thing is to instantly draw forth the "I AM Presence," and set It to work.

Jesus said: "Ask and ye shall receive."

"Seek and ye shall find."

"Knock: it shall be opened unto you."

Say to your Divine Self: "See here, God! come forth and take care of this." *God wants you to set him to work*. This releases a flood of the God-Energy, Intelligence, and Substance which flows forth to do the command.

BENEDICTION: Thou Mighty, Commanding, "I AM Presence"! assert Thy Dominion within the heart and consciousness of each student, command the Life Activity to express Its fulness, set Thyself as a guard at the door of the mind of each one, that he admits only that which is helpful and harmonious. Bless each one with that power to hold fast, and to go forth to harmonious attainment. We thank Thee.

DISCOURSE XXVII

December 24, 1933

CHRISTMAS EVE

SAINT GERMAIN

INVOCATION: Thou Mighty, Majestic Christ-Power, now grown to Full Stature! we salute Thee by the Sign of the Heart and Head, accepting the Fulness of Thy Mighty Power, made manifest in the hearts of the students and of the people of America. We accept the Fulness of the Light and Its illuminating Presence within the heart and mind of each one, surging forward with such intensity that It carries the courage and strength for everyone, to make the needed conscious effort, that will enable the "Mighty I AM Presence" to raise the atomic structure into its Full Ascension.

Now I will step aside, and let our Beloved Brother speak his heart.

JESUS' DISCOURSE

I bring you Love and Salutations from many of the Ascended Host—some of whom you know, and others of whom you are yet to know.

"I AM the Light, the Way, and the Truth," is the Christmas Bell that is still ringing throughout the field of Cosmic Activity. In the understanding that has been brought to you, in the meaning and power of the words, "I AM," you will find a Charmed Circle in which you may move untouched by human discordant operation. It is not only a matter of *knowing* the Presence, but in *practicing* the Presence in even the simplest activity; for as you attempt an unfamiliar experience, you many times feel timid and uncertain, but as you learn to use the "I AM" in the solving of your desire or problem, you find growing a confidence that you can apply with a definite assurance.

The students should always understand that it is in the "Great Silence," or stillness of the outer, that the Inner Power flows in its ever-increasing accomplishment, and soon they will come to know that even as they think of their "Mighty Source, the I AM," they will *feel* an increase of strength, vitality, and wisdom that will enable them to go forward with a *feeling* of Mastery, that will surely one day open wide the door through the limitations of their human creation, into the *Vastness of their True Freedom.*

We so often see in the heart the craving for proof—some remarkable manifestation that will strengthen them on the way. I assure you, blessed children of the Light, any proof given outside of yourself is but temporary; but every step proved in and through your own conscious application, is an eternal accomplishment, and as you continue to gain the Mastery through your Self-conscious application, you are not only accomplishing the things in hand, but you are raising the consciousness, until presently you will find that all barriers have gone down.

It is in this manner that the door of human limitation is forever nailed back, and as my outer form was nailed to the cross, so do you, by your ascending consciousness, nail back the door of self-created limitations, and feel and know your Dominion.

To the many students so vitally interested in making the Ascension, I would urge you to use the statement often: "I AM the Ascension in the LIGHT." This will enable your consciousness to more quickly rise out of the maya of human creation.

It cannot be stressed too urgently, that as you live in, and accept more fully the Transcendent Power of the "I AM Presence," you will find that not only the outer struggle ceases, but that as you have entered deeper into the Light, *the outer things that you have sought so earnestly will really and truly begin to seek you;* because by that time, you will truly and fully realize the unreality of form and its transitory activity. You will then *know, that within you and the Light about you* is everything you can possibly desire, and the outer that has seemed so very important will have lost its great binding power upon you. Then, in the outer things that come to you, will come joyous freedom. This is the true activity of outer things.

As you become more conscious of the Transcendent Powers that are at your command, you will *know* that you can quickly draw to yourself anything you require without harming or affecting another of God's children.

This Truth must be established within the consciousness, for conscientious souls must know this unwaveringly, that they may not at intervals find themselves wondering, if it is right for them to succeed, when others around them are not succeeding, for your greatest service, I assure you, is to gain the Mastery and Freedom for yourself.

Then, you are prepared to dispense the Light without being affected by the human creation in which you must move. Never feel sad or distressed, if another of God's Children is not ready to accept the Light, for, if he does not come to the Light of his own choosing, it is rarely but a temporary step.

As one begins to gain a conscious freedom from the body, he understands how temporal these outer things are, and how unimportant; but when one enters into the Universal Consciousness, or the Great Cosmic Activity, *one finds to enter into the Light is of all importance.* Then he will know the joy of the Inner Presence and Its Invincible Activity, for which his heart will leap with joy.

Shortly before I became aware of my Full Mission, the statement stood out vividly before me: "I

AM the Presence that never fails or makes a mistake." This I knew later was the sustaining power, that enabled me to BE the resurrection and the Life.

It is unfortunate indeed, that some of the scriptural statements have been clouded by human concept; yet I AM thankful indeed that many have remained unaltered. Another statement I used constantly, for more than three years, was: "I AM always the Majestic Power of Pure Love that transcends every human concept, and opens the door to me to the Light within its heart." I knew later that this greatly intensified my True Inner Vision.

In response to the earnest desire within the hearts of many, I wish to say, that during the years in which the scriptures seem to have been unaware of my activity, I was going from place to place in search of the explanation of the *Light and Presence* which I *felt* within myself; and I assure you beloved students, not with the ease and speed with which you are able to seek to-day. Those of that day in my association were joyous to receive the knowledge of those unchronicled experiences; but, owing to the unusual nature of them, it was thought unwise to place them before the multitude.

So it has been through the ages, when the period of transcendent experiences has begun to fade into the yesterdays, and those who followed were not sufficiently advanced to realize this Truth, they have shut out from humanity glories—beautiful and wonderful.

However, at this time, there has come to the assistance of humanity, the Cosmic Christ Power, which became so real to me. This, through its natural impulse for expression, is steadily and surely finding its way into the hearts and minds of a large per cent of mankind, to the extent, that great hope is present that this activity will enable the veil of human creation to be lifted, so great numbers of humanity will see signs and wonders, and feel them within their own hearts. Then, they cannot be turned aside from the Truth by human doubts and fears.

I spent some time in Arabia, Persia, and Tibet, and closed my pilgrimage in India where I met the Beloved Master, who had then made the Ascension, although I did not know it at the time. Through the Power of His Radiation, revelation after revelation came to me through which *I was given expressions or statements which enabled me to hold steady the outer activity of my mind,* until it no longer had power to disturb or retard me.

It was then, the full glory of my mission was revealed and the Eternal Cosmic Record it was to make, which was to be established at that time, for the blessing and enlightenment of the humanity that was to follow.

You might be interested to know, that, this became an Active Cosmic Record which is quite different from any other record made, *in that it contains within it, and does to-day,* the forward urge or impulse for which the human mind was and is a magnet.

This accounts for the expressions and statements I gave forth becoming more and more vivid through the centuries, and with the forward impulse of that activity, assisted by other Powerful Rays of Radiation, focused upon the earth, it will enable a great number of humanity to become so anchored in the Truth and Its conscious application that a transcendent accomplishment will be achieved.

There is no one single step so vitally important, as getting before mankind the knowledge of the "I AM"—their Source of Life and Its Transcendent Power—which can be brought into the conscious use of the individual. Within three years it will be amazing how this simple, yet All-powerful Truth, will have spread among humanity; for all, who will think upon it, practice its Presence, and consciously direct its energy, through the power of Divine Love, will find a new world of peace, Love, health and prosperity open to them.

Those, who understand applying the knowledge of the "I AM" need never, never be beset by inharmony or disturbance in their homes, worlds, or activities; for *it is only by a lack of acknowledgment and acceptance of the Full Power* of this Mighty Presence, that individuals allow human concepts and creations to disturb them.

The student should constantly look within his human self, and see what habits or creations are there, that need to be plucked out and disposed of; for, only by refusing to any longer allow habits of judging, condemning, and criticizing to exist, can he be free. The true activity of the student is only to perfect his own world, and he cannot do it as long as he sees imperfection in the world of another of God's children.

You have been given marvelous statements to harmoniously govern your Life and world. Apply them with determination, and you will succeed.

Another correction many of you wish me to make is this: "I did not say on the cross: 'Father why hast thou forsaken me?' but I did say: 'Father! how thou hast glorified me,' and I did receive into the glories with me the brother who was on my right on the cross."

There are a number of these beloved students whom I knew personally at the time of the crucifixion, and in giving this message forth to them I feel like talking to old friends; for in that Great Ascended Presence, centuries are but an incident, and only as we come into contact with human events is there a cognizance of time.

Beloved students, who are so earnestly seeking the Light, try to *feel* yourselves held in my loving embrace; try to *feel* yourselves clothed in that Light, Dazzling as the noon-day sun. So anchor within your consciousness the *feeling* of your ability to make the Ascension, that each day brings you closer and closer to the Fulness of That Realization.

Cut loose all things of earth that bind you. Know that in the Love, Wisdom, and Power that you accept from your "Mighty I AM Presence," is the power that does this transcendent service.

Always remind yourselves that: "God in you is your certain victory; The 'I AM Presence' which beats your heart, is the 'Light of God that never fails'; and that your power, by the acceptance of this Presence, to loose Its energy and direct It, is limitless."

It is my great joy and privilege to continue in association with my Beloved Brother, Saint Germain, in pouring forth, through my Conscious Radiation, a definite assistance to the students who can accept the instruction of Saint Germain. This will continue during the entire year of 1934. Do not misunderstand me, I AM pouring out to all mankind, but in this radiation to the students, I AM privileged to give a special service.

With my Love I enfold you. With my Light I clothe you. With my energy I sustain you, that you may go forth dauntless in your quest for happiness and the perfecting of yourselves and your world.

I trust this will bring a radiation that you may feel at will throughout the year, and that your attainment may bring you boundless joy.

"I AM the Enlightening, Revealing Presence manifest with full power."

JESUS THE CHRIST

SAINT GERMAIN:

I wish to convey my enfolding Love as a gift to each of the beloved students, for *Love is the Greatest Gift that can be given.*

DISCOURSE XXVIII

CHRISTMAS DAY

SAINT GERMAIN

INVOCATION: Thou Mighty, Infinite, Active Presence of the Christ everywhere! we bow before Thy Majesty and Power. Assert Thy Dominion in the heart and mind of every individual throughout the land, causing Thy Wondrous Perfection to express everywhere.

I bring you greetings of Love, the Comprehending Consciousness and Mastery from the Great Host of Ascended Masters, who have looked with favor upon my humble efforts to dispense the Light, and Who bring to you their Love and clothe you in Their Mantle of Light this Christmas Day.

THE DISCOURSE

Oh, Love Divine! in Thy Magic Power of Transmutation, we assert Thy Power in cleansing and purifying the world of human mistakes and human creations.

Thou art the Eternal Victory—the Golden Pathway of Attainment for every student of the Light, and through Thy Transcendent Power, the Kumaras start forth Their Mighty Radiation for the blessing of the earth and mankind for the entire year of 1934.

Thus, will mankind find many desirable changes taking place—greater health, happiness, and prosperity being restored, a deeper sense of Love, and a greater desire for justice in the hearts of mankind everywhere.

In many channels, human selfishness will be greatly transcended through the feeling of Pure Love that will generate within the heart, enable them to govern the human sense, and cause them to involuntarily desire to bless.

It is my wish that every one of the students send forth this Truth in conscious radiation at least once a day: "God, the 'Mighty I AM Presence,' is governing with Invincible Power *everywhere* in the hearts and minds of mankind."

Those Masters from Venus, who visited the Royal Teton, and Who will again visit it this New Year, will start forth a *definite activity* to consume the subtle attempt to generate and bring into outer activity, another war.

Shamballa is loosing Its Powers, that for many years have been drawn within Its own compass.

The Golden City, Whose Rays are sent in all directions—like the spokes from a wheel—is performing a service for mankind, that It alone can do.

If mankind could know and understand these activities for what they are, such marvelous changes would take place in the outer world, as even the advanced would hardly conceive possible.

On New Year's Day, the Cosmic Wheel of progress will have reached a point where in personal activity, much of the free will of individuals can be set aside. This brings a joy and hope unspeakable to the consciousness of those serving from these transcendent spheres of activity.

Thus, O students of Light! can you understand the magnificent assistance that is yours, to be had by stilling the outer and reaching forth for it. *I plead with you, dear students, shut your minds against the ignorance and inharmonious suggestions of human beings everywhere.* I say to every one of you: "Freedom in every way, stands at your door, if you will but keep your personality harmonized, and refuse to accept inharmonious, sinister suggestions from the atmosphere and from those you contact in mortal form."

It is imperative that this be done, if you wish to bring into your world, joy, beauty, opulence, and Perfection of every kind. It is not our intent or desire to intrude a single thing upon your free will, but Oh the joy! that leaps within our hearts, when we see the students taking hold, comprehending, and applying these Transcendent Laws that *we know* mean their Certain Victory; and may I reiterate what we have said before: "There is no single thing so vicious in the human activity as that personality or suggestion which would try to turn the student from the Truth and Light which would be his freedom."

In connection with this Mighty Cosmic Activity, the student should work with great determination, consuming all past and present inharmonious creation. Every time your thought and desire reach forth in this manner, *great currents of energy will come to your assistance to sustain and help you.* This is part of the present amazing assistance sent forth to the earth. The Silent Watcher has waited for 200,000 years for the Cosmic Wheel to reach this point—the coming New Year.

Again, I assert that never in the history of mankind, has such Transcendent Activity been ready to rush to your assistance. I plead with you, O beloved students! is it not worth all your determined effort to act in accordance with this great blessing, that makes your struggle for freedom from human-self-creations so much easier?

Beloved students, how deeply my heart rejoices to see within you the intense desire for the Light, and your determined effort to apply these Unerring Laws, which will as surely give you your freedom as you apply them.

I wish to thank all the students for that joyous desire for the limitless distribution of "Unveiled

Mysteries" and "The Magic Presence." In this great desire, beloved ones, is a service that you can little comprehend as yet, its far-reaching blessing.

I feel greatly blest this day of devotion to the Christ, to feel the Love from the many pouring out to me, and I assure you, blessed ones, that I shall come back to you with all the Loving Power at my command to assist, enlighten, and bless you.

In the special service that Jesus has decided to give forth, you are surely blest indeed. Try to *feel* this Wonderful Truth with the deepest intense feeling you can command. Open your arms, hearts, and minds to the Glory of This Radiation, and as you can do this more fully and completely, you will see how quickly all disturbing and limiting conditions about you will disappear.

I plead with you, beloved students, do not continue to limit yourselves by human concepts. *Declare and feel your amazing ability* to use these Laws and direct this Mighty Energy to your Freedom and Perfection. Try to realize that your human form is not a dense creation, difficult to manipulate. Try to *feel* it a transparent substance that follows your slightest direction. Speak to your body. Command it to be strong, receptive only to the Ascended Master Consciousness, to be a Perfect Expression of the Divine Power of the "Mighty I AM," and to take on Its Beauty of Form and Expression.

Review in your experience, the *powerful determination* you have had at times to accomplish success in the outer activity of things, and then realize how much *more powerful* your determination can generate to attain your Eternal Freedom.

Believe me, beloved ones, when I say to you: "There is but your human creation that stands between you and your freedom from all limitation. *That creation is no greater an obstacle than you accept it to be.* If you take away from that creation its power to limit you, *any hour—any day,* you may joyously step through that veil into your world of the "Electronic Presence"—so beautiful—so joyous—so filled with the Dazzling Light of Its Glorious Presence, and move there forever in that Light of Eternal Glory. Then, as you step back through that human veil, for service in the outer activity, you will continue to still *feel* the Glory of that Transcendent Being, *which you are.* Then naught of your own outer conditions or those about you will touch you or affect you in any way.

My whole being thrills with this joyous anticipation for you, as I know with a definite certainty your attainment. To any, who would let the suggestion of the ignorance of other human beings turn them aside from the Path, I wish to say: "Just remember what awaits you—that it is within your ability to achieve and *be.*"

Remember again, again and again: that as you grow into more and more intense acceptance of your "Mighty I AM Presence," the outer problems that have seemed so terrifying will surely fade from appearance.

Thus, not only is your problem solved, but every step gained in this way, does not reappear. Instead, it becomes your Eternal Freedom. If it is financial freedom you crave, I plead with you to take the outer activity of your mind off the appearance, and place it upon your "Mighty I AM Presence," the only Giver of all the Mighty Opulence there is. Stand firm and determined in this, and you will have all the money you desire to use.

Life does not limit you. *Opulence* does not limit you. *Love* does not limit you. Therefore, why allow your human limiting concepts to bind you longer?

Beloved Children of the Light! Arise! in the Mighty Glory of your True Being. Go forth! a Mighty Conquering Presence. Be! "the Light of God that never fails." Move! clothed in the Light of the Transcendent Glory of your God-Self—and Be Free!

BENEDICTION: "Mighty I AM Presence!" Transcendent in this Christ Activity! we give to Thee our eternal thanks and gratitude for Thy Love, Glory, Freedom and our conscious ability and power to accept the Fulness of Thy Glory made manifest in the outer activity of our lives; that we *stand* with firm determination in Thy Light—*directed* by Thy Wisdom, and *forever sustained* by Thy Transcendent Love, anchored within our hearts.

DISCOURSE XXIX

August 19, 1934

It is Saint Germain's request, that I voice to you the Mighty Accomplishment at the Music Festival last night.

May I first refer to my own humble efforts in conjunction with those at the Royal Teton, on New Year's day two years ago. It was then decreed that the Century of Progress Exposition should be a focus for a constructive activity, that should ever expand and increase in intensity during the next one hundred years.

The opening and lighting of it was the initiatory step that is to usher in the beautiful, magnificent Golden Age, which is signalized in that activity.

This has made Soldiers' Field sacred ground—a Sacred Altar of Divine Activity in the Western World, and so far as humanity at large is concerned, the hub of the whole of America.

A volume could be voiced on all that took place and that which led up to last evening, but owing to the human sense of time, this must be greatly condensed, and but an outline given.

Before proceeding to this description, I wish to call your attention to the unparalleled number of pageants of all kinds, of many nationalities, that are being held in Soldier's Field this summer. These cover the period from the Ascension of Jesus down to the present time. They give acknowledgment of the Ascension which is the most vital thing and the culmination of all human experience.

These pageants from the human standpoint are a calling forth of the latent memory in humanity at large, and are a raising of the Essence of that activity.

How easy it is for humanity to pass over transcendent activities because of their unbelief, acknowledgment, or acceptance of the True Perfection of Life, for all Life in manifestation is *God in Action*. Unfortunately, however, It is more often colored by human concepts of limitation and destructive qualities, which through the individual's power of free will everyone is at liberty to do.

This ere long, however, will be greatly remedied by the setting aside of the greater part of the human free will, as it is known to-day. This will enable much of humanity to be awakened and saved from their own destruction.

Here may I say, that the students who think they can play with the Great Law, because of their unwillingness to give the necessary Self-discipline, will find themselves unfortunate indeed, if they attempt it when once having entered upon the conscious path.

The Great Law, that does not discriminate, takes individuals at their words and feelings. Those who think they can escape this are but deceiving themselves.

The coming pageant of the Celts is really of great importance, for it enters into the vibratory action from the time of Jesus up to the present.

The Inner activity within and above Soldier's Field last night, was one of the most Divine Activities since the advent of the Kumaras into the presence of the earth.

Circle upon circle rose above the surface of the earth and those seated within the field. The first circle was formed by the Members of the Great White Brotherhood in their Golden Robes, being those whose outer forms have not yet made the Ascension.

Next came the Ascended Host of Masters who have made the Ascension. Then came the Angel Devas and seven of the Cherubim. The circle above them contained four of the Gods of the Mountains, three of whom you know, the other you shall know. Around these were the Archangels of whom the Archangel Michael was the Director.

Surrounding the "Core of Light" within the center of the Field, extending for two hundred feet within the earth and to five thousand feet above, were Saint Germain, Jesus, the Tall Master from Venus, and the Great Divine Director. They were the Dispensers of the Mighty Currents of Energy sent to all parts of the earth to do their work with no uncertainty.

During the singing of the "Holy City," the Divine Pattern of that which is to become the "Holy City upon earth" was lowered into Its position, where It shall remain, until It becomes a visible, vibrant City of Light to the westward. The exact position of this I may not disclose at the present time, but I assure you It was a Mighty Activity, which will become a Mighty Reality to the humanity of earth.

During Mr. Thomas' solos, that great vibratory action was taken up and re-echoed by a Great, Majestic, Celestial Chorus, whose radiance poured forth over America like a glistening shower of Light to consume and bless.

During the singing of the Hallelujah Chorus, the entire activity was turned over to the direct dispensation of Jesus Himself.

I wish to assure you that the set pieces in color were not just a human idea, but those responsible for their presence were inspired by the Ascended Masters, principally Saint Germain, in order to establish their renewed, powerful activity, which was intensified a thousand-fold or more to again act within the Life, the Soul, the Light, from the heart to the periphery of America and the world.

The representation of signing the Declaration of

Independence was to bring before the conscious attention of the earth, and especially America, its unparalleled activity upon the earth, and *to call the attention of the people of America that they might hold close to and stand by the original constitution of the United States, which was and is a Divine Creation,* until such time as the complete. Ascended Master Constitution of the United States shall come forth, as the advance of the Golden Age proceeds.

The Golden Eagle and the Shield represent the Height of Divine Protection for America again re-established.

The Bell of Liberty, in the power color of blue, represents the Glorious Liberty and Freedom forever for America and the earth, from all human selfishness, the instigator of which in every case is private profit, and the cause has been the same throughout the ages.

The four powerful blue rays that formed a canopy over the field, thought to be ordinary by the mass of humanity, represented that Fourth Dimensional Activity brought into visibility upon earth, and *if it be necessary for the protection of America, the Jewel in the Heart of God, then that "Blazing Light as of a Thousand Suns" shall descend upon earth and consume all human inharmony and selfishness from the planet.*

The fan of pink Light at the beginning was qualified to serve in the entire activity, and the Great Love Star stood above all, shedding its Rays through the tier above tier of Great Beings.

I congratulate you and this good Brother, and those many students of our Beloved Saint Germain, and I thank you all for your earnest, sincere work in behalf of the freedom of America. I also congratulate and thank the Beloved Messenger, Margaret Pettit, and her beloved students for their splendid work. May the activity of these beloved students of Light ever continue to expand until from this nucleus the Light of Its Radiance covers America.

I also congratulate our Beloved Saint Germain for his great accomplishment in establishing this nucleus and focus in America; and *for his Wonderful Love, His Light, His Work for America for nearly two hundred years, which, ere-long, will begin to bear fruit of such Perfect Kind as has not been heretofore in any civilization.*

I bow in acknowledgment of His Great Love, Wisdom, and Strength. I congratulate you, my beloved Sister and Brother, for your Love, steadfastness, patience, and activity for the students that have been and those that are to follow. Ever know that: "I AM the Only Acting Presence," and you will find that *all* activity will conform to the *"Perfection of That Presence."* I bid you adieu but not good-bye.

ARCTURUS.

DISCOURSE XXX

November 29, 1934

BELOVED STUDENTS OF THE LIGHT:

To-day is indeed one of the greatest days of thanksgiving that I have experienced in one hundred years. To see how the Light, acknowledgment, and acceptance of the "Mighty I AM Presence" is being received, and utilized by the hundreds of students in America, is truly a time of rejoicing and thanksgiving.

Not only do I pour forth my Love and Blessings, to the students, but the Entire Host of Ascended Masters, the Great Cosmic Masters, the Great White Brotherhood, the Legion of Light, and Those ministering from Venus, join in this praise and thanksgiving for the True Light that is being spread among mankind.

I do and shall deeply appreciate every assistance of the students under this radiation in getting the books into print and spreading them before humanity, for it is the greatest service at present that can be rendered.

The greatest need to-day is in calling the outer attention of mankind to the "One Great Source" that can give the needed assistance, and that is the "Mighty

335

I AM Presence" and the Host of Ascended Masters.
The *attention of individuals* fixed upon This Great
Source, *gives the opening needed* for the outpouring
of the Great, Eternal, Cosmic Light, to flood forth
into the outer world, reaching not only the consciousness of individuals, but into conditions that greatly
need re-adjusting.

It is my wish that all the students under this radiation, feel their individual responsibility in this respect, to keep their minds and bodies harmonized,
and to keep charging their minds and emotional
worlds with the Directing Wisdom and Perfection of
the "Mighty I AM Presence." This will enable assistance to be given humanity which the outer could not
possibly conceive of in its heretofore limited condition.

I wish each student to understand and feel deeply,
that the Great Ascended Masters and Myself stand
ready to give every assistance to the individual that
the Law of his Being permits. The need of the students is always to stand firm and unyielding in the
Presence, until the outer human creation about them
is dissolved—consumed—and then the Mighty Light,
Wisdom, and Power of the "Mighty I AM Presence"
will flood their minds, Beings, and worlds with this
Glorious Radiance, filling them and their worlds
with that harmony, happiness, and Perfection which
every heart so much craves.

I urge ALL to do definite, conscious, protective work for America, that the Cosmic Light and Eternal Perfection enfold the earth, removing and consuming all discord, and continue: "To bless persons, places, conditions and things, for It is the Mighty Miracle-Working Activity that will usher in the prosperity and happiness that all so much desire."

It is my great joy to report to you, that already great protection has been given to the eastern coast from Philadelphia to Maine. If this protection had not been given, some of your cities would have been in ruins to-day.

This Beloved Ones, is what it means to bring a Mighty Focus of the Ascended Masters into your midst. Only as your Inner Sight is opened to see and know the True Reality, can you have a small concept of the Truth which I have just spoken.

May your hearts fill with joy and may you work earnestly for the health, success, and prosperity of the Messengers, who have been the channels through whom this focus of protection has been given. Unfortunate indeed are those who criticize the Messengers or the work. Better had they never been born in this embodiment.

Beloved students, try with all sincerity to feel the Reality and Infinite Blessings of this work, that your world and America may reap the great reward of that blessing.

Words are inadequate to tell you the fulness of my gratitude for your earnest sincere effort. Your ability and power to bless and prosper will ever increase, as you hold firmly to and within your "Mighty I AM Presence."

My Love enfolds you, My Light illumines you, and the Wisdom of the "Mighty I AM Presence" prospers you unto the Fulness of All Perfection.

The Love of the Mighty Host of Ascended Masters, the Great White Brotherhood, and The Legion of Light enfold you always.

I AM sincerely in "The Light"

SAINT GERMAIN.

DISCOURSE XXXI

December 25, 1934

It is with great joy that we are observant of the tremendous accomplishment—individually, nationally, and Cosmically-speaking: for when we have the use of and can co-operate with those Great and Mighty Cosmic Currents of Energy, directed by that Great, Wise Intelligence, then we know that every step moved forward brings us nearer and nearer to That Mighty Glory and Freedom, which many are learning to feel and rejoice in.

How different all activities are when working in conjunction with That Great, Cosmic Wisdom, that is no longer compelled to withhold Its Mighty Energy, because of the free-will of the individual; for now the Cosmic Activities of the nations are of first consideration. Then comes the individual.

Heretofore, because of the individual, certain Cosmic Activities had to wait. Now the Great Cosmic Wheel has turned, bringing all national, emotional, and mental activities into that Great Preparation where every cog of the wheel must fit into the Cosmic Reality.

The free will of the individual still binds and limits the outer sufficiently, so there will be many

339

individuals and conditions in which it will be as though they were being run through great rollers, in which all undesirable qualities are pressed out, and by the power of the Consciously-Directed Flame are consumed.

The Mighty Radiance, consciously directed, by the Great Host of Ascended Masters from the Great Central Sun, is not only having tremendous effect on the minds and feelings of mankind on the surface of the earth, but far within the crust of the earth itself. Hence, it has been possible to avert many great disasters.

Here I want to say in Great Love, gratitude, and blessing to the hundreds of students who have been projecting the Mighty Love, Wisdom, and Power of the "Mighty I AM Presence" into the mental and emotional world, and assure them, that a gigantic work has been accomplished; for if mankind and the beloved students can once understand, that all cause rests within the mental and emotional worlds, then they will have reached a point of understanding, wherein they know with complete assurance that the outer activity of mankind must and will come into Perfect Order when the only cause—the mental and emotional activities—are corrected and held in subjection.

This is how so much has been accomplished even since last June. Here, I want to assure those who have had some questioning in their minds: "Was it really true that great devastation had been averted"? that one day they will see and know the Truth of which I have spoken.

Since three hundred years after Jesus' ministry, mankind steadily and surely drifted back into dealing with effects instead of causes, and that is why no permanent assistance has been possible to be given. Now, with the assistance that the turn of the Cosmic Wheel permits, it is possible to bring the consciousness of mankind back into dealing with the cause, and the effect, if out of order, must disappear.

This is why the knowing of the "Mighty I AM Presence," Its Powers, and Whereabouts is bringing the students to deal only with *That One and Mighty Presence, whose Cause is Full Perfection,* as hundreds of these students are proving for themselves. When their attention is fixed upon the "Mighty I AM Presence," they are dealing with the *One and Mightiest Cause, Whose One and Only Expression is Perfection.* Therefore, their worlds first become filled with ease and rest, and through that, they begin to feel the Glory of That Mighty Presence. As they begin to feel this, they realize that they can reach forth to this "Mighty Presence" consciously, and release such a Mighty Avalanche of Its Mighty Energy, that the human does not even have time to re-qualify but a fragmentary part, with its limitations and inharmonies. Therefore, the strength, that is required to give the Eternal Proof to the individual, is sustained. Thus, through the individual's own Self-conscious effort, comes the Greater and Greater recognition of the possibilities within his conscious grasp. Mark you, I say *conscious* grasp, for it is only through first conscious acknowledgment: second, acceptance: and third, application, or in other words *consciously directing this Mighty Intelligence* and Pure Energy, that the outer or human is kept dissolved enough, for the outer to truly grasp these Mighty Activities.

Oh! the pity that mankind has believed so long, and many individuals very sincerely, that they could cure hate, condemnation, and criticism with those same qualities. How futile and tragic has been this false concept. Believe me, O Children of the Light! hate never cured hate and never will. Condemnation and criticism never cured their kind, for as we have so often said to you: "That which your attention and vision is held upon you are qualifying, and compelling to come into your world—abide and act there."

With all we have said and given forth, so little has been grasped of how much the personality is constantly qualifying the very atmosphere and conditions about it, with the things it does not want, through the belief, that it can continue to have any kind of feeling and speak words of discord, hate, and limitation, and still be unaffected by it. This stubborn, false concept of mankind has filled the world with all kinds of tragedy.

Now, this Mighty, Eternal Light is being released to show mankind *why* the outer world has been so filled with tragedy. If I were to show you for one half hour, how much selfishness has been removed from the mental and feeling world of humanity, since these classes of the "I AM," began, you would scarcely believe that so much accomplishment, in so short a time could have been possible. It could not and would not have been possible, except for this *"Mighty, Eternal Radiation of Light from the Great Host of Ascended Masters, from the Great Central Sun, the Masters from Venus, the Silent Watcher, Cyclopea, and the Mighty Gods of the Mountains."*

All this is making possible the achievement for which the Legion of Light and the Great White Brotherhood have labored for centuries. For over fourteen thousand years this work has continued without cessation, the Great Ascended Ones seeing the victory from the beginning; but Oh! the infinite patience, to wait upon the waywardness of mankind century after century, yet was there no single thought of impatience or: "Why does not humanity change?" It is only within the compass of human thought and feeling that judgment and impatience enter in.

Not for seven thousand years has there been such rejoicing at the Inner Octaves of Activity for mankind, as comes with the ushering in of 1935. While it is true there will be some great extremes in both constructive and destructive activity, yet the forward impulse is so great, that many of the destructive things will pass with much less notice than otherwise would have been.

As more and more of the students of the "Mighty I AM Presence" realize that their thought and feeling are the only causes in their worlds, and that it is entirely within their province—within their ability and dominion, to govern their thought and feeling, then they will know that to govern these harmoniously, sustaining this activity, will fill their worlds with Eternal Perfection.

This day, when the great feeling and thought are fixed upon the Christ Activity, it has made possible as never before the filling of the mind and feeling world of mankind, with this "Mighty Cosmic Christ Presence."

Thus can you understand how great is our happiness on this Christmas Day, to see the Goal of the Freedom of mankind in sight. Once they learn to withhold all power, they have given the screaming human appearances, then individuals will see how quickly those appearances will disappear; for no kind of discord nor human limitation can be sustained unless by the thought and feeling of individuals.

Therefore, O beloved students of Light! to every discordant limiting appearance, say: "Get thee hence, thou powerless human creation! I know thee not, my world is filled only with the 'Mighty Perfection of my Mighty I AM Presence.' I take away from you— foolish appearance—all power to harm or disturb. *I walk henceforth, in the 'Light of the Mighty I AM Presence,' in which there is no shadow and I am free, forever free."*

I say to you, O beloved students! "Do not fail to charge your mind, body, home, world, and activity with the 'Mighty Love, Perfection, and Intelligent Activity of your Mighty I AM Presence.'"

Send forth through conscious projection—like the belching forth of a great cannon—the Mighty Violet Consuming Flame, consuming everything undesirable and imperfect in your world of activity. *Consciously qualify this with the "Full Power of Divine Love in Action,"* then see and feel what great beauty, happiness and Perfection you will experience as you move forward.

I urge the students with all the earnestness of my Being to constantly charge *everything* within the activity of their thought and feeling with Love, Opulence, and Perfect Achievement.

Do this qualifying with dynamic energy! Put great feeling and sureness back of it, and you will find such

*changes taking place in your world of activity and
environment as almost to compare with the rubbing
of "Aladdin's Lamp."*

I say to you, beloved students, with all the Love
of my heart: *"Use,—use—use this Mighty Application
to your Freedom."*

When you call the Mighty "I AM Presence" into
action, into your Life, environment, and activity, all
struggle ceases. The undesirable moves out, and the
"I AM Presence" moves in, and you find that you
have truly entered into a new world, filled with the
happiness and Perfection you have always known
existed somewhere, within your own heart.

Beloved Ones, no matter how humble your present position seems to be, by calling your "I AM Presence" into action, you can transform everything
within your world, and fill it with the Perfection that
you desire to have there.

VERY IMPORTANT

Train yourselves to still the outer, if only for five
minutes three times a day. At the end of that stillness with all the calm earnestness of your Being, call
the "Mighty I AM Presence" into action, and you
will have all the proof in the world that you wish,
of the Presence, Power, and Dominion of your own
"Mighty God-Self."

The Beloved Master Jesus, wishes me to extend his

Love and Assurance that He will give forth His Special Radiance to the students under this Radiation for the entire year of 1935. He will not dictate over the Ray to-day, but will on New Year's Day.

This is the Christmas Message which the Host of Great Ascended Masters, the Legion of Light, and the Great White Brotherhood give to you to-day.

May your hearts, O beloved students! be filled with that Eternal Presence of Divine Love, and may you become so charged with its Active Presence, that Its very Radiance becomes an Eternal, Consuming Activity, keeping out everything but the Eternal Light of Perfection.

I charge the mental and emotional world of humanity with that Eternal, Active Presence of Divine Love, manifest everywhere in the hearts and minds of mankind. In the Name, in the Power, in the Love of That Eternal Light and Perfection of the Universe, I send forth the Consuming, Purifying Flame throughout the earth, freeing mankind, controlling the feelings of mankind, and holding them in the Governing Presence and Perfection of Divine Love, now and forever.

With all the Love of my Being,

SAINT GERMAIN.

DISCOURSE XXXII

January 1, 1935

As we look upon the accomplishment of the past year from the Higher Octaves of Light, and then come into your octave of human activity, we see and feel the great change that has taken place, even in one year. It is truly most encouraging, most assuring, of the ultimate goal of victory in the freedom of mankind from the chains and limitations of their own creation. After all, the pity is that mankind does not understand that the human activity alone is the only creator of limitation and inharmony there is.

In other words, through the ungoverned activity of the outer, personalities allow themselves to constantly re-qualify the Perfect Energy, the Pure Essence of their own "Mighty I AM Presence" producing all that is undesirable, when it is within their ability to keep themselves so harmonized that the Perfect Intelligence and Energy, flowing through the human form, could not and would not be re-qualified. Therefore, it would constantly do Its Perfect Work, not only in perfecting the human form, causing it to express Divine Perfection, but it would allow that Purity and Perfection to flow out into the individual's

348

world, producing the beauty, harmony, and success each heart so much craves.

Q. Why does almost everyone desire greater beauty, Perfection and abundance of every good thing?

A. Because it is an Inner Recognition of each one's own God-given Dominion which everyone can assert at any time. I assure you, beloved Children of Light, that every individual can assert his Dominion at any time, *if he only will, by his recognition and acceptance of his own "Mighty I AM Presence,"* for that enables this Mighty, Invincible Presence to become the Mighty, Directing Intelligence.

Therefore, do you not see that to this Mighty Presence there is no obstruction, therefore no *struggle,* no interference of any kind? This is how the old scriptural statement, so long used: "Be still and know that I AM God," can be made a dynamic power in one's outer mind. In the past year, we have drawn attention to many of the scriptural statements, giving more explanation of their true meaning. This year, we hope to bring forth a full and complete explanation of all the "I AM" statements used through the centuries, that mankind may have the evidence before their own eyes, of the Freedom and Dominion which is within their own grasp.

We rejoice and give thanks that this year will release such abundant, financial support for this work, that Boundless Light and Blessings will be brought to mankind. In all past Golden Ages, when the Great Light of the Higher Octaves descended into the earth, enfolding and dissolving the human creation about individuals, they were so enabled to reach into the Higher Octaves through the Inner Sight, Hearing, and Feeling that they knew, first hand, the True Reality, and that the outer form was but the garment of this All-wise, Supreme Intelligence which the "Mighty I AM Presence" used to find expression in the denser octave into which the human had drawn itself.

Can you, O beloved students of the Light! even for a few moments, realize what joy this brings to the hearts of the Host of Ascended Masters, who have freed themselves through Self-conscious effort from these same human limitations, that you are now experiencing? As these Beloved Messengers have come to know with full assurance that freedom, so all mankind will one day understand that everyone can make the necessary, Self-conscious effort in the recognition and acceptance of this "Mighty I AM Presence" and have this same freedom.

Do not let anyone of the beloved students make such a mistake, as to think that the "Mighty I AM Presence" is going to act independently of the individual's own Self-conscious effort. *This never is and cannot be done.* It is true that after the student has reached a certain point of attainment, the Law seems to begin to act almost automatically, but this is only because a charged momentum has been built and established about the individual. Let me make clear to you now, that *never until you have made the Ascension, do you cease to make conscious application for your own Freedom.*

To-day I am going over some of these simple, yet All-powerful, acknowledgments of the Truth, because I wish every student under this radiation to have a copy of this, that each one may read it once a day; for to those who will do this earnestly and conscientiously, I will give forth my own individual radiation to bless them and assist them to their Freedom.

You have been asked, throughout the past year, to charge your mind, body, home, world and activity with the Perfection of the "Mighty I AM Presence." Now with your permission, I shall assist you, and also charge your Being and World with this "Mighty Perfection and Abundance."

I AM offering this assistance to you, O beloved students! Let no one be so foolish as to doubt, for I AM the Jesus, the Christ of Galilee, that you have known of for the past two thousand years, that is dictating this discourse and offering this assistance to you.

Again, let me assure you that this work of Saint Germain and Myself is entirely different from anything that has been given forth to the Western World, because in this work there are no human concepts or opinions. It has not been possible to do this heretofore, until the Visible Light and Sound Rays could be established, through which knowledge and instruction could be given. If you, beloved ones, as students, can realize this, how great will be your blessing and benefit.

The protection that has been given America and certain other parts of the world, during the past few months, has transcended anything I have ever known in my experience. Oh! if humanity could but realize this, how gladly and willingly would they co-operate to their utmost to sustain it, that its All-powerful Activity might ever increase.

We can but call your attention to the Truth, the Reality, as we know it to be. When you can fully accept this Truth and apply It in your world and activity, you will have all the proof required, in your own experience to enable you to know the Full Power of the Truth of which I have spoken.

To all who can accept this Truth, it will enable me to charge their consciousness and fill their worlds and activity with this Truth. They who doubt must wait, for doubt and fear are the two doors through which every human being must pass, to know and have his Full and Complete Freedom. The key that unlocks these doors is Divine Love in each one's acknowledgment of his own "Mighty I AM Presence," as the Fulness of this Power of Divine Love Acting.

The Door to the Seventh Octave of Light stands open to every one of the beloved students under this radiation who will make sincere, earnest, Self-conscious application. This, my beloved Brothers and Sisters, means your freedom. *Can you—will you—grasp this with the full power of your "I AM Consciousness" and be free?*

As I AM dictating these words to the Messengers, through amplifiers which your outer world has not yet known, these words and this radiation are going forth into the mental and feeling world of humanity, which will immediately start into operation, and as the students and individuals contact these words from time to time, they will find an immediate response that will enable them to *feel* the Truth and the Reality of which I speak.

Oh! that humanity, who through church service after church service is acknowledging my Ascension, Oh! why can it not feel the True Reality and know that in my Ascended, Eternal, Light Body, I can and do reach all who will open their hearts to my reception? Oh, children of earth! learn to couple your *feeling* of the Truth with the acknowledgment of the Truth that you wish to have manifest in your Life. Then, you will be enabled to go forth to any height of achievement in your quest for freedom.

I AM the Open Doorway which no man can shut. Your "Mighty I AM Presence" is the Light that lighteth every man that cometh into the world. Your "Mighty I AM Presence" is your Directing Intelligence, your Exhaustless, Sustaining Energy. Your "Mighty I AM Presence" is the Voice of Truth speaking within your heart, the Light enfolding you in Its Luminous Presence, your Eternal Belt of protection through which no human creation can pass, your Eternal Reservoir of Exhaustless Energy which you can release at will through your conscious charging. Your "Mighty I AM Presence" is the Fountain of Eternal Youth and Beauty, which you can call into action and expression in your human form to-day. Your "Mighty I AM Presence" is your Resurrection and the Life of your body, of your world of action into that Perfection which the heart of every human being so much desires.

Listen, O beloved students of Light! When you are uttering these decrees for yourselves and I AM uttering them for you, do you not see that we are doing it for all the rest of mankind as well as ourselves? That when you issue a decree of and through the "I AM," you are issuing that for everyone else as well as yourselves? This is how the application and expression of the "I AM" becomes all-powerful, exhaustless in Its activity, and forever acts beyond the realm of human selfishness. Why? Because you are asking for every one of God's children that same Perfection which you are calling into action for yourselves.

This is not possible except in the use of the "I AM" statements and application, for acting within the "I AM Presence" takes you *instantly* out of the activity wherein there is human selfishness. This is why the earnest, sincere student who will cast out all doubt and fear will find himself or herself acting within a sphere of positive, definite activity that knows no delay or lack of accomplishment in anything. Then O beloved ones! do you not see how you are then acting in a world of Infallibility, wherein your decrees enable the Full Power of the "I AM" to move into action, causing all human inharmony and limitation to move out?

I now voice the decree that the Host of Ascended Masters and students issued last night at the Royal Teton: *"Such freedom, health, prosperity, and harmonious action shall come forth for America and the world, as have never before been experienced on earth."*

The students who will join us in this decree will render a service which will bless them throughout the ages. *Only because America is the Cup—the Holy Grail—do we often speak of America first.* All should know without question that what blesses America blesses the world.

An Activity, a Radiance, such as has not been known since the height of the last Golden Age on Atlantis, was sent forth from the Conclave at the Royal Teton, the description of which Saint Germain will give you later.

The Fulness of my Love, Light, and Blessing I leave with yourselves, all the students, and all mankind, that the Light within each heart may be so quickened, that you and they will no longer know limitation of any kind, and that That Light becomes so powerful that Its very Radiance consumes all human creation, accumulated through the past or present, setting all forever free.

My Love enfolds all forever,

JESUS THE CHRIST.

DISCOURSE XXXIII

July 4, 1932

SAINT GERMAIN

INVOCATION: Mighty, Sustaining, Enfolding Presence! we give praise and thanks for Thy Life Everlasting, Thy Youth Eternal, Thy Light Illumining.

THE DISCOURSE

O America! WE LOVE YOU. Mighty Seed of God's Eternal Manifestation, we give praise and thanks that Thou art sustained and governed by God alone. The day on which independence within thy heart was established, thou didst become a Radiating Center of Light to all humanity. We give praise and thanks that out of all, will come peace and prosperity to mankind in thy embrace. *Back of thee is the Power that will sustain and maintain the Reign of God on earth.* His Light *shall* illumine and strengthen the hearts of thy children in all ruling places, and out of all shall come Love, Justice, and Wisdom. America! we love you. America! we love you. America! we love you. America! we love you. America! we love you. To-day, O America, those Mighty Messengers of God who have passed before look upon thee with their hearts filled with Love and strength, the Love

357

of the "Mighty I AM Presence," flowing forth to heal, to bless and to prosper thy inhabitants. The very substance of earth is being quickened into greater activity, and as the Children of God walk the earth, so shall they feel the *Current of God* flowing in, quickening them into greater Love, Loyalty and desire for thy freedom, O America! Thou dost seem to have become bound, but thou art not. Thou art entering into thy Great Freedom. Thou dost seem in the throes of pain, but thou wilt be born into that great peace, health, happiness and prosperity. We give praise and thanks that this is God's Wisdom— "The Mighty I AM Presence"—speaking.

The Christ Child enfolding thee, America, has grown into Majesty and Power. It no longer pleads but commands obedience of all that is of the outer, to the service of the Inner Presence. The Power of Divine Love governs thee and consumes all unlike Itself. America, we give praise and thanks that thou art a Great Jewel within the Heart of God, the Lamp of Illumination, lighted by the "Mighty I AM Presence," the Chalice, the Crystal Cup, holding within its Pure Radiance the freedom, peace, health, prosperity and illumination of those who dwell within thy embrace. May all the world feel thy Radiance and be blest by it. Peace, peace, peace, and on earth good-will to man.

ARCTURUS.

NOTES

I would suggest that sometime each day, you think of yourself as a radio station sending forth peace and good-will to all mankind. Know that in this Mighty Consciousness, the Limitless Power of the "Mighty I AM Presence" flows forth to each individual and gives that which he is ready to receive, bringing enlightenment and decision to everyone. Be conscious that your own minds are such powerful Divine Centers, that at any time you can make quick, unerring decisions through the power of Divine Love. Recognize that your mind is but a vehicle of the Great Master Presence of the "Mighty I AM Presence" within, and that it is to obey that Inner Presence at all times. Command it always to act with decision, alertness, and quickness, and that all human sense of wavering be forever consumed.

THE NEW CYCLE

To-day is a focal point of ten thousand years, the beginning of another cycle of ten thousand years in which the Great Ones from Venus, who have always been instrumental in the uplift of humanity and our earth, this day come forth and pour out to humanity throughout the earth a Mighty Radiance. This will bring about more quickly a greater stabilization and confidence in the hearts of many public officials. It will cause them to have a strong unwavering desire to reestablish America in confidence and prosperity, and make them feel a deeper Love and loyalty for her progress than ever before. Many will have learned that they cannot rule humanity with a ruthless hand, for they are seeing that the inroad of control, which they had desired to gain over others, is returning to themselves for redemption. If this lesson can be impressed upon them sufficiently, a great calamity will have been averted. In this quickening period, things can be done, in the short period of twenty years, that would ordinarily require a hundred years.

SAINT GERMAIN'S DESCRIPTION

OF

NEW YEAR'S EVE CONCLAVE AT THE ROYAL TETON—

JANUARY 1, 1935

It is with great joy that I relate to you briefly some of the activity that took place at the Royal Teton last night.

Two hundred fourteen of the Ascended Masters were present and the twelve from Venus. The All-Seeing-Eye was in the most powerful action known thus far.

Great Rays of Light are made permanent to our national capital, and the capital of each state that a Constant Radiation may pour forth to these focal points, and also to the principal cities of Europe, India, China, Japan, Australia, New Zealand, South America, Africa and Mexico.

A similar activity or Radiation from the Golden City and Shamballa was also poured forth, making a Triple Activity for the blessing of mankind. *Every effort is being made to avoid as much destructive activity as possible throughout the world.*

The activity of the past three months has been tremendously encouraging, and we do have high expectation for this year. Being so well aware of the free will of humanity, we can but trust for their harmonious co-operation with the Conscious Radiation pouring forth from the above-mentioned Triple Activity.

There were out-pourings of Light from the Tall Master from Venus, Jesus, and the Great Divine Director, such as I have not known before in my experience.

The many who have been fully aware of my sincere efforts for the blessing of America, have now joined me in full power to achieve all possible that the Cosmic Law and the law of the individual will permit. The Cosmic Laws are daily giving greater freedom in this activity which is the thing that gives us such great encouragement.

There were many students present last night, for which I AM very grateful. There is much detail of the activity which took place that I may not reveal at this time; but I assure all the students that it was marvelous beyond description.

The Great Host of Ascended Masters join me in their Love, Light, Blessing and Opulence to the students, to America, and to the world, that this year may be unparalleled in its happiness to mankind.

In the Fulness of My Love,

SAINT GERMAIN

FINIS

THE SAINT GERMAIN SERIES

By GODFRÉ RAY KING

UNVEILED MYSTERIES—VOLUME I

Contains the first group of experiences under the Ascended Master, Saint Germain, in America in 1929, 1930, and 1931

THE MAGIC PRESENCE—VOLUME II

Contains the second group of experiences under the Ascended Master, Saint Germain, and explains the use of "The Mighty I AM Presence."

THE "I AM" DISCOURSES—VOLUME III

Contains thirty-three discourses explaining the Ascended Master's application of the "I AM"

THE "I AM" ADORATIONS AND AFFIRMATIONS— VOLUME IV

A selection of salutations, Adorations, and Powerful Affirmations of "The Mighty I AM Presence." Ready in the summer of 1935

A PICTURE OF "THE MAGIC PRESENCE"

A color chart of "The Magic Presence" lithographed beautifully and prepared for meditation or class instruction, suitable for framing. Size approximately 12 x 20 inches.

A PICTURE OF THE MASTER JESUS

A hand colored steel engraving of an etching by Charles Sindelar, to whom Jesus has personally appeared. It is an exact likeness of Him as He stood in consultation with Saint Germain and the Tall Master from Venus at the Retreat in the Royal Teton, last New Year's Eve.

Size approximately 12 x 16 inches—on heavy cardboard.

A NEW PICTURE OF THE ASCENDED MASTER SAINT GERMAIN

A hand colored steel engraving of an etching by Charles Sindelar. An Exact likeness as He has appeared on many occasions in the Retreat. A companion piece to that of Jesus and meant for the student's meditation.

Size approximately 12 x 17 inches—on heavy cardboard.